GW01003755

POVERTY AND PIETY
IN AN ENGLISH VILLAGE
Terling, 1525–1700

This is a volume in

STUDIES IN SOCIAL DISCONTINUITY

A complete list of titles in this series appears at the end of this volume.

POVERTY AND PIETY IN AN ENGLISH VILLAGE

Terling, 1525–1700

Keith Wrightson

Department of Modern History
St. Salvator's College
University of St. Andrews, St. Andrews, Scotland

David Levine

Department of History and Philosophy
The Ontario Institute for Studies in Education
Toronto, Ontario, Canada

Academic Press

New York   San Francisco   London   1979

A Subsidiary of Harcourt Brace Jovanovich, Publishers

ACADEMIC PRESS, INC.
111 Fifth Avenue, New York, New York 10003

United Kingdom Edition published by
ACADEMIC PRESS, INC. (LONDON) LTD.
24/28 Oval Road, London NW1 7DX

Library of Congress Cataloging in Publication Data

Wrightson, Keith.
  Poverty and piety in an English village.

  (Studies in social discontinuity)
  Bibliography: p.
  1. Terling, Eng. – – Rural conditions. 2. Villages– –
England– –History– –Case studies. 3. Poor– –England– –
Terling– –Case studies. 4. Reformation– –England– –Terling.
I. Levine, David, Date   joint author. II. Title.
III. Series.
HN398.T45W74   301.35'2'094267   78–22536
ISBN 0–12–765950–1

PRINTED IN THE UNITED STATES OF AMERICA

79 80 81 82   9 8 7 6 5 4 3 2 1

TO EVA AND JENNIFER

For reasons that don't need to be spelled out

Contents

Preface

In the summer of 1974, we decided to join forces in an effort to dove-
tail our converging interests in the problem of illegitimacy in early-modern
England. In the course of the following twelve months, our attention
became focused on the lives of the villagers of Terling, Essex—a sample
parish originally selected for the exceptional quality of its parish register. In
time, the subject of our initial investigation was gradually subsumed within
a larger, more comprehensive framework. Our efforts became harnessed to
a more ambitious project. To a large degree, this extension of the scope of
our collaboration was forced upon us. As a result of our friendship and frequent discussions, we had long realized that our backgrounds and experience as historians complemented one another. We hoped that our dissatis-
factions with the limitations of our own individual styles of analysis might
be overcome through a joint effort. With these objectives in mind, we ap-
proached the records of Terling. But the records themselves and the problems which they raised led us much further than we had anticipated.

Our work on Terling is based upon seven of the principal sources for
historical community studies recently described in Alan Macfarlane's *Reconstructing Historical Communities*.[1] These are: the parish register of
Terling; the wills of the villagers; manorial and estate records; parish ac-

---

[1] A. Macfarlane, in collaboration with S. Harrison and C. Jardine, *Reconstructing
Historical Communities*.

count books; taxation records; the records of Quarter Sessions and Assizes; the records of the ecclesiastical courts. In addition, we have drawn upon contemporary printed books as well as a variety of other locally and centrally kept records, and, to a limited extent, the records of the central courts of the kingdom. We have also benefited, from time to time, from the help of other researchers who have generously communicated to us their occasional findings of Terling material, often from quite unexpected sources.

We would certainly not claim to have established a complete archive of Terling records for our period; to do so would be virtually impossible. What we have done is to build up a large body of material from the principal local sources available for the study of a village community in the past, supplementing it from other sources as need arose. Some central collections may very well contain additional material. We recognize this. But on the basis of our experience with the records of the Star Chamber and of the Court of Requests, we concluded that the time and labor necessary to sift thoroughly through other massive and still relatively inaccessible central collections was unlikely to be justified for the sake of recovering the occasional Terling records which might be uncovered. We have had neither the time nor the finances to aim at such total coverage. Again, it was never our intention to attempt to write "total history." We came to our task with certain questions in mind. In seeking answers, however, we let the records speak to us. As our work progressed, our range of questions and of source materials grew. The emerging picture of society in Terling sometimes crystallized and confirmed, sometimes modified or challenged the ideas and prejudices of our earlier work on the social structure of preindustrial England. Moreover, we gradually became aware of an unexpected social drama in which the players' roles subtly changed and their self-consciousness was subject to novel strains and tensions. Yet we have not sought to discuss every aspect of rural life in the period. We have simply tried to deal thoroughly with the materials most relevant to our concerns.

Our methods have been laborious, but relatively simple. We made considerable use of microfilm and Xerox photography in gathering material from the principal sources. From 1974 through 1976, David Levine undertook the family reconstitution of the parish. Meanwhile, Keith Wrightson worked his way through the other sources, noting their contents as fully as possible and adding additional material. He gradually constructed a name index containing all references to particular individuals in the period 1524 to 1700, together with all evidence of their linkage to other individuals. In the subsequent process of analyzing the material in order to answer particular questions, it proved possible to move constantly from index and family reconstitution forms to notes and, where necessary, to the copies of the original records. Our study is thus based upon the analysis of the individual classes of records, amplified by the use of the material rendered accessible through the name index and family reconstitution forms to explore the suggestions thrown up by each particular section of the study. We have tried to be inventive in our use of the sources in order to pursue questions which are rarely answered directly by historical records. At the same time, however, we have been constantly preoccupied with the need to avoid straining the evidence. We hope that we have succeeded in this, but our readers must judge that for themselves.

By the autumn of 1975, we were separated by the Atlantic Ocean, but the work progressed and ideas continued to be regularly exchanged. Having produced a series of working papers, we finally wrote up our respective sections in the spring and summer of 1977, indulged in some sharp mutual criticism, and produced our manuscript.

Our research and writing has led us to incur many debts. We would like to take this opportunity to acknowledge the help and courtesy of the staffs of the several record offices listed in our bibliography. In particular, the staff of the Essex Record Office provided invaluable help. Further aid was forthcoming from the Hon. C. R. Strutt of Berwick Place, Hatfield Peverel, who generously made available to us his own collection of materials for the history of the parish. At various points we were aided financially by the Twenty Seven Foundation and the University of St. Andrews Research Fund.

We were fortunate to find ourselves in Cambridge during the years 1970–1975. The period was an exciting one. As in all intellectual conjunctures, we were heavily influenced by and are indebted to those others who were themselves engaged in studying complementary problems. Andy Appleby, John Brewer, Ann Kussmaul Cooper, David Cressy, Viv Brodsky Elliot, Derek Hirst, Martin Ingram, Alan Macfarlane, David Sabean, Roger Schofield, Simon Stevenson, Emmanuel Todd, John Walter, and Tony Wrigley have all made subterranean contributions to our effort which they will be able to detect. We count ourselves lucky that Peter Laslett was there, too. Peter was a constant source of inspiration, criticism, and encouragement—a truly dialectical friend and mentor. Beyond individuals, Cambridge provided two wonderful forums for debate and discussion—the King's College Seminars in Social History and the bimonthly meetings of the Cambridge Group for the History of Population and Social Structure.

Within this percolating world of cold rooms and warm beer, fast talk and idle chatter, we first found our interests moving along converging lines. Since leaving Cambridge, others have had their part in our thinking through of the problems raised as the study developed. Keith Wrightson's special subject class in St. Andrews in 1976–1977 proved that the customary acknowledgments made by teachers to their students are more than lip-service. Brian Crook, Dave Duncan, Andy Gailey, John Hill, Rab Houston, John Martin, Liz Walker, and Katie Walsh contributed more to this book than they will ever know. Finally, the manuscript was read in its entirety by Martin Cherry, Peter Laslett, Jack Plumb, Richard Smith, Lawrence Stone, C. R. Strutt, John Walter, and Susan Watkins. We thank them all.

This book represents our attempt to understand how the villagers of Terling experienced and came to terms with their places in an important period of England's history. It has been a work of collaboration in the fullest sense, which could not have been completed—indeed, would not have been undertaken—by either of us as individuals. The project has been immensely stimulating while the opportunity to work together has been educative and rewarding. It was also fun.

POVERTY AND PIETY
IN AN ENGLISH VILLAGE
Terling, 1525–1700

1

THE NATIONAL CONTEXT[1]

England has many histories. There is the history of court and cabinet, of high policy, politics, and diplomacy. There are the histories of the great institutions of national life, of churches, Parliament, and courts of law. In the world outside Westminster there are the histories of counties, towns and villages, of local administration, of trades and industries, of classes, of the land itself. Each of these histories has its own dynamics and its own integrity, its own elements of distinctiveness. Yet all are in a powerful sense interdependent, however much the degree of interdependence might vary with place and period. Our concern here is with the history of a single village and its people. But in telling its story we have a larger aim. In its experience we are seeking to discern the manner in which national and local development intersected in a period in which the evolution of English society was peculiarly influenced by the nature of their interaction. If we are to fully understand the convergence of forces that shaped the nation in the later sixteenth and the seventeenth centuries, we must uncover the processes of change at work in the smaller worlds of county and village. If we

---

[1] This introductory chapter seeks to synthesize the very extensive literature on the economic, administrative, religious, and educational history of early-modern England. To cite every work which has influenced its arguments would be both pointless and obstructive to the reader. We have therefore adopted the convention of providing footnotes only in the case of sources drawn upon for examples, or quoted from directly.

are to make sense of the experience of our village, however, we must begin with that of the nation.

Our theme is that the century and a half between the Reformation and the Revolution of 1688 witnessed, against a background of continuity in some of the principal characteristics of the social structure, a complex of demographic, economic, political, social, and cutural changes that reinforced one another in such a way as to produce two major developments in English rural society. First, there was a significant weakening of the localism of provincial society. There was a slow shift from a situation in which long-active forces of integration were still somewhat weaker than the forces of local autonomy, toward one in which centripetal forces gained precedence. Persisting economic diversity came to reflect specialization within an emerging national economy. Local loyalties and identities slowly gave way before the increased participation of those of yeoman status and above in the political and cultural life of the nation. Second, a new complexity emerged in the social differentiation of rural communities. Such elements of local cultural homogeneity as had overlain the already broad differences of wealth and status between villagers were slowly broken down. They gave place to a more marked differentiation of rich and poor, observable in terms of attitudes, education, and manners. Those at the bottom of the social scale became not simply poor, but culturally different. These interconnected developments might be described as a process of slow incorporation that had both geographical and social dimensions and was highly selective in its impact. Different areas of the kingdom were involved to different degrees and at different times in the overall process of change. Within particular localities the direct impact of change was felt more strongly by particular social groups.

Change of this kind was cumulative rather than catastrophic, selective rather than all-embracing. It left untouched some of the basic features of preindustrial society in England. Indeed, it was to a considerable degree shaped by such persisting structural characteristics. Society remained predominantly agrarian. The conditions of life—in particular its insecurity, its vulnerability to fluctuations in the quality of the harvest or to the ravages of epidemic disease—persisted largely unchanged. The scale of life was generally small. The age-old hierarchies of wealth, status, and power were modified to a degree but survived fundamentally unchanged. All this and more endured; yet there was change. It was considerable and it was significant, for it marked the transition to a new stage in the development of preindustrial society in England. It occurred in response to four principal forces: socioeconomic adjustment to demographic expansion, the integrating influence of a more aggressive state, the impact of religious reformation, and the expansion of educational opportunity. Let us examine each of these factors in turn.

Between 1520 and 1700 the population of England doubled. Estimates of national population are, of course, exceedingly difficult to make, but it seems likely that a total population of perhaps two and a half million in the 1520s had swelled to one of five million by the close of the seventeenth century.[2] More reliable local estimates bear out the general picture. In Cambridgeshire and Essex, in Worcestershire and Shropshire, in Lancashire and Devon, the course of change was broadly similar.

This demographic expansion, coming as it did after a century and a half of stable or declining population, is difficult to explain. It was not an English but a European phenomenon. It seems possible that it resulted from the twin influences of economic conditions favorable to younger marriages and a consequently higher marital fertility, coupled with a drop in mortality rates brought about by a decreased incidence of epidemic diseases in the countryside. But whatever its causes, it continued unabated to the end of the sixteenth century, slowed somewhat in the early decades of the seventeenth century and finally stabilized in the period after 1630. Its consequences were many and varied.

Perhaps the most notable consequence was inflation. Contemporaries who failed in general to appreciate either the extent or the dynamics of population growth were much more sharply aware of the unprecedented price rise. The average prices of foodstuffs in southern England remained fairly stable between 1450 and the early sixteenth century. By the 1540s they had doubled, by the 1570s they had trebled and by the early decades of the seventeenth century they had risen sixfold.[3] While historians continue to debate the role in the price rise of a variety of short-term or secondary factors, there is general agreement that beneath all lay the steady pressure of a prolific population upon inelastic resources. The prices of foodstuffs rose more quickly than did those of manufactured products. The prices of cheaper grains rose more swiftly than did those of dearer grains. Wages limped lamely behind prices in an overstocked labor market. Real wages were probably halved in the period between the Reformation and the Civil War. Those dependent on wages saw their living standards steadily eroded, while in years of harvest failure when prices rocketed their situation became desperate. By the second, third, and fourth decades of the seventeenth century, when prices were at last stabilizing, the situation was such that a student of the problem has called these "among the most terrible years through which the country has ever passed."[4]

A further consequence of demographic expansion was a redistribution of population. The shortage of tenants for holdings, decay of buildings, and

---

[2] J. D. Chambers, *Population, Economy and Society in Pre-Industrial England*, p. 19.

[3] R. B. Outhwaite, *Inflation in Tudor and Early Stuart England*, p. 10.

[4] P. J. Bowden, "Agricultural Prices, Farm Profits and Rents," p. 621.

reversion of arable land to the waste that had characterized much of rural England prior to 1520, and the declining population of some towns, were rapidly reversed. Surplus population that could not be absorbed in crowded fielden parishes was channelled toward those rural areas that retained some capacity to support a greater population. The Cambridgeshire fens, for example, became the most densely peopled part of that county, since their extensive pastures and opportunities for fishing and wildfowling provided a living for families whose tiny holdings of land would have been inadequate for their support in the corn-growing uplands. In the Cumbrian forest of Inglewood, numerous encroachments on the waste produced a multiplicity or marginal agricultural holdings. In Rossendale, Lancashire, the inhabitants survived on subdivided holdings by seeking employment in the expanding domestic textile industry of the area.[5] Here, as elsewhere, the expansion of rural industry was facilitated by the existence of a pool of underemployed cheap labor. But above all the expansion of population stimulated urban growth. The population of Norwich rose from some 12,000 in 1520 to almost 30,000 in 1695, that of Bristol from 10,000 to almost 20,000 in the same period. London increased massively in size, from a city of about 60,000 inhabitants in 1520 to one of almost 600,000 at the close of the seventeenth century—and this despite a death rate which meant that the city needed a constant influx of immigrants merely to maintain numbers.[6]

The concentration of a larger proportion of the national population in either the towns of those "dependent areas" of the countryside unable to fully produce their own foodstuffs, together with the steady inflation of food prices, led to a significant expansion of internal trade in England to supply their needs. Specialized production for the market was stimulated and as a result myriad rural communites were gradually integrated more deeply into broader regional economies centered on the cities. The London food market alone extended its tentacles deep into the home counties and beyond, encouraging specialized market gardening, dairying, and corn production. By the mid-seventeenth century a regular carrying trade had been established between the capital and the rest of the kingdom, pulling in cloth for export, coal for fuel, and food for the teeming population of the metropolis, disseminating other manufactures, fashions, books, news, and ideas. And what London did at a national level, provincial cities did for their smaller hinterlands. Preston extended its influence to whittle away

---

[5] M. Spufford, *Contrasting Communities. English Villagers in the Sixteenth and Seventeenth Centuries*, Chapters 1 and 5; A. B. Appleby, "Agrarian Capitalism of Seigneurial Reaction? The Northwest of England, 1500–1700," p. 578; G. H. Tupling, *The Economic History of Rossendale*, p. 167.

[6] P. Clark and P. Slack, *English Towns in Transition, 1500–1700*, p. 83.

and concentrate the trade of small Lancashire market towns, integrating more fully the economies of highland and lowland Lancashire. Worcester channeled exchange between Bristol and the Severn valley and between the fielden and pastoral regions of its hinterland.[7]

This growing trade was carried on by a swelling army of middlemen of curious appellation: "badgers" and "broggers," maltsters and drovers. They were enterprising and, not uncommonly, hard-fisted bargainers who bought in bulk from farmers and bypassed, if they could, the traditional open market and its regulations. Such men were marginal figures, suspected by both the government and the poor of the areas where they bought up supplies. In years of dearth they were invariably blamed by the one and, on occasion, attacked by the other. But they were both symptomatic of the increasing interdependence of regional economies and important agents of their integration.

The conditions which gave them their opportunity also underlay other changes in rural society. Population pressure created a greater demand both for existing agricultural holdings and for such new holdings as could be taken from the wastes and forests, which tilted the balance of power between landlords and tenants in favor of the former. At the same time the price rise forced landlords to take steps to maintain or improve the real value of their income from rents, while expanded marketing opportunity encouraged them to improve the output of their home farms. Their response varied. Some concentrated on the more efficient exploitation of lands farmed directly. Others granted favorable "improvement" leases to their larger tenants. Many enclosed the open fields and commons of their manors, sometimes against the opposition of their tenants, but commonly with the consent and cooperation of at least the more substantial men among them. Most devoted a good deal of energy to transforming customary medieval tenures into short, frequently renegotiable leases. Most also increased their rents, sometimes reasonably, sometimes drastically. While some gentry families foundered as a result of incompetence, extravagance, or demographic misfortune, most prospered—at least until the later seventeenth century when stabilizing or declining prices placed a new premium upon higher output and reduction of costs. Indeed, the period saw an overall expansion in the absolute numbers of gentle families.

Lower in the social scale, the fortunes of English countrymen depended to a large degree on the balance that was obtained between family subsistence and commercial enterprise in their farming. This in turn depended above all on the size of their landholdings. The yeoman or

---

[7] F. J. Fisher, "The Development of the London Food Market, 1540–1640"; H. B. Rogers, "The Market Area of Preston in the Sixteenth and Seventeenth Centuries"; A. D. Dyer, *The City of Worcester in the sixteenth century*, Chapter 6.

substantial husbandman farming an acreage well in excess of that needed to support his family was excellently placed to prosper, the more so if he held his land by freehold. With a substantial surplus to market he reaped the benefit of the inflation of food prices. Their wills and inventories of goods testify to the prosperity of the yeomanry in every part of England, as does the surviving physical evidence of their farmhouses, many of them extended and reconstructed after 1570. And domestic goods and housing were but part of their expenditure. More went on land, bought up from the unfortunate or the improvident, or rented at market rates to which few of their neighbors could aspire. Some sent their children off to the universities, to trade, or the professions. Others established them on the land—sometimes as gentlemen.

Less fortunate were the smallholders, the mere husbandmen and cottagers who had little enough surplus to market in a good year and none at all in a year of poor harvests. Some prospered if they had the good fortune to be near enough to an urban market to turn their hands to intensive marketgardening or the like. For others, mounting rents wiped out such profits as they made, while a series of bad harvests might even force them to buy their own food at inflated prices, fall behind on their rents, mortgage future crops, and sink into chronic indebtedness. Many failed to survive these pressures and were gradually depressed into the ranks of cottagers or landless laborers, while their lands were snapped up by engrossing yeomen. Margaret Spufford has shown in detail how the failure of this group to survive the indebtedness that resulted from the catastrophic harvests of the 1590s resulted in the polarization of rural society in the fielden parishes of Cambridgeshire. In the fenlands, by way of contrast, the gradual subdivision of their fifteen to forty-five acre holdings in order to meet population pressure kept this group on the land but at a reduced standard of living.[8] Similar long-term processes have been described for other areas of England. They represented a major stage in the disappearance of the English small landholders fully five generations before the age of parliamentary enclosures. Their gradual demise owed less to seigneurial oppression than to their inability to benefit from either the market opportunities or the technical improvements of the age, coupled with their lack of withholding power under pressures slowly forcing or tempting them to sell out. By 1700 much of rural England, though by no means all, had advanced far along the road towards the classic agrarian pattern of the eighteenth century: that of the squire, his tenant farmers, and a vast army of agricultural laborers.

Of those countrymen without land at the beginning of our period, the

---

[8] M. Spufford, *Contrasting Communities,* Chapters 2 to 5.

landless laborers and cottagers, little need be said. Their numbers rose both absolutely and relatively to other social groups, while their real wages steadily fell up to the mid-seventeenth century. The laborers of a part of seventeenth-century Essex were described as "so extream poor that they are scarcely able to put bread in their childrens bellys." They and their fellows formed the majority of those whom Gregory King classed in 1688 as "decreasing the wealth of the kingdom": those, that is, whose necessary expenditure exceeded their pitiful incomes. By then they constituted around half the rural population.[9]

The socioeconomic adjustment to the demographic pressure of the sixteenth and earlier seventeenth centuries thus resulted on the one hand in considerable progress towards the emergence of an integrated national economy but on the other hand in a marked intensification of the existing tendencies towards the polarisation of wealth and poverty. We must now turn to the noneconomic developments that reinforced these changes.

Whether or not there was a "Tudor despotism," it is undoubtedly true to say that the sixteenth and seventeenth centuries saw a considerable augmentation of the effective power of the central government and in particular of its power to control local administration. The monarchs of medieval England had to a large extent created the machinery of centralized monarchical power. Their problem, as the disintegration of the mid-fifteenth century had shown, was that of retaining the service and obedience of their over-mighty subjects among the nobility and through them that of their clientages of county gentry. In this the early Tudors succeeded to a considerable extent. Rebellion, when it appeared, was crushed. A renewed judiciousness in the exercise of royal patronage once more brought the interests of territorial magnates into closer alignment with those of the crown. While they continued to nurse their clientages and to exercise great govermental power, they did so increasingly by the king's license or at the king's command. Indeed, the members of the political nation were brought to heel less by their exclusion from power than by the steady multiplication of the administrative tasks that were entrusted to them and by a continuous governmental pressure for the satisfactory performance of these tasks. The justices of the peace, in particular, began their transition from their role as judges to that of ubiquitous agents of the central government in local administration. Finally, the political unification of the kingdom was completed by the abolition of internal "liberties," the nationalization of the church, the establishment of royal councils charged with the good govern-

---

[9] E. R. O. Q/SR 227/28; J. Thirsk and J. P. Cooper, eds., *Seventeenth Century Economic Documents*, pp. 780–781.

ment of the north and of the Welsh marches and the steady extension of parliamentary representation.

On these foundations the governments of Elizabeth and of the early Stuarts built. In 1569, the last major outbreak of aristocratic rebellion—the rising of the northern earls—was crushed: a fiasco that served as a final reminder that the day of semi-independent magnate power was over. Henceforward even the local power of the nobility was to rest not on the numbers of their armed tenantry but on the influence that they commanded at the center of affairs, on their ability to channel a share of royal power and bounty towards their personal clients. Meanwhile the trend towards the intensification of local administration continued. From the Henrician Reformation to the middle years of James I's reign over eighty regulative statutes were enacted in Parliament and handed down to the justices of the peace for enforcement.[10] Local administrators staggered under the weight of the "stacks of statutes," in Lambarde's phrase, which were piled upon their shoulders: statutes concened with social and economic regulation, with the enforcement of public order at the local level, with the establishment of conformity to the religious changes of the period, and the rest. And yet they gradually learned to enforce them—not as well as the government would have liked, no doubt, but well enough. Throughout the reign of Elizabeth and those of the early Stuarts, local administrators were pressured, exhorted, and reprimanded into more conscientious performance of their duties. Stinging rebukes from the Privy Council were dispatched to the negligent, backed up where necessary with a reshuffle of the commission of the peace. Assize judges, instructed on royal policy before their departure on circuit, delivered, after the awesome ritual of their reception in the counties, their "charge" to the assembled justices and grand jurymen in which they explained royal policy and demanded its effective implementation. They also took note of local diligence in the royal service. Negligent justices of the peace were likely to find themselves excluded from the next commission, while the deserving received the accolade of inclusion.[11]

This process of steadily increasing the burden borne directly by local officials reached its peak under Charles I, with the final establishment in the 1630s of monthly meetings of justices for the better enforcement of the poor laws and of regulative statutes. No better testimony to its long-term results exists than the steadily augmenting bulk of the surviving records of local administration as one passes from the early reign of Elizabeth to that of Charles II—a bulk that speaks volumes for the growing willingness of justices, of lesser officers, and indeed of private individuals to participate in

---

[10] M. W. Beresford, "The Common Informer, the Penal Statutes and Economic Regulation," p. 222.

[11] J. S. Cockburn, *A History of English Assizes, 1558–1714*, Chapter 8.

the "increase of governance." The burdens imposed by Crown and Parliament became gradually accepted, regularized, while their enforcement (though it fluctuated considerably in intensity) involved the activity of an expanded proportion of the upper ranks of society. Between 1625 and 1640, for example, members of 161 out of the 750 gentle families of Yorkshire were involved in local government in the prestigious roles of deputy lieutenant, sheriff, or justice of the peace.[12] Many more served in the humbler offices of high constable, grand juryman, and the like. And below the level of the gentry, the upper ranks of the villages found themselves more active in administration both in traditional offices and in the new offices created by the Tudor statutes: as overseers of the poor, for example. By 1660 the quarter sessions and petty sessions of the king's justices had replaced the seigneurial manor court as the focus of the administrative activity of village notables.

One should not, of course, overestimate the local effectiveness of central authority. Policy still had to pass through a filter of local interests before it found implementation. The relationship between central government and unpaid local officers at all levels involved a constant balancing out of local and national interests. Yet there can be no mistaking the general direction of the trend towards augmented governmental authority and intensified administrative activity. By the later seventeenth century, when governmental pressure was relaxed, a great deal had been achieved and was to endure.

Equally significant was the effect that the increased presence of authority had in stimulating local desire to exercise a voice in the shaping of governmental policy. Grand jurymen not only listened to the charges of the Assize judges, they also presented (sometimes in vehement terms) their own statements of their opinions and grievances. Justices of the peace did not simply implement royal directives. They sought also to influence the policies they were called on to enforce. In their increasingly frequent meetings they formulated the opinion of the county and expressed it in letters to the Council. A wise monarch listened. Moreover some of them made, as well as enforced, laws. The Somerset justices of Charles I's reign, for example, included thirty-two former members of Parliament.[13] In Parliament, an institution that steadily grew in importance and initiative throughout our period, the expanded political nation had its opportunity to express its views on matters of national significance. It was a forum for the expression of grievances, an instrument for the resolution of conflicts. It was national, unlike the provincial estates of some European monarchies. Moreover, it was increasingly educative. Its more frequent meetings in the

[12] J. T. Cliffe, *The Yorkshire Gentry from the Reformation to the Civil War*, p. 233.
[13] T. G. Barnes, *Somerset, 1625-1640. A county government during "the personal rule,"* p. 30.

seventeenth century saw the development of a core of experienced parliamentarians. The more frequent and more commonly disputed elections of the century saw the steady political education of an expanded body of voters. Derek Hirst has suggested that, as the result of the effects of inflation in lowering the property qualification for the county franchise and of the deliberate extension of some borough franchises, perhaps 27–40% of the adult male population had been enfranchised by 1640.[14] Though the small "parochial" gentry and the "middling sort" of town and country might still tend largely to follow the lead of the traditional ruling class in their political activity, they nonetheless enjoyed new opportunities to formulate opinions on national affairs and to express them.

The development of a more effective and more aggressive machinery of government in the sixteenth and earlier seventeenth centuries thus played its part in the integration of the provinces into the nation state. At the same time it transformed both the level and the nature of the administrative and political participation of not only the gentry but also their immediate social inferiors. The cavalry of Fairfax and Cromwell was recruited voluntarily from all over eastern England; its ranks were filled with yeomen farmers who knew what they fought for and loved what they knew.[15] That was a far cry from the semifeudal tenantry who rode from Durham with the northern earls in 1569.

If the "increase of governance" of the sixteenth and earlier seventeenth centuries brought men into closer contact with the state, the Protestant Reformation had an equal, perhaps even a greater, role to play in the incorporation of the nation as the immediate enforcement of the Protestant victory in 1559 gave way to the slow penetration of the provinces by Protestantism. A minority of villages contained a resident justice of the peace. Most, though not all, had a church.

The initial establishment of a broad conformity to the Elizabethan settlement was relatively easily accomplished. It was steadily consolidated by the activities of the ecclesiastical courts in enforcing conformity in church furniture and ritual, in punishing failure to attend church or to participate in the sacraments. Success in the attainment of even these minimum standards of conformity, however, was never total. Weekly church attendance in particular was an unfamiliar ideal to the mass of the population and was rarely wholly achieved at parish level. Moreover, in certain areas—most notably in parts of the northwest—a substantial proportion of the popula-

---

[14] D. Hirst, *The representative of the people? Voters and voting in England under the early Stuarts*, p. 105.

[15] The phrase is, of course, Cromwell's. For the original words, see C. Hill, *God's Englishman. Oliver Cromwell and the English Revolution*, p. 67.

tion remained Catholic. But Catholicism was not the fundamental problem faced by the Anglican Church; nor, for that matter, was Puritanism. More serious was the problem faced by every church of the post-Reformation era, be it Anglican, Lutheran, Presbyterian, or reformed Catholic. This was the task of transforming the devotional habits of the rural population as inherited from the medieval church: of replacing the performance of ritual duties with the internalization of specific theological beliefs, of substituting doctrinal affirmation for ingrained observances as the hallmark of a Christian.

In the case of the Church of England, this task was inhibited by a number of factors. One was the low quality of many of the clergy. Only twelve of the ninety-three clergy of the Archdeaconry of Leicester in 1576, for example, were regarded as having sufficient scriptural knowledge to adequately perform their duties. Many were written off as "utterly ignorant."[16] Again, ignorance of the basic texts of the faith might be compounded by low standards of professional conduct. Too many of the clergy shared too much the mental attitudes and behavioral habits of their flocks to be effective agents of godly reformation. A related problem was that of the inadequacy of clerical stipends. The tithes of many parishes were impropriated by laymen who allowed only a pittance to the vicars of the parishes concerned. Poverty encouraged pluralism and pluralism meant nonresidence. Again, some areas of the kingdom lacked an adequate parochial structure. In Cheshire there were some 500 townships but only seventy parishes. The Lancashire uplands had many vast parishes containing numerous settlements whose inhabitants had little enough contact with the church at all. Admarsh in Bleasdale, Lancashire, as late as 1650 had a chapel but "neither minister nor maintenance and . . . the people thereabouts are an ignorant and careles people knowing nothing of the worship of God, but live in ignorance and superstition and six miles from any church or chapell."[17]

These problems were never fully solved within our period. Nevertheless, considerable advances were made. Above all, there was a steady improvement in the quality of the clergy. Whereas only 19% of the clergy of the diocese of Worcester had been university graduates in 1560, for example, this figure had risen to 23% in 1580, 52% in 1620, and 84% in 1640.[18] Efforts were also made to improve clerical stipends. Bequests came from the pious and concerned. The Puritan feoffees for impropriations attempted the systematic buying up of impropriated tithes for the augmentation of the livings of godly preaching ministers. Their adversary, Arch-

---

[16] W. G. Hoskins, "The Leicestershire Country Parson in the Sixteenth Century," p. 19.

[17] J. S. Morrill, *Cheshire, 1630–1660. County Government and Society During the "English Revolution,"* p. 6; H. Fishwick, ed., *Lancashire and Cheshire Church Surveys*, p. 126.

[18] A. G. Dickens, *The English Reformation*, p. 419.

bishop Laud, planned a not dissimilar effort within the church, though for the benefit of conforming ministers.[19] Meanwhile, both private and official efforts were made to supply ministers and places of worship for the neglected "dark corners of the land." Groups of London merchants banded together to place preachers in their counties of origin. The Earl of Huntingdon, as Lord President of the Council of the North, placed powerful preachers in Yorkshire market towns.[20] Four itinerant "King's Preachers" were established in Lancashire, a county in which lay initiative, either local or on the part of successful emigrants to London, resulted in the building of thirty-eight much needed chapels between 1610 and 1650.[21] These gradual efforts were markedly reinforced between 1645 and 1662 by state action. Godly preachers and money to augment their livings were poured into needy areas by the Puritan governors of the Interregnum. Pluralism was abolished and plans were laid for parochial reorganization and for the building of new churches in order to facilitate church attendance. Though these plans were blasted by the Restoration, it is probably true to say that by 1660 the English parish clergy were of higher quality and were more adequately financed than they had ever been before. Not even the purge of the clergy that followed the Restoration could turn back the clock. Lanterns of learning and piety had been lit to illuminate the dark corners of the land.

This gradual improvement of the quality of the clergy was a matter of considerable significance. For perhaps the first time in their history many parishes gained a resident intellectual. These were men who, as often as not, made some efforts to keep in touch with contemporary religious debates. Again, many of them, be they puritanically inclined or not, were to some degree committed to improving the religious education and moral standards of their flocks. At the same time these frontiersmen of university civilization were backed by a reinvigorated apparatus of ecclesiastical discipline. The church courts, however much they were to become unpopular with their Puritan victims in later years, labored steadily to enforce parochial conformity, to combat magical beliefs and practices, and to inculcate stricter moral standards.

Yet success was always severely limited. Though the preaching ministers winnowed out their converts, they failed in the greater task of winning over the mass of the people to either enthusiastic Protestant devotion (as distinct from virulent anti-Catholicism) or reformation of life. At first they tended to blame their limited progress upon the hangover of "popish ig-

---

[19] C. Hill, *Economic Problems of the Church, from Archbishop Whitgift to the Long Parliament*, Chapters XI and XIV.

[20] C. Hill, "Puritans and 'the dark corners of the land'."

[21] W. K. Jordan, *The Social Institutions of Lancashire*, p. 87.

norance." Next they demanded still more preaching ministers. In time some came identify popular ignorance of scripture and doctrine as the root cause of the limited success of even good preaching and advocated more effective catechizing. Others blamed the distracting and undermining influence of the godless institutions of the popular culture and called for a war on Sunday sports and pastimes, alehouses, and sabbath-breaking. In this they sought to eradicate the customary rivals to the hegemony of the reformed church.

By the turn of the century, however, the tone of clerical comment on the common people was souring. Where they had been prone to see fields ripe for the harvest, hungry sheep left unfed, they tended increasingly to see "silly ignorants" or an "earthly minded" multitude. Their stubborn flocks were people "not able to lift up their mindes to any heavenly meditation" who sat through the plainest, soundest sermons "more like stockes than men, conceiving no more than the very stooles they sit upon." Impervious to godly teaching, they lived "of custom or example or necessity, as beasts do, and not of faith," imprisoned, in Robert Bolton's words, "in the darkness of their natural ignorance and dung of their own corruption."[22]

While the ecclesiastical hierarchy was prepared to content itself with the ritual conformity of the common people, the remedy favored by the more radical preachers was a blend of punishment and preaching, of "sword and words," as they put it. As regards "the stupidity and profaneness of the multitude," advised the preacher Nicholas Proffett in terms only marginally more severe than the norm: "In as much as no instructions noe admonitions will work upon such men, the blueness of the wound might be applied."[23] After the disappointing failure of the pulsating interregnum efforts to implement this policy and the wave of spontaneous profaneness which greeted the king's return in 1660, even this was abandoned. Henceforward, until the advent of Methodism, the incorrigible profanity of the multitude was simply accepted.

Such success as was achieved in building up a firm popular base of informed and committed Protestantism tended to be among particular social groups. The response was readiest among the gentry, the yeomen and craftsmen of the villages, the merchants, tradesmen and artisans of the towns. These were above all those who possessed the education necessary to appreciate the significance of theological niceties and the contrast between biblical precept and popular custom. Of course it was not excusively

[22] The quotations are drawn from R. Baxter, *The Reformed Pastor*, p. 254; N. Bownde, *The Doctrine of the Sabbath plainely layde forthe*, pp. 197, 230; T. F. Merrill, ed., *William Perkins, 1558–1602; English Puritanist, His Pioneer Works on Casuistry*, p. 43; R. Bolton, *Two Sermons Preached at Northampton*, p. 81.

[23] N. Proffett, *Englands Impenitencie under Smiting*, p. 46.

so; there are plenty of examples of godly laborers and servants. But it was an undeniable trend (and one that was by no means peculiar either to England or to Protestantism). This was partial success, but it should not be undervalued. By 1662, after the spiritual efflorescence of the Interregnum, the diversity and vitality of English religion had become too great ever again to be contained within even the flexible walls of the Anglican Church. But we should not mistake the experience of some for that of most. Ralph Josselin, godly minister of Earles Colne, Essex, distinguished in his diary between three groups of parishioners. There was "our society," a group of deeply pious individuals drawn largely, though not exclusively, from among the most substantial villagers. Then came "my sleepy hearers," the great majority of simple church attenders. Finally came "the families that seldom heare"—later distinguished as "the ruder sort."[24] His comments are to a large degree descriptive of the state of English Protestantism as the impulse of the Reformation reached its high-water mark in the 1650s.

If the limited success of the Reformation opened up something of a cultural divide within local communities, that development was at once facilitated and reinforced by the significant spread of educational opportunity and achievement within the period.

Among the gentry the sixteenth century saw the transition from education by service in a noble household to education in grammar schools, private schools, the universities, and the Inns of Court. The ruling class were accommodating themselves both to the humanistic ideal of the cultured ruler and to the simple fact that a degree of educational achievement had become a necessity for the aspirant to office and power, be it local or national. Once in the universities, they rarely pursued the formal curriculum of studies and rarely obtained degrees. They acquired instead a smattering of the classics, some knowledge of modern languages and history, and passed on to the Inns of Court, where they picked up the modicum of legal training which was as important to the justice and landowner as a patina of humanism was to the courtier. This movement was of considerable significance, for by their adoption of formal education in central institutions a firm basis was laid for the growth of a common national culture among the English ruling class. Thus, whereas in 1563 only sixty-three members of Parliament were university educated, the number who had attended Oxford or Cambridge had risen to 161 by 1593 and was to continue to rise. In 1608 one-third of the justices of the peace of Kent had attended university; in 1636, two-thirds. Of the 247 heads of Yorkshire gentry families in 1642, 172 had been university educated, 164 had at-

---

[24] A. Macfarlane, *The Diary of Ralph Josselin, 1616–1683*, pp. 252, 376, 424, 500.

tended the Inns of Court and six had attended Catholic colleges abroad.[25]
The situation in other countries was much the same.

Nor were the gentry the only social group to benefit from the expanding
educational opportunities of the period. The growing numbers of endowed
grammar schools and of parish petty schools provided educational opportunity for children of humbler origins. Over the whole of the sixteenth and
early seventeenth centuries, there was a marked swing of charitable
benefactions toward educational provision. In Lancashire, for example,
there were three endowed schools in 1480, twelve in 1540, twenty-eight in
1600 and fifty-seven in 1660. The endowed grammar schools, however,
which offered a training in humanistic rhetoric and a firm grounding in
religion, were only part of the expansion of educational facilities. Beneath
them in the educational hierarchy were the much more numerous petty
schools which concentrated upon the basic skills of literacy, while still further opportunities were provided by the instruction given at the village
level by the occasional resident schoolmaster or by the clergy. Margaret
Spufford has shown that, while some twenty-three Cambridgeshire villages
had schools in the period 1574 to 1628, a further nine provide continuous
references to the existence of village schoolmasters, while fifty-five more
provide occasional references to schoolmasters. In the diocese of Canterbury, where the major expansion of educational facilities came before 1600,
some 42% of settlements had a school of one kind or another at some point
between 1561 and 1600. In the succeeding forty years, the percentage rose
to exactly 50%.[26]

Such evidence puts beyond doubt the argument that the period saw
something of a revolution in the provision of educational facilities. Yet if
there was an educational revolution, as Lawrence Stone has argued,[27] it
was one that was highly selective socially in its impact. For access to education diminished sharply as the social scale was descended. Education, at
whatever level, cost money and it also cost time. Many families could afford neither for their children. This fact is made abundantly clear by such
research as has been undertaken on the extent of popular literacy in this
period and on its variation between different social groups. The evidence of
subscriptions to the Protestation Oath of 1641, for example, indicates that
adult men were by this time perhaps 66% illiterate overall, though their
performance varied much, not only from region to region but from village

---

[25] M. H. Curtis, *Oxford and Cambridge in Transition, 1558-1642*, p. 59; P. Clark, *English Provincial Society from the Reformation to the Revolution: Religion, Politics and Society in Kent 1500-1640*, p. 206; J. T. Cliffe, *The Yorkshire Gentry*, p. 73.

[26] W. K. Jordan, *The Social Institutions of Lancashire*, pp. 30-71; M. Spufford, *Contrasting Communities*, Chapter 6; P. Clark, *English Provincial Society*, p. 200.

[27] L. Stone, "The Educational Revolution in England, 1560-1640."

to village. This in itself might be seen as a not inconsiderable achievement.
The analysis of wills and depositions providing evidence of the social status
of signatories, however, reveals that while the sixteenth and early seventeenth centuries had seen the annihilation of gentry illiteracy and very
substantial improvements among yeomen and craftsmen, little progress at
all had been made lower in the social scale or among women. The yeomen
of Leicestershire were only 55% illiterate by 1640, but the husbandmen of
that county remained more than 80%, and the laborers and servants more
than 90% illiterate.[28] Similar results have been reported for East Anglia,
Durham, parts of Cambridgeshire and elsewhere.

The inescapable conclusion is that, while a massive breakthrough had
been made in educating the upper strata of society, those below the middling ranks had scarcely been touched. One qualification, however, must
be made to this argument. In the towns the illiteracy of the lower orders
would appear to have been much reduced. David Cressy has found the
laborers and servants of London to have been only 33% illiterate, as compared with the 92% illiteracy of their East Anglian counterparts, in the
years 1580–1640.[29] The obvious conclusion is that urban life provided both
the incentive and the opportunity for the poor to acquire basic reading and
writing skills.

The use to which these new skills were put were many and varied. Some
may have been primarily concerned with the making of bonds and wills
and the keeping of accounts. Reading as a leisure activity, however, must
not be discounted even though cheap works were not yet so available to the
common people as was to be the case in the eighteenth century. The sixteenth and seventeenth centuries had their ballads and almanacs, their
tracts and, above all, their sermons and devotional works. Some were
perhaps beyond both the pockets and the comprehension of those countrymen who could read, but others had their audience. Even the illiterate
might buy ballads and stick them on their cottage walls where literate
neighbors could read them aloud.[30] Almanacs were produced in very large
numbers and presumably had a ready market. There were also those with a
taste for more substantial stuff. As early as 1598 on mercer of Colne in Lancashire had a Bible, two psalm books, a few primers and grammars, eight
volumes of *Aesop's Fables* and a dozen "Catoes" among his stock,
presumably in response to local demand. A Warrington bookseller in 1648

---

[28] We owe these illiteracy figures to the generosity of Dr. R. S. Schofield in allowing us to
quote unpublished material contained in the literacy files of the Cambridge Group for the
History of Population and Social Structure.

[29] D. Cressy, "Education and Literacy in London and East Anglia, 1580–1700," p. 311. We
wish to thank Dr. Cressy for permission to refer to his unpublished dissertation.

[30] Such a practice is described in N. Bownde, *The Doctrine of the Sabbath*, pp. 241–242.

had a stock of over 1200 volumes. It included primers, psalters and Bibles, works of classical literature, a good selection of Puritan sermons and devotional guides, and a stock of the works of Erasmus. Presumably his market was large and extended beyond the local gentry. One Lincolnshire yeoman of the period had a copy of Lyttelton's *Tenures*, doubtless for reference, and the *Canterbury Tales*, certainly for diversion. Adam Eyre, a yeoman farmer of upland Yorkshire who fought in Fairfax's cavalry, had a small library in 1647 that he lent out to his neighbors. It included Dalton's *The County Justice*, which was much in request, several works of astrology by Lilly, a variety of Puritan sermons, Foxe's *Acts and Monuments*, Raleigh's *History of the World*, and Erasmus' *Praise of Folly*. Reading was one of Eyre's principal recreations.[31]

Although the advent of true mass literacy was to await the nineteenth century, there can be no doubt that the educational expansion of the later sixteenth and the seventeenth centuries did much to broaden the cultural horizons of the fortunate minority who were both able and willing to benefit from the new opportunities of the age. By 1700, illiteracy was a characteristic not of lay society as a whole but of the poor.

These various forces of change were not, of course, equally strong in all parts of the kingdom. But they were at least active in the nation at large. Where they acted together they were able to reinforce one another in such a way as to promote integration nationally, but differentiation locally. By the earlier seventeenth century it could be said that England had gone far toward the development of what might almost be termed a series of superimposed cultures. When all due allowance is made for regional variations in conditions, the culture of the gentleman, of the yeoman farmer, of the artisan or laborer was to a large degree the same across the nation. Within particular communities, however, significant differences had emerged between the cultures of these different groups. These might be dampened by deference and social imitation, overlaid by vertical ties of patronage and clientage; they were nonetheless real. It may be doubted whether the parish notables of England, the yeomen and substantial tradesmen, possessed like the gentry a sense of belonging to any social grouping broader than the ruling group of their own locality. Their social identity belonged to a specific local context. But our argument is that they had been detached from the world of their poorer neighbors and assimilated more closely to the interests, attitudes, and values of their social superiors and religious mentors.

---

[31] M. Brigg, "The Forest of Pendle in the Seventeenth Century, Part II," p. 83; W. H. Rylands, "Booksellers and Stationers in Warrington," pp. 72 and 77–115; M. Campbell, *The English Yeoman under Elizabeth and the Early Stuarts*, pp. 266–267.

In putting forward this argument we are not trying to caricature preceding social formations. We hold no sentimental view of village life in the later Middle Ages. In the light of recent research on this period it can scarcely be doubted that village society of the medieval period was both mobile and heavily stratified in terms of wealth, status, and power. Within the local community, social relations seem to have been as marked by conflict as by cooperation.[32] All these well-attested features of village life existed before our period and were to persist throughout it. The continuities of rural society are indeed striking but no less impressive are the discontinuities, and it is with these that we are principally concerned. Our thesis is simply that the sixteenth and seventeenth centuries saw processes at work that gave a new edge to the existing stratification or rural communities, largely by introducing new forms of cultural differentiation. Inequalities of wealth became more marked and produced intergroup conflicts of interest charged with ideological passions. Distinctions of education, religion, attitudes, and manners emerged to reinforce the polarizing effects of demographic and economic development. Changes of great significance took place in English rural society that were to culminate in the sharp dissociation of polite and plebeian cultures of the eighteenth century.[33] What distinguished our period was the conflict and strain of the transitional process. For in these years men and women involved on the winning side had not yet abandoned the struggle to create a social world in their own image.

In the subsequent chapters of this book we shall be concerned with the history of a single village: Terling, in Essex. Only by thus concentrating our attention, we would contend, can we hope to fully taste the subtle blend of continuity and change, to fully capture the processes of transition that made the sixteenth and seventeenth centuries what they were for the common people of the English countryside. We have reviewed the national context within which the particular experience of the villagers or Terling must be placed. Our purpose now is to attempt to recapture that experience and in so doing to give a more human face to the broader processes and interpretative abstractions of historical change.

---

[32] See, e.g., J. A. Raftis, *Tenure and Mobility*; E. B. Dewindt, *Land and People in Holywell-cum-Needingworth*; R. H. Hilton, *The English Peasantry in the Later Middle Ages*; E. Britton, *The Community of the Vill.*

[33] E. P. Thompson, "Patrician Society, Plebeian Culture."

2

PROSPERITY AND POVERTY: THE RURAL ECONOMY OF TERLING

The parish of Terling lies on the undulating boulder–clay plateau of central Essex, some thirty-eight miles from the city of London. Its situation was described in 1597 by the surveyor John Walker as "verye pleasante and comodious," being in "the most principalle parte of the Countye of Essex."[1] "Pleasante and comodious" it undoubtedly was, its lands being fertile and well watered both by the river Ter which bisects the parish from north to south and by numerous springs. Moreover, Terling was fortunate in its neighbors. Two miles to the east lay the busy market and weaving town of Witham. Five miles to the north was Braintree, another market and the nearest of a further belt of weaving towns in the densely-populated north Essex hundreds of Hinckford and Lexden. Maldon, one of the principal ports for the export of Essex grain to London, lay six miles to the southeast of Terling. Chelmsford, the administrative center of Essex and one of the principal market towns on the highway from Colchester to London, lay some five miles to the southwest. These simple geographical facts were to be of profound significance for the economic development of the parish within our period.

In the course of the later sixteenth and the seventeenth centuries, the development of the village economy, like that of the county of Essex

---

[1] Essex Record Office T/M 63.

generally, was shaped by four basic factors. First there were the simple facts of topography and soil type; second, the agricultural technology available to the villagers and the practice of husbandry associated with it; third, the system of landholding inherited from the medieval past; and, finally, the influence of market opportunities. For much of the period of this study the available evidence would suggest that there was little change in the first three of these factors in Essex as a whole. Dr. Hull has characterized the agriculture of the clayland heart of the county in the sixteenth and early seventeenth centuries as based on mixed farming and wheat production for the most part, with smaller areas of specialization being found along the Thames shore (meat production) and the marshy eastern coast (dairy farming).[2] For the later seventeenth century, Dr. Burley finds these established patterns of land use essentially unchanged and goes on to comment that after the modifications introduced at the end of the seventeenth century "the agrarian pattern so determined has persisted until the present day."[3] Agricultural technique was again largely stable. Essex was, for the most part, a county of ancient enclosure. This very fact gave the agriculture of the county an air of precocity in the sixteenth century and made easy the early adoption of convertible husbandry, but does not appear to have stimulated experiment or change in basic husbandry methods before the end of the seventeenth century. Though the early seventeenth century saw the bringing into cultivation of many of the county's numerous parks, only the last years of our period saw the introduction of improved ploughs and undersoil draining, a new preoccupation with methods of improving soil fertility, and efforts to produce fodder crops that would enable more stock to be kept.[4] In regard to the system of landholding, Essex was and remained—by contemporary standards—"a county of large farms interpersed with many smaller ones," while in the seventeenth century there seems clear evidence that the average farm size was growing still larger.[5] From at least the late sixteenth century, most land was held in large units by leasehold and let at market rents. Copyhold tenure remained as a minor element in landholding. The copyholders of Essex were fortunate in that income from copyhold fines and rents was too marginal for many Essex landlords to make efforts to augment the rents or

---

[2] F. Hull, "Agriculture and Rural Society in Essex, 1560–1640," Chapter 3. We would like to thank Dr. Hull for permission to refer to his unpublished dissertation.

[3] K. H. Burley, "The Economic Development of Essex in the Later Seventeenth and Early Eighteenth Centuries," pp. 35, 42. We would like to thank Professor Burley for permission to refer to his unpublished dissertation.

[4] F. Hull, "Agriculture and Rural Society," Chapters 2 and 3; K. H. Burley, "The Economic Development of Essex," pp. 50–62.

[5] F. Hull, "Agriculture and Rural Society," p. 82; K. H. Burley, "The Economic Development of Essex," pp. 45–48.

fines of copyhold land in that manner complained of eleswhere in England.[6]

Such change as did take place in the rural economy of Essex can be very largely attributed to the influence of changing market trends, for while the husbandry of the remaining smallholders of Essex may have been aimed primarily at family subsistence, that of the farmers who held the bulk of the land was emphatically commercial. Little wonder that this should be so when one considers the excellent marketing opportunities that existed to stimulate the Essex farmer. In the northeast of the county lay not only the city of Colchester, but also a belt of densely populated weaving towns. Much more important than these, however, was the steadily growing demand of the London food market. The bulk of the produce that traveled along the highways of Essex was bound for the capital city. Still more was shipped from the numerous havens of the county's long coastline. London demand during the long inflationary trend of the sixteenth and early seventeenth centuries underlay the prosperity of Essex farmers in those years. Competition for the London market during the years of sagging prices after 1650 stimulated the efforts to reduce costs and improve efficiency thereafter.[7]

Terling shared fully these characteristics of the rural economy of Essex. Though the village lay close to the weaving town of Braintree, its own economy in the sixteenth and seventeenth centuries was almost wholly agricultural. This point is abundantly demonstrated by a survey of occupations in Terling in this period. A search of the entire range of documents available for the village, for the century and a half after 1550, yields specific occupational designations for over 400 individual villagers below the rank of gentleman. Of these, only one was a weaver and one other a clothier.

This occupational survey is of real, though strictly limited, usefulness. It must be said immediately that it provides a collection of occupations rather than a statistically meaningful sample, and that the sources providing details of occupation are socially biased in different ways—wills toward the middling and upper ranks of village society, court records toward the lowest ranks. Nevertheless it is useful in giving an impression of the range of occupations recognized in the village, though to go beyond this to quantify the relative proportions of villagers employed in different ways would be to strain the evidence. A number of general points can be made.

Women are rarely accorded specific occupational designations. The few who appear in our survey were either female servants, alehousekeepers, or

---

[6] F. Hull "Agriculture and Rural Society," Chapters 7, 8, 9.

[7] F. Hull, "Agricultural and Rural Society," Chapters 4 and 5; K. H. Burley, "The Economic Development of Essex," Chapters 2 and 8.

midwives. Women were presumably engaged for the most part either in domestic work or in unspecialized agricultural labor. Though it might have been expected that some might be involved in the spinning of yarn for the looms of the nearby cloth townships, there is no firm evidence that this was the case. The term "spinster" seems to have implied no more than an unmarried woman in Terling.

Male occupations can be broken down into three broad groups: those directly involved in agriculture (yeomen, husbandmen, laborers, and male servants in husbandry); a handful of professional men (clergymen, schoolmasters, the parish clerk); a mixed bag of ancillary crafts, trades, and services. Of the first group little more can be said save that it provided the great bulk of occupations recovered for the entire period surveyed and that the impression given is that permanent agricultural laborers rather than living-in male servants provided the bulk of the labor force of the farms of the parish. Of the professions it can be noted that the range of professional services available in the village was minimal and that, in the first half of the period at least, the clergy were also engaged in agriculture. Craftsmen and tradesmen can be further broken down into subgroups. There were those involved in the manufacture and maintenance of agricultural equipment—blacksmiths, carpenters, wheelwrights and ploughwrights, coopers, and millwrights. A second group was composed of those involved in the processing or retailing of foodstuffs—millers, butchers, maltsters, and alehousekeepers being present throughout the period studied, while a grocer and several shopkeepers made their appearance in the later seventeenth century. Those concerned with the provision of clothing—tailors, shoemakers, tanners, and glovers—are found throughout the period. The building trades—bricklayers, masons, a tiler, and a plumber—are found mostly in the early seventeenth century. Finally, scattered at random over the whole period are a variety of miscellaneous occupations—ropemaker, cutler, barber, chandler, and even "fiddler," for example.

The economic activities of some of these craftsmen and tradesmen seem sometimes to have been very largely, if not wholly, confined to their particular trade—especially where this involved a skill that one might expect to have been in constant demand as, for example, with some carpenters and blacksmiths. The available evidence, however, would suggest that this was not usually the case. The more prominent tradesmen can frequently be shown to have owned or held land that they either worked themselves or let to others. Daniel Wilshire was both a yeoman and a butcher in the 1630s; John Aldridge an innkeeper and a farmer at the same period. Mathew Raven, one of the biggest farmers of the later seventeenth century, was nonetheless designated a "tanner" for much of his life. Multiple occupations of this kind were commonest among the wealthier tradesmen who had diversified their activities, and the poorer men who had to make shift by turning their hands to many tasks. Thus in the lower reaches of the social scale we have Edward Melford, laborer and fiddler; John Clark, laborer and cowleech; William Thompson, laborer, cooper, and tinker; Mathew Mitchell, laborer, tailor, and alehousekeeper. Alehouse-keeping was an employment involving many of the poor at the turn of the sixteenth and seventeenth centuries. Some had become licensed alehouse-keepers in widowhood or old age, while others operated as unlicensed alesellers for brief periods from time to time when they were able to raise the small capital necessary to set themselves up. Essentially, many of the poorer "tradesmen" were almost certainly agricultural laborers for much of the year and they were sometimes so described by outsiders or social superiors such as sessions clerks, gentlemen, clergymen, and overseers of the poor. When described by themselves or by their closer neighbors, however, they aspired to the dignity of a craft or a skill. This recognition of individual worth was accorded by those close enough to the laboring poor to see them as more than an undifferentiated mass.[8]

Terling was then an entirely agricultural village. The nature of that agriculture can be firmly, if only briefly, sketched in. In the first place, the lands of the parish were of good quality, lying on the boulder–clay plateau which was the heartland of mixed farming in Essex. In the second place, the parish was entirely enclosed. All references to arable, pasture, and meadow in the various records of landholding are unanimous in referring only to "closes" and there is no evidence of any form of communal husbandry. The map drawn in 1597 of the principal manor of Terling Place shows a crazy quilt of fields surrounding the village, manor house, and park, all held in severalty and half of them over ten acres in size.[9] The precise proportions devoted to arable or pasture at any given point in time are hard to assess. In the mid-nineteenth century some 500 acres out of a parish of about 3000 acres was given over to pasture, while there were 185 acres of woodland.[10] In the seventeenth century, after a substantial part of the park of 1597 had been leased out to a farmer, it would appear that the situation was not dramatically different. The only precise information on the proportions of arable and pasture comes in a description of the farm held by John Fletcher

---

[8] A more discipline estimate of the proportions of village men primarily involved in particular occupations in the eighteenth century can be obtained from the parish registers for the years 1754–60, when occupations were regularly recorded. Farmers, yeomen, and husbandmen, 37.5%; craftsmen and tradesmen, 6.25%; laborers, 56.25%. These figures described a situation little removed from that obtaining in the later seventeenth century.

[9] E. R. O. T/M 63.

[10] C. A. Barton, *Historical Notes and Records of the Parish of Terling, Essex*, p. 139.

in 1614. It contained 237 acres of arable, twenty-one of pasture, and three of meadow.[11] Elsewhere, surveys, rentals, and wills show a marked tendency to speak of "arable and pasture" in describing holdings, all of which suggests the practice of convertible husbandry, as does the will of John Godbold of 1672 which mentions "two fields . . . newly laid for pasture."[12] If this interpertation is correct, then doubtless the acreage given to pasture varied from time to time.

Whatever the proportion of the land under grass at any given point in time, animal husbandry in Terling was supplementary, though complementary, to the main business of the farmers of the parish, grain production. Terling, unfortunately, lacks more than a handful of the inventories of goods that have proved so valuable to agrarian historians for the reconstruction of local husbandry. The wills of the villagers do, however, mention crops and stock sufficiently often and in sufficient detail for a clear picture to emerge. With the single exception of an early will that refers to peas, the field crops mentioned by testators are invariably of grain. Over time, there is clear evidence of a change in the nature of the principal grain crop. Before 1570 both barley and wheat are mentioned equally commonly, while in the very earliest wills barley appears to be the principal crop. After 1570 it is clear that wheat has come to the fore, barley being mentioned less often. It is difficult to interpret this change other than as a response to the demands of the market. The wills further clarify that grain production was complemented by the keeping of a good number of sheep and smaller numbers of cattle and pigs. These findings from sixteenth- and seventeenth-century wills alike are confirmed by a tithe account of 1713 that lists flocks of up to eighty sheep, herds of up to thirty cattle and numerous pigs.[13] The produce of this corn–sheep husbandry was further supplemented by that of the orchards (usually of apple trees) and gardens, frequently mentioned in wills and deeds and visible on the 1597 map.

As will be evident from this brief description of the husbandry of Terling, this was a parish well able to feed itself with grain, meat, milk, butter, and cheese. As will be equally evident, mere subsistence was not the main concern of any but the smallest of Terling's farmers, for there is good evidence that they were deeply involved with the market. This evidence is of various kinds. In the 1560s the rent of one farm was to be partly paid in "good, sweet and marchantable" wheat and barley. In 1574, one Terling yeoman was prosecuted for engrossing large quantities of grain, butter, and cheese for export, while the same year provides an incidental reference to the fact that another had contracted to supply hides in large numbers to a

[11] E. R. O. D/DRa T 59.
[12] E. R. O. D/ACR 9/127.
[13] E. R. O. T/B 54.

Bardfield tanner. The surveyor of 1597 made pointed reference to the "goodly Market Townes" that lay near to the parish, while the late sixteenth and early seventeenth centuries provide several cases of complaints of decay in the roads to Braintree, Witham, and Chelmsford, which hindered the inhabitants in their marketing. In 1590, for example, some were "greatly annoyed and some hurt with the overthrow of a cart" on the way to Braintree. In 1636, a confidence trickster from Southminster successfully persuaded a Kelvedon dealer to part with money for a large quantity of grain (which failed to materialize) by pretending to be a yeoman from Terling. Clearly the dealer found his story plausible. Finally, two Terling men were accused by the inhabitants of Chelmsford in 1647 of buying up butter and cheese by the cartload in nearby parishes to sell in Chelmsford at profits of almost 50% on a pound (much of this produce being bought up in Chelmsford by London dealers), and Terling men were again prosecuted for marketing offences in Chelmsford in the 1690s.[14] These odd references and incidents serve to point up the various opportunities open to the farmers of a parish well-placed geographically and well-adapted in its husbandry to benefit from the expanding opportunities for profit that the age afforded.

Opportunity certainly existed, but the ability to take advantage of it depended upon access to the land—and to a substantial acreage, at that. Dr. Bowden has calculated that an arable farmer of thirty acres in the conditions of the early seventeenth century might make an annual net farming profit in normal years of some £14–£15, ensuring a margin of £3–£5 once the subsistence needs of his family were met: "a tolerable, though by no means easy existence." In bad harvest years, this margin would be wiped out and the small farmer might be forced to dip into savings or else fall into debt. Only the man farming between fifty and one hundred acres could regard himself as not only secure from such misfortune but even likely to profit from the soaring prices of dearth years. In more normal years, on the other hand, the profit margins of the bigger farmer, who of necessity employed labor and thereby had greater production costs, would depend largely upon the extent to which he was able to keep down labor costs, adopt methods to improve his yields, or both.[15] The husbandman needed land; the yeoman farmer needed both land and cheap labor and aspired to improvement.

Essex, as has already been observed, was a county of large farms. On the manors sampled by Dr. Hull, some two-thirds of the available land was

---

[14] Public Record Office Req. 2 107/47; E. R. O. Assize Calendar 35/17/2/55; E. R. O. D/ACA 3 fo. 84; E. R. O. Q/SR 112/70, 127/23, 157/19, 272/25, 304/57, 332/106, 435/33, 440/73, 443/34.

[15] P. J. Bowden, "Agricultural Prices, Farm Profits, and Rents," pp. 657–663.

farmed in units of over fifty acres, this pattern being particularly marked in the southern and central areas of the county.[16] Terling was no exception to this general picture. The land of the parish was divided between five manors—again, not an unusual situation in Essex. The manors of Terling Place, Ridley Hall, Terling Hall, and Ringers each included demesne, copyhold, and freehold land, while the manor of Ockendon Fee consisted entirely of freeholds. The surviving records of these manors for the seventeenth century allow a full account to be made of freehold and copyhold land and reveal that there were some 450 acres of freehold (16% of the arable, pasture, and meadow of the parish) and some 250 acres of copyhold (approximately 9%). The remainder formed the demesne lands of the four larger manors, over half belonging to the manor of Terling Place.[17]

By the 1690s, for which period an estate survey survives, the demesne lands of the manor of Terling Place were being let out in five large farms—the smallest over one hundred acres, the largest over 300 acres—in addition to which several smaller parcels of land were separately let. Incidental references to particular farms suggest that this pattern was already established—certainly in the 1660s and probably in the 1610s also. The only major change that can be pointed to in the seventeenth century was that much of the park stocked with game, which is shown on the 1597 map of the manor, was also being leased out to a farmer by the 1690s. Whether these circumstances also prevailed in the sixteenth century is impossible to say. Two leases of 1581 and 1582 of closes, which were later incorporated into larger farms, provide a suggestion that demesne land may have been leased in smaller units of thirty to sixty acres at that time, but this is a suggestion only, based on scraps of evidence. For the seventeenth century, at least, the pattern of large-scale farms held sway.

References to the terms on which demesne land was leased are few but are unanimous in showing that at the end of the sixteenth and in the early seventeenth centuries a twenty-one year lease was the norm. Details of rents are equally sparse but it is clear that throughout the seventeenth century, market rents were charged on the farms of the manor Terling

---

[16] F. Hull, "Agriculture and Rural Society," p. 81.

[17] These manors included some land lying outside the parish of Terling. Such outlying land has been excluded from consideration. The following discussion of landholding in Terling is based on the surviving tolls, surveys, and rentals of the manors of Terling Place (E. R. O. D/DM M 170; D/DQS 64; T/M 63; T/P87), Ringers (E. R. O. D/DRa M 79), Terling Hall (E. R. O. D/DRa M 89, 90), Ockendon Fee (E. R. O. D/DRa M 91–94), and Ridley Hall (E. R. O. D/DRa M 98, 102–4). These have been supplemented with the available deeds of the parish (E. R. O. D/DRa T 59–251), with the wills of the villagers (as listed in F. G. Emmison ed., *Wills at Chelmsford*, vols. I and II) and with taxation records (P. R. O. E 179 110/419, 111/509, 111/523, 112/588, 112/607, 112/638).

Place—about 6s. 8d. per acre per annum in the first two decades of the seventeenth century and varying between 4s. and 9s. per acre per annum in the 1690s on different farms. In both the 1620s and the 1690s, it would appear that the smaller the farm, the higher the rent but, in the absence of details of land quality and use, one hesitates to say more. As with the question of units leased, there is a little evidence that conditions may have been different in the sixteenth century. One lease of 1581 was clearly granted for three lives in return for a fine and then a small annual rent of about 1s. per acre. If a change had taken place to larger annual rents, however, it had been accomplished before the first decade of the seventeenth century. Of the demesne farms of the smaller manors little can be said, save that they also were of substantial size—over one hundred acres where information is available.

Examination of the freehold lands of the parish presents a somewhat different picture. In the seventeenth century, almost two-thirds of the freehold land was held in six units of middling size—two of about sixty acres and four of about forty acres. The rest consisted of a patchwork of small units, mostly under eight acres in size. On the manors of Terling Place, Ridley Hall, and Ockendon Fee, the court rolls show that the annual rents of freeholders were nominal and that the relief paid by new tenants was equal to one year's rent.

Copyhold land was clearly a marginal element on all the Terling manors, though equally clearly it was of great significance to the small husbandman. The overall acreage of copyhold was small but, even so, it was not evenly distributed among tenants. On the manor of Terling Place in 1597, 136 acres were held by seventeen tenants. Of these, one held over fifty acres and six held between five and fifteen acres. The others held small plots more in the nature of allotments than of holdings on which to support a family. Of the eighty acres of copyhold on the two manors of Ringers and Terling Hall, the Wistock family held almost a third at the turn of the sixteenth and seventeenth centuries. Only one other holding seems to have been of any size.

Most copyholders, then, were small husbandmen who must often have needed to supplement their income from husbandry in order to subsist (or alternatively whose land supplemented an income based on laboring or a craft); hence, the multiple occupations that can be ascribed to some of them. Their lives can scarcely have been comfortable, but at least they were spared in general from rent exploitation. Annual rents for the copyhold lands of Ridley Hall in 1678 ranged from 4d. to 1s. 6d. per acre only, while three of the four tenants were expected to provide their lord with three days' work in corn harvest, three in hay harvest, and three during weeding and to pay him one hen at shrovetide and fifteen eggs at

Easter! This extraordinary survival of the medieval past is perhaps indicative of the lack of attention paid by the landlord to his tiny income from copyhold land. It sits uneasily with the leasing policy of the demesne farms. On the manor of Terling Place, copyhold was more extensive and the income from fines and rents, though small, was not negligible. Entry fines seem to have been arbitrary but were not high, and annual rents per acre were low in comparison with demesne land—standing at about 6d. to 9d. an acre in 1597. There is some evidence of an upward trend in the copyhold rents of this manor—one holding paying 6d. an acre per annum in 1597, for example, yielded 1s. an acre after 1610—but such increases can be regarded as reasonable by contemporary standards.

In proceeding further with the discussion of landholding in Terling, we are very much limited by the nature of the surviving evidence. The manorial surveys, rentals, and rolls for the various manors cannot, unfortunately, be brought together in order to provide a full cross section of landholding at any one point in time. Nevertheless, the broad picture is clear enough and can be briefly reemphasized. Most of the land of the parish was in the hands of perhaps ten large farmers holding by lease and paying market rents. In addition, there were a number of smaller leasehold farms and half-a-dozen fairly substantial freehold farms. Finally there came a varying but quite large number of small holdings held by free or copyhold tenure.[18] Only a combination of surveys and rolls, which would yield not only a full profile of landholding but also details of subtenancy, would fully reveal the manner in which the smaller men pieced together the holdings that they worked. Of this, we have only tantalizing glimpses. William Burchard, for example, held in 1632 five acres of freehold and also two acres of copyhold on the manor of Ridley Hall, in addition to one-and-a-half acres of freehold on Ockendon Fee. Such detail is unfortunately beyond us for the most part, but serves to show that the small patches of land available to the husbandman were not held individually. Even if they had been, it seems improbable that more than half the adult men in seventeenth-century Terling could have held land other than the garden plots attached to houses and cottages. The smallholders or petty craftsmen needing occasional laboring work to eke out a living, and the larger group of wholly landless laborers lived in symbiosis with the gentry rentiers and

---

[18] The evidence of landholding within the parish of Terling must, of course, be qualified by the fact that some of the villagers (in particular the relatively wealthy) also held land in other parishes that might be either let out or farmed directly by them. The yeoman farmer Jeremy Cosen, for example, had eighty acres in neighboring Hatfield Peverel as well as his farm in Terling in 1634. (E. R. O. Q/SR 285/12).

the yeomen farmers or freeholders who formed the elite of rural society in Terling.

This broad pattern of landholding was already established by the end of the sixteenth century, when the documentation becomes fuller, and showed an essential stability during the seventeenth century. Such modification as took place affected mainly the freehold land and can be interpreted as a consolidation of the tenant system within the parish. This process is revealed in the evidence that an increasing proportion of non-demesne land was gradually passing out of the hands of peasant cultivators and into the hands of the gentry. The beginnings of this process may have belonged to the later sixteenth century. In 1567, fifteen villagers had owned sufficient land to be taxed on it in the subsidy of that year. In 1599, only eight villagers were taxed on land, and this number was repeated in 1600 and 1629. Subsidy assessments, however, are notoriously problematic sources, and this evidence is introduced only for the sake of raising the question of whether some consolidation of ownership might have taken place in the later sixteenth century. The course of change in the seventeenth century is much clearer. The manorial records make it plain that, while some freehold and copyhold land had been held by frequently nonresident gentry who let it to villagers from the beginning of our period, their share of such land was increasing over time. A good proportion of Terling freehold was on the manor of Ockendon Fee, for which a complete series of records survives. In 1601, gentlemen held 14% of this land; in 1632 they held 67% and in 1670 the proportion had reached 94%, falling to 90% in 1705. For other manors the position is less clear, though on the manor of Ringers at least 75% of the freehold was in gentry hands by 1650. On Terling Hall, half of the freehold and half the copyhold land was held by gentry by the early eighteenth century but it is hard to say how long this had been so. Ridley Hall seems to have been less affected than other manors by this process.

In the case of the land affected on Ockendon Fee and Ringers, it is possible to show quite clearly that this land had been held in 1600 by owner–occupiers, yeomen, and husbandmen whose names will recur in this book: Richard Mason, Robert Hare, Richard Gaymer, and John Wood, for example. By 1670 it was held by the tenants of gentry owners. Again, in both cases, the period of change seems to have been the first three decades of the seventeenth century. In every case the land concerned had passed by sale, though the circumstances prompting yeoman and husbandman families to sell and gentlemen to buy are unknown in detail. There was, as we shall see, an active market for small landholdings in seventeenth-century Terling. It may be indicative of both the pressures and the opportunities of the period that over time it resulted in the transfer of ownership from small farmers to gentlemen rentiers. Some of the land involved may have been added onto larger farms—there were a number of prosecutions under the statute against the erection of cottages without four acres of land in the 1620s, such evidence often being indicative of the consolidation of holdings.[19] Most, however, seems simply to have been let out to tenants. There was little enough need or opportunity for the consolidation of further large farms in this parish. What we see, rather, is the consolidation of the *tenant system*, a decline of the independent yeomen freeholders and the metamorphosis of their successors into tenant farmers.

This process becomes clear only because of the opportunity afforded by some records to take stock at particular points in time. For the rest, the evidence of land transmission presents a bewilderingly volatile picture for, in contrast to the relative stability of the broad pattern of landholding, the pace of turnover of land from family to family was intense. By bringing together manorial records, deeds, and wills it proved possible to trace the turnover of approximately half the freehold and one-quarter of the copyhold land in the parish over the period about 1600 to about 1700.

The twenty-one freehold holdings traced experienced a total of 118 changes of ownership in the course of the seventeenth century, some changing hands as rarely as twice, eleven changing hands six or more times. The six copyholds changed hands a total of thirty-six times, two changing hands four times, the others witnessing five, six, seven, and ten transfers of ownership. The nature of these changes of ownership is of some interest. Inheritance by children, widows, siblings, or other kin of the owner accounted for 52% of the freehold and 55% of the copyhold transfers of ownership. Marriage to a widow or an heiress was involved in 11% of freehold and 3% of copyhold transfers. Thirty-five percent of freehold and 39% of copyhold transfers were simply by sale. Finally, two of the freehold (2%) and one of the copyhold transfers (3%) resulted from mortgage foreclosures.

On both free- and copyhold, sale was almost as significant a factor as inheritance in the transmission of land. This suggests either that the attachment of the villagers to particular landholdings was not strong, or that the pressure upon the small landowner to sell was intense in this period—or perhaps both. In fact, not a single freehold or copyhold holding in this sample remained "in the name" in the sense of passing by inheritance in the male line. Only two freeholds and one copyhold remained within the same family in 1700 as in 1600, however broadly one defines it. All three of these holdings originally belonged to the Burchard family. They passed twice by marriage to an heiress and ended by being owned by a great-grandchild

---

[19] E. R. O. Q/SR 227/24; Assize Calendar 35/71/H/90, 92.

resident in Little Baddow, five miles from Terling. For the rest, there were very few examples of either a freehold or a copyhold holding remaining in the same family for more than two generations, though two generations on the same land was not uncommon. Inheritance by an heir who in a number of years would sell the land was a common pattern. The turnover of Terling's small farmers was, in fact, as rapid as that of the merchant classes of sixteenth- and seventeenth-century cities.[20] The impression gained is that the important thing was to have land. The question of which bit of land was of little importance. As we shall see, many children left Terling early to make their own way in the world. Many were married and set up elsewhere when their fathers died; they were often happy enough to sell their inheritance in order to raise cash to consolidate the positions they had carved for themselves elsewhere. There is abundant evidence that Terling villagers wished to see their children independently established in life and at a social level akin to that of their parents. Whether their own seed remained on their own land seems to have been of no real significance to them.

We have, then, a community wholly agricultural, practicing mixed farming in enclosed fields and supplying grain, and to some extent dairy produce, for both local and distant markets. The various elements of rural society have been identified as gentry landowners (some resident, some not), large-scale tenant farmers, a number of independent yeomen farmers whose independence was giving way to tenant status, craftsmen, small husbandmen, agricultural laborers, and servants in husbandry. This brief account of the village economy has been provided primarily in order to set in context the discussion of the changing patterns of social relations in Terling which is the principal theme of this study. It must now be complemented by an analysis of the distribution of wealth and of living standards in Terling that will enable us to delineate the broad shape of village society, to assess the relative size of the various groups that existed within it, and to gain some insight into their varying economic experience.

The examination of the distribution of wealth is, of course, only one way of looking at the structure of local society. Nevertheless, it is an essential prolegomenon to the discussions of status, power, and interpersonal relations that will follow in later chapters. Evidence of the distribution of wealth survives primarily in a number of taxation assessments that were sufficiently comprehensive to include representatives of most of the village families. The application of this criterion immediately excludes the use of most of the Subsidy assessments of the sixteenth and seventeenth centuries,

---

[20] P. Clark and P. Slack, *English Towns in Transition, 1500–1700*, pp. 117–120.

which included only a minority of the wealthier villagers. We are left with the snapshots of the distribution of wealth provided by the returns of assessment for the "Great Subsidy" of 1524/5 and for the Hearth Tax levied a century and a half later.

The Lay Subsidy of 1524/5 is outstanding among sixteenth-century taxes in that it involved a genuine attempt to take account of the whole taxable wealth of the kingdom. It was based on an assessment by the most substantial inhabitants of the villages of individual wealth of one of three kinds (whichever promised the greater yield in individual cases). These were lands to an annual value of £1 or more, the capital value of goods worth £2 or more (excluding standing corn and personal attire) and finally the wages of those aged sixteen years or over which amounted to or were in excess of £1 per annum. The tax was virtually a poll tax on those above the age of sixteen, and, in the words of a recent scholar, "it is probably safe to assume that a picture of England based on the lay subsidy returns, while neither complete nor accurate in all its details, does reflect some of the major elements in the distribution of wealth in the 1520s."[21]

Essex was one of the richest counties of England as measured by the yield of this tax, and within Essex the half-hundred of Witham, which included Terling, was one of the richer divisions of the county. Within the half-hundred of Witham, Terling was one of the wealthier villages in terms of both total tax yield and tax yield per taxpayer.[22] Thus Terling was one of the wealthier rural communities in the England of Wolsey and Henry VIII. In all, eighty-five men and three widows from Terling paid this tax, ten being assessed on land, forty-nine on goods, twelve on wages, and seventeen on "ernyngs."[23] The distinction made by the assessors between wages and earnings would appear to have been a real one. Those persons assessed on wages appear in small groups placed immediately after the names of substantial taxpayers. Thus, four of them follow the name of Robert Frank who was assessed on goods to the value of £31, two more follow John Boosy, Senior, who paid on goods worth £10, and so on. All persons assessed on wages can be accounted for in this way, whereas those paying on earnings are almost all grouped at the end of the list of taxpayers. These facts suggest the hypothesis that the tax list is to some extent hierarchically arranged and that those paying on wages were living-in farm servants, whilst those paying on earnings were agricultural laborers, the lowest

[21] J. Sheail, "The Regional Distribution of Wealth in England as Indicated in the Lay Subsidy Returns of 1524/5," pp. 16–17, 22–23, 30, 33–34, 73. We would like to thank Dr. Sheail for permission to refer to his unpublished dissertation.

[22] J. Sheail, "The Regional Distribution of Wealth in England," pp. 188–189, and Gazetteer.

[23] P. R. O. E 179 108/154.

stratum of the *permanent* population. This hypothesis receives further support from the will of Robert Frank's father, dated 1522; of the four wage
earners listed after Robert Frank in 1524, two of them are named in his
father's will as receiving small legacies of the kind sometimes left to servants.[24] The assessment suggests that the farms of Terling in 1524 were
worked with the assistance of twelve servants in husbandry and seventeen
laborers. Wage earners already made up slightly more than one-third of the
male taxpayers as a whole. Putting it another way and excluding assumed
servants, laborers constituted about one-quarter of the settled male taxpayers.

Wills and other incidental information can assist in the interpretation of
the distribution of wealth revealed in the tax list as a whole. Starting at the
top, two men paid on lands to the value of over £50 per annum; both were
gentlemen of the Rochester family, the only resident gentry in 1524/5. Next
came seven men assessed on goods to the value of between £10 and £31.
One of these men farmed the demesne of the Manor of Terling Hall, while
another is known to have possessed at least sixty acres of freehold land.
These men were probably large farmers, the greater yeomanry of the
parish. Another seven taxpayers paid on goods (or, in one case, lands) to
the value of five to eight pounds. By analogy with Margaret Spufford's findings for Cambridgeshire, these may perhaps have been fairly substantial
yeomen; [25] only one of these men kept servants.

Below this level the pyramid of wealth began to broaden. Twenty-one
taxpayers paid on goods or land valued at between £2 and £5. Of these,
two left wills that included bequests of grain and stock. Were these perhaps
the lesser yeomen, greater husbandmen and more substantial craftsmen? A
further twenty-one taxpayers paid on goods or wages of £2 exactly. Two of
them left houses in their wills; one had a freehold croft. These were most
probably small husbandmen, craftsmen, and principal servants—bailiffs in
husbandry, for example. Finally, thirty men paid on land, wages, and earnings of under £2. Of the five landowners in this category, three were young
men of the Boosy family who had been left a toehold on the land; the other
two were aged and perhaps retired men who had relatives higher up the
ranking of wealth. The remainder were servants and laborers, only one of
whom seems to have had kin higher up the social scale. On the basis of this
interpretation and *excluding assumed servants*, the list of taxpayers can be
divided up (in a manner which must, of course, be somewhat arbitrary) to
suggest the following broad socioeconomic levels or categories:

---

[24] E. R. O. D/ACR 2/128.
[25] M. Spufford, *Contrasting Communities*, pp. 34–36.

Category	Wealth assessment	Social position	Number and percentages of taxpayers	
I	£10–£54 land or goods	Gentry and very large farmers	9	11.8
II	Over £2–£8 land or goods	Yeoman, substantial husbandmen, and craftsmen	28	36.8
III	£2 goods	Husbandmen, craftsmen	18	23.7
IV	Under £2 land or earnings	Laborers, cottagers	21	27.6
Total			76	99.9

This breakdown of the taxpayers into four broad categories was originally arrived at out of a sense of its appropriateness as a simplification of the finely graded hierarchy of wealth and social position within the village. It is also valuable as a basis for comparison with the recognizably similar, yet very significantly modified, picture that results from analysis of the Hearth Tax assessment of 1671.

Several Hearth Tax assessments for Terling survive for the years 1662 to 1673, of which that of 1671 is undoubtedly the best both for Terling and for the county of Essex as a whole. This superiority derives from the fact that the listing of 1671 alone includes the names of those householders excused from payment on the grounds of their chronic poverty. The completeness of the list of householders in the case of Terling can be easily demonstrated by comparison with some near contemporary accounts of payments by the overseers of the poor of the parish. All those receiving relief from the overseers appear on the tax list among the excused householders.[26]

The assessment of 1671 has been analyzed by Dr. Burley in such a way as to highlight the variations in the incidence of severe poverty within the county of Essex as a whole. Overall, he finds that some 38% of Essex householders were excused from the tax for poverty, though the experience of different disricts varied from the 23.2% excused in the south of the county to the 53.2% excused in the weaving districts of the north of Essex. The central area in which Terling lay was relatively fortunate in that 30.4% of householders were considered too poor to pay.[27] In Terling itself, forty out of 122 listed householders were excused (32.8%). These can confidently be taken to have been the chronically poor since the assessment of 1673, though not giving the names of persons excused, gives the criterion on which the Terling assessors based their judgment as those "that receves

---

[26] E. R. O. Q/R Th 5; D/P 299/5/A, fo. 3v.
[27] K. H. Burley, "The Economic Development of Essex," p. 335.

constant allmes therfore omitted."[28] Whatever Terling's relative position in comparison with other villages, the problem of poverty in 1671 was severe. One household in three was unable to maintain itself without recourse to charity. These cold statistics convey something of the reality of seventeenth-century life that needs no verbal embroidery.

Turning to the assessment as a whole, it is clear that the number of hearths on which individual householders were assessed provides a guide to housing standards within the village, ranging from the twenty-hearth mansion of the squire, Robert Mildmay, to the one-hearth cottages of the poor. Again, the assessments provide a broad guide to the relative wealth of the villagers. Margaret Spufford has argued convincingly that "in general an incontrovertible association existed between wealth and house size" and that Hearth Tax assessments can provide "a guide to status and wealth in general."[29] In the case of Terling, comparison of the 1671 assessment with other independent evidence of social standing, wealth, and poverty provides a number of exceptions among the middling ranks of village society but satisfactorily upholds the general validity of Spufford's argument. On the basis of the assessment and supplementary evidence, the Terling householders of 1671 have again been divided into four broad categories:[30]

Category	Number of Hearths	Social position	Number and percentage of households	
I	6–20	Gentry and very large farmers	10	8.2
II	3–5	Yeomen, wealthy craftsmen	29	23.8
III	2	Husbandmen, craftsmen	21	17.2
IV	1 and excused[a]	Laborers, poor craftsmen, poor widows	62	50.8
Total			122	100.0

[a] 40 of 62 were excused from tax on the grounds of severe poverty.

A number of limited though useful comparisons can be made between this analysis and that of the Subsidy of 1524/5. In the first place, though the Subsidy was assessed on individuals rather than households, our analysis suggests that—servants excluded—it indicates a population of

---

[28] E. R. O. Q/R Th 8/9.

[29] M. Spufford, *Contrasting Communities*, pp. 39, 41.

[30] For the half-hundred of Witham as a whole, the distribution of hearths assessed was as follows: 6+ hearths, 6.9%; 3–5 hearths, 25.9%; 2 hearths, 17.9%; 1 hearth, 49.3%. (Calculated from figures provided in K. H. Burley, "The Economic Development of Essex," Appendix I, p. 398.)

something in the region of seventy households. By 1671 the population had
clearly expanded very considerably. Secondly, the two analyses suggest
something about the nature and effects of this demographic expansion. It is
striking that the absolute numbers of persons in Categories I to III seem to
have remained remarkably stable, whereas those in Category IV underwent
an equally remarkable expansion. The parish would appear to have filled
at the bottom.[31] Though the broad structure of society in 1671 remained
recognizably that of 1524, the relative size of the different social strata that
constituted it had undergone very marked change, the full significance of
which will be discussed later.

Exactly how the expanded numbers of the laboring poor supported
themselves is a difficult question. They must have found work as and when
they could in Terling and the surrounding parishes, and we must assume
that local employment opportunities had grown. Perhaps a more intensive
cultivation was being practiced on the larger farms of the parish. Perhaps
the rising prosperity of the farmers provided more employment for petty
craftsmen. Perhaps again the servants in husbandry, living with the
farmers, were giving way to laborers dwelling in their own cottages. All of
these factors may have played some part. What is equally evident is that
many laborers were unable to maintain themselves fully, as we shall see
when we turn to the analysis of the position of the poor in the later seventeenth century. But before engaging in what will be an analysis of the
economics of mere survival, something more can be said of the experience
of more fortunate villagers for whom the period saw not impoverishment
but a real, if modest, prosperity.

It is by now generally agreed among historians that the later sixteenth
and early seventeenth centuries witnessed significant improvements in the
living standards of the "middling sort" of English countrymen. In a justly
famous passage written in the middle years of the reign of Elizabeth,
William Harrison, parson of the Essex parish of Radwinter, described how
in his time, despite the inflation of the period, farmers and artificers "doo
yet find the means to obtein and atchive such furniture as heretofore hathe
beene unpossible." The greybeards of Harrison's own village "noted three
things to be marvellouslie altred in England within their sound remem-
brance": first, "the multitude of chimnies latelie erected"; second, "the great
(although not generall) amendment of lodging" (i.e., bedding); third, "the
exchange of vessell" (i.e., tableware) from wood to pewter and even

---

[31] The enduring pattern of the distribution of wealth in social categories I to III is further
confirmed by analysis of the Ship Money assessment of 1636 (printed in C. A. Barton,
Historical Notes and Records of the Parish of Terling, Essex, Appendix III) and of the rates
assessed by the overseers of the poor of Terling in the 1690s (E. R. O. D/P 299/12/0). The
laboring poor were, of course, excused from both.

silver.[32] The study of both inventories and physical evidence by historians has abundantly confirmed Harrison's testimony concerning the improvement of both housing and furniture among the yeomanry of the period.

Only two inventories survive for Terling in this period. The wills of the villagers, however, are sufficiently specific about personal possessions and refer commonly enough to the rooms of their houses for us to form an impression of living standards that broadly confirms the improvements discovered elsewhere. This evidence, however, relates only to the middling ranks of village society, Terling testators being overwhelmingly drawn from what we have called Categories II and III: yeomen, husbandmen, and the more substantial craftsmen. This qualification accepted, the evidence speaks clearly.[33]

Housing standards certainly seem to have improved around the turn of the century. The map of 1597 shows the houses of the village as being for the most part single-story dwellings, though some have an upper story built at one end. Many have chimneys, a significant contribution to domestic comfort. Where internal arrangements are referred to in wills of the later sixteenth century, the rooms mentioned are usually the hall and the chamber (an upper room), though there are infrequent references to "the parlor." The yeomen and husbandmen of the period would seem to have lived in dwellings already improved beyond the standards of the medieval hall house but not yet up to the standards that became established in the seventeenth century. By 1650, references to hall, chamber *and* parlor were commonplace, while by 1700 a wide variety of rooms might be mentioned. John Humphrey's will of 1655, for example, contains references to hall, parlor, parlor chamber, and the chamber above the buttery, and is not atypical.[34] Confirmation of the impression of improving standards given by the wills of villagers comes from the report made on the village in 1921 by the Royal Commission on Historical Monuments. Several late-medieval houses are listed that had seen the division of the hall to provide two stories and the addition of chimneys in the late sixteenth and early seventeenth centuries. Even more prominent are the many fine houses of the earlier seventeenth century. These buildings provide living evidence of the prosperity of the upper levels of village society in this period.[35]

If the wills offer us only a glimpse of the progress of the "great rebuilding" of rural England in which Terling shared, they allow us to chart

[32] R. H. Tawney and E. Power eds., *Tudor Economic Documents*, vol. III, pp. 69–70.

[33] The following discussion is based on the examination of all Terling wills, 1522 to 1700, listed in F. G. Emmison ed., *Wills at Chelmsford*, vols. I and II.

[34] E. R. O. D/ACW 16/158.

[35] *Royal Commission on Historical Monuments. An Inventory of the Historical Monuments in Essex*, vol. II, p. 227 ff.

the improvement of furnishings more exactly. Bedding was sufficiently valuable to be frequently listed in detail by testators. From the 1550s through to the 1580s, flockbeds and even featherbeds, together with sheets and bolsters, are commonly mentioned, but there is only a single reference to an actual bedstead below the level of the gentry. Between 1590 and 1610, "joyned" bedsteads begin to appear, usually standing in the parlor and commonly containing the testator himself while the will was dictated! From the 1610s onward, bedsteads with all their "furniture" become commonplace, while the wealthier villagers might even possess two or more and distribute them among their heirs. In the 1660s and 1670s "high beds" complete with curtains appear among the wealthier, while the latter decade saw the first appearance of a further element of sophistication—the warming pan.

Improvements in other furnishings followed a similar chronology. Cupboards and "hutches" seem to have been widely owned since at least 1550, but "joyned" tables and chairs appear regularly only after 1600. Earlier references are to trestle or "foylding" tables accompanied by stools and forms. The only joined table found before 1600 was in the will of a carpenter who died in 1592. Pewter tableware is occasionally mentioned even before 1550, but became commonplace in the later sixteenth century, as did brass cooking pots. Before 1600 there were occasional yeomen who left a silver spoon or two but in the early seventeenth century the possession of such treasured items became fairly common amongst yeomen. Brass candlesticks also appeared in these years to grace the tables of the prosperous. In the later seventeenth century, testators gave much less detail of such possessions, perhaps an indication that they were now sufficiently normal to be simply taken for granted and lumped together with other goods and chattels.

Finally, a word can be said about clothing. Clothes were valuable enough to be passed on from generation to generation. In 1566, for example, Agnes Biggen left her daughter "my kyrtell that I had of Mother Lerner"; she herself had been left the garment ten years before: It had been Margery Learner's best gown too.[36] This practice was assisted by the fact that there appears to have been little change of fashion in the main items of clothing between 1550 and 1650. Throughout the period, women's costume seems to have consisted of underlinen, smock and petticoat (very often red, sometimes green or blue), gown, "crosse cloths," apron, neckerchief, and coat. Men had their doublets, hose or (later) breeches and stockings, jerkins, and coats. One yeoman, for example, left in 1551 "a coot, a doublett of fustian, a pere hose . . . and a gyrken," and another husband-

---

[36] E. R. O. D/ACR 5/126; D/ABW 23/103.

man in 1622 left his best suit of apparel "that is, my dublett, britches and Jerkin,"[37] The contents of the wardrobe had changed little by 1660, but one has the impression that more clothes were possessed—some testators were leaving several sets of clothing.

These matters are not trivial. These various goods were their owners' pride, lovingly detailed in will after will. The fine table laid with pewter and brass, the great bedstead in the parlor with its featherbed, pillows, and coverlet, even the best "stuffe dublet lined with bayes" were the outward and very visible signs of success among those best placed to take advantage of the opportunities of the age. The prestige that they conferred was perhaps the more important because these comforts were new and because they were not usually available to the mass of the villagers. The century of improving standards for the middling sort of the village, 1550–1650, was a century of impoverishment for the laboring poor.

In 1622 Richard Sizer, a laborer, died and his goods were inventoried. He possessed two bullocks and one hog, an old chest, some tools, his purse, and his clothing. The total value of his goods came to £4 8s. 8d., of which £3 15s. 4d. was earmarked by those who took the inventory to pay his debts. They noted at the same time that all other goods in his cottage had come with his wife from an earlier marriage to the village schoolmaster. Three years later she died. Her children were left to the care of the parish and her goods too were inventoried. She possessed an old bedstead, two blankets, three sheets, and one "old fether bolster." In addition there was "a little boord table," a form, two hutches and a cupboard with wool in it, two pots, two kettles, a spit, five wooden dishes, six pewter dishes, a pair of tongs and a kneading trough. Her clothing included only one gown, two aprons, a hat, and a pair of pattens. Running about the cottage and noted down as the valuers moved about were one hen and seven chickens.[38]

These inventories present one vivid picture of the living conditions of the laboring poor in the 1620s. Another comes from the confession of Robert Whitehead, who stole and ate a sheep in the winter of 1623/4, "beinge a verie poore man and haveinge a wiefe and seaven smale children and being very hungery."[39] Direct evidence of this kind is rare, but something can be done to fill out the picture of the lives of those families that by the mid-seventeenth century made up half the population of the village.

Constructing a "typical" budget for a poor family is fraught with difficulties, but is perhaps less difficult for Terling than for some other villages. For the last six years of the seventeenth century very detailed overseers of the poor accounts survive that enable us to gain some insight

[37] E. R. O. D/ABW 25/97; D/ACW 9/81.
[38] E. R. O. D/ACW 9/62; D/ACW 10/115.
[39] E. R. O. Q/S Ba 2/7.

into the costs of maintaining a pauper at the end of our period.[40] Adult paupers received varying sums for their relief, but a fairly typical regular payment was 2s. per fortnight (£2 12s. per annum). A pauper child would appear to have cost £1 10s. per annum. These payments can be taken to represent the costs of food and drink only, since additional sums were also granted to those receiving regular relief for clothing, fuel, and rent. Clothing an adult man with coat, shirt, breeches, shoes, and stockings cost about 18s. A woman's linen, gown, shoes, and stockings cost 15s. A child's shirt or shift, breeches or undercoat, and shoes cost around 5s. Some of these items were the subject of annual expenditure, others were needed more rarely. Nevertheless a man, wife and three children might well need £2 a year for clothing as well as £9 14s. for food. In addition, the overseers spent about £1 a year on wood for each pauper and paid rents for them of £1 to £1 10s. a year. Whether these rents were typical one cannot easily tell. The housing stock of the village must have been expanded in the later sixteenth and earlier seventeenth centuries in order to meet population expansion, and many of the one-hearth cottages on which the poor were assessed in 1671 must have been erected in this period. Some were possibly tied cottages with negligible rents. However, an allowance of £1 a year can be made for rent. The following expenditure might be typical for a poor family of five in the 1690s:

Food	£ 9 14s.
Clothing	2
Fuel	1
Rent	1
Total	£13 14s.

Other expenses may also have been incurred, of course, but this hypothetical budget is intended only to give an idea of the minimum costs of keeping a family at the level that the parish overseers considered appropriate for paupers.

Our next question must be to ask what the typical laborer earned. According to official wage assessments, an Essex laborer in 1599 should receive 8d. or 10d. a day, without food and drink, depending on the season. In the 1610s the official rate, without food and drink, varied from 8d. to 16d. a day, depending on the task, with higher payments for harvest work. For comparison, tailors and collarmakers were assessed at 10d. to 14d. a day, carpenters at 12d. to 16d. In 1661 laborers were to have 12d. to 14d. a day for normal work, tailors the same, collarmakers, sawyers, and coopers

---

14d. to 16d., and carpenters 16d. to 20d. Details of *actual* payments for a day's labor from the Terling churchwardens' accounts show that common laborers in the last two decades of the seventeenth century received a usual payment of 1s. a day, though sums paid could be higher on occasion.[41] Let us assume that our hypothetical laborer worked six days a week every week, giving a total of 312 days a year. This is, of course, an unwarranted assumption since the underemployment of labor in this period was notorious. However, this assumption may make some allowance for extra earnings in harvest time and for the occasional earnings of wives and children. On this assumption, laborers and craftsmen working for wages may have had the following maximum incomes at different points in the course of the seventeenth century:

Years	Employment	Wages per diem	Income per annum
1599	Laborer	9d.	£11 14s.
1610s	Laborer	12	15 12
	Tailor or collarmaker	12	15 12
	Carpenter	13	16 18
1661	Laborer	13	16 18
	Tailor	13	16 18
	Collarmaker, sawyer, or cooper	15	19 10
	Carpenter	18	23 8
1680–1700	Terling laborer	12	15 12
1688	Gregory King's estimate of total income of a laboring family[42]		15.0.0

On these estimates, then, (which are, if anything, likely to be too high), a Terling laborer in the 1690s (or, for that matter, some of the petty craftsmen who largely shared his position) would be able to maintain his family at a level slightly above that at which the overseers of the poor maintained the village paupers. These estimates, of course, assume that laboring families were entirely dependent on wages for their subsistence. Certainly the laborers of Terling had no common pasture on which to keep animals. Yet we might consider that some would have the produce of at least garden plots to ease their burdens, while others may have been partly paid in kind

---

[41] Wage assessments: E. R. O. Q/SR 145/58, Q/AA 1, Q/S 0 1, fos. 254-7. Churchwardens' Accounts, E. R. O. D/P 299/5/1A.

[42] Gregory King's estimates of family income and expenditure in 1688 are printed in J. Thirsk and J. P. Cooper eds., *Seventeenth Century Economic Documents*, pp. 780–781.

or allowed to buy foodstuffs at cheap rates from their employers. Of these matters we have no evidence. What is certain is that the laborer's lot was hard enough at the best of times. Any additional expense over and above mere subsistence needs, any period of bad luck in finding work, any period of illness, would threaten to push him (and his family) under. Above all, any severe rise in the price of foodstuffs would have disastrous results. The family expenditure calculated above is based upon the overseers' accounts of the year 1697/8, which tell us that barley—the principal breadcorn of the poor in seventeenth-century England—was priced at 2s. 6d. a bushel. Earlier in the century, occasional references reveal that barley had stood at about 3s. 4d. in some normal years and even higher in years of bad harvest such as the later 1590s, 1631, and 1647–1650. In 1599, for example, in the aftermath of the terrible dearth years of the later 1590s, an Essex jury presented to the justices of the county "that the rate [of wages] for laborers in husbandrie be to smale" and suggested that they be raised. In 1604/5 a much less drastic enhancement of the price of corn led the authorities to predict that the laboring poor were "like to suffer great want and penury." In 1631 the poor of Witham hundred, unable to afford their normal bread-corns, "were constreyned to buy Branke and Teares which was brought by shipping . . . to serve their necessities for bread." Eighteen years later barley cost 5s. a bushel in north Essex, other grains still more, and one clergyman described his people as "pincht with want of food."[43] In the later decades of the seventeenth century it is likely that the laboring poor of Terling were experiencing their first rise in real wages after a century and a half of steady inflation in which wages had lagged behind food prices. Their existence remained marginal enough but had probably actually improved since 1650.

There were elements of real stability in the economic and social history of Terling between 1520 and 1700 but there were also major elements of change. The villagers of 1700 knew both a greater prosperity and a more widespread, more abject poverty and dependence than had those of 1524. The former can be seen in the uses to which the yeomen and more substantial husbandmen and craftsmen put their greater wealth. The latter is less directly visible in historical documents. Yet it forms the essential background against which the petty dramas of village life were acted out.

---

[43] E. R. O. Q/SR 344/22, 145/58, 171/57; P. R. O. SP 16 203/89; A. Macfarlane ed., *The Diary of Ralph Josselin*, pp. 154, 181.

3

DEMOGRAPHIC STRUCTURES

The century before 1625 was characterized, as we have seen, by a growing polarization in the distribution of wealth in Terling, a polarization that resulted above all from an expansion of the laboring population of the village. A crucial element in the process of social change in seventeenth-century Terling was to be the necessity of coming to terms with this development. Vital to both the emergence of the greatly expanded laboring class and its continuance as a permanent feature of village society in Terling was the demographic structure of the village community, and it is to this issue that we will now turn.

Our study of the population of Terling was conducted by applying the technique of "family reconstitution" to the entries of baptisms, burials, and marriages recorded in the parish register between its inception in 1538 and the middle of the eighteenth century.[1] This methodology is slow, careful, and arduous, yet provides a means of approaching demographic issues otherwise inaccessible to the historian. Essentially the procedure of reconstituting families is simple: first, separate forms are made out for each event recorded in the register and, second, each event is allocated to its

---

[1] Because the original of the Terling parish register is still kept in the parish chest we used a trascript, made by the Hon. C.R. Strutt, which was checked for accuracy and found to be of the highest quality. (Essex Record Office, T/R 60).

"family of origin." Thus, the primary problem is to find an appropriate family for each baptism, burial, or marriage, thereby reconstituting the origin, growth, and ultimate dissolution of each family unit. Once this difficulty has been surmounted, it is possible to go about the demographic analysis of the resulting body of data.[2] The use of computer programs devised by the Social Science Research Council, Cambridge Group for the History of Population and Social Structure greatly facilitated this stage of our research program. Before embarking on our presentation of the results, however, it will be useful to survey briefly the broad outlines of population change in our period, both in Terling and the county of Essex as a whole.

Any estimate of the rural population of Essex in our period must be an approximation, given the nature of the evidence at our disposal. The taxation records from Essex for 1524/5 and 1671 do, however, suggest that the county's population rose very substantially between these two dates. On the basis of the figures provided by Dr. Sheail's analysis of the Subsidy returns of 1524/5, we would estimate that the maximum rural population of the county at that time was in the region of 50,000. A century and a half later the maximum rural population was in the neighborhood of 100,000. Not only had the population increased markedly over the period, but a number of changes had also taken place in its distribution within Essex. Whereas the areas of the county bordering most closely on Middlesex and London were the most densely peopled and the coastal fringes of the county the most thinly peopled districts in both 1524/5 and 1671, shifts had taken place in the relative positions of the hundreds of north and central Essex. In 1524/5 the population of these districts had been concentrated in a belt stretching from the Cambridgeshire border in the northwest down to the central hundreds of the county. By 1671 this area had been overtaken by the hundreds along the Hertfordshire border on the west of the county (in particular the forest hundreds of Waltham and Ongar) and by the hundreds of Lexden and Hinckford in the northeast that were deeply involved in protoindustrial textile production. Though the total population of the half-hundred of Witham, within which Terling lay, had risen by something like 70% during this period, the district had fallen in the table of population density from a high to a middling point.[3] The population of Essex,

---

[2] A lengthy discussion of this methodology has been presented by E.A. Wrigley who pioneered its development in England, "Family Reconstitution." Wrigley has published the two major works which have contributed toward a redefinition of the preindustrial demographic regime. ("Family Limitation in Pre-Industrial England" and "Mortality in Pre-Industrial England"). In addition, the S.S.R.C. Cambridge Group for the History of Population and Social Structure has filed another dozen completed village studies which have not yet been discussed in a public forum.

[3] This discussion is based on information provided in J. Sheail, "The Regional Distribution of Wealth in England", pp. 186–189, F. Hull, "Agriculture and Rural Society in Essex," p. 123,

then, had virtually doubled and had been significantly modified in its distribution in the course of the demographic expansion of the sixteenth and early seventeenth centuries.

How was this development worked out at the local level in Terling? We have already seen that in 1524/5 Terling was a village of perhaps seventy households. In 1671 the village had 122 households. Using the multiplier of 4.75 persons per household suggested by Peter Laslett's researches,[4] we would estimate that the population of 1524/5 was about 330, while by 1671 it had expanded by some 75% to approximately 580. Between these two dates the actual course of population change is suggested by the annual totals of baptisms, burials, and marriages provided by the parish registers of Terling. In Figure 3.1 a simple annual series has been plotted.

As is immediately apparent, the variability of the annual figures obscures any trends that may have been in evidence. For this reason a second graph, Figure 3.2, has been provided. This second graph is a weighted, nine-year moving average and it tends to smooth out the annual variations so that the longer-term trends are thrown into relief.

Several aspects of Terling's population history come immediately to the fore from a perusal of these graphs. Perhaps the most obvious characteristic of the village population is its extreme volatility from year to year. Nowhere is this more evident than in the burial curve, where seismographic eruptions are interspersed with smaller, more frequent peaks

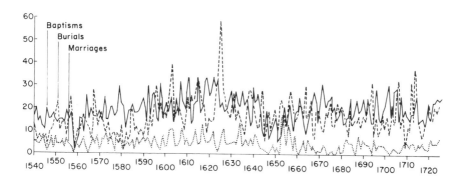

Figure 3.1   Annual totals of baptisms, burials, and marriages.

and K.H. Burley, "The Economic Development of Essex," pp. 21, 398. The hundreds for which no information is available for 1524/5 have been accorded estimated populations based upon the assumption of a relatively high population density by Essex standards. Unlike Dr. Burley, we have preferred a multiplier of 4.75 for the conversion of the numbers of households to total population estimates.

⁴ P. Laslett, "Mean household size in England since the sixteenth century."

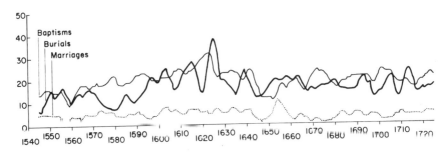

Figure 3.2 Weighted 9-year moving average of baptisms, burials, and marriages.

and valleys. Only one year–1625—experienced anything approaching disaster levels. In 1625 the plague was mentioned in the parish register. Approximately one person in twelve was carried away, about three times the annual figure. The next highest peak in the burial curve—1603—was also a plague year but no mention of the pestilence was made by the clerk. Famine, on the other hand, seems to have been of no significance in the demographic history of Terling. While it is remarked by the scribe in the 1590s that poor, wayfaring strangers were being found dead in the yeomen's barns, the overall effect of the harvest disasters of these years is muted. Other "famous" dearths likewise seen to have little effect on the life chances of the villagers.[5] To be sure, there was deprivation and a crying need in such years, but we have no evidence that there was death by starvation among the settled population of the village.

In more normal years the extreme volatility of the village's yearly burial figures is explicable in terms of the small size of the community. Death was not a random event: It tended to strike the young and old with particular ferocity but due to the small numbers "at risk," as it were, it was improbable statistically that an annual pattern would be immediately visible. Rather, there was a great deal of fluctuation around the average. And, moreover, the fact that one year was a bad one was no guarantee that its successor would be milder.

Given this situation, it is only by submerging the annual variations that a pattern can be discerned. In Figure 3.2 we can see that in the later sixteenth century a gap persisted between baptisms and burials. This surplus population, over and above replacement levels, seems to have been absorbed into the broader local community, for the population of the village, like that of neighboring settlements with which it exchanged young people, swelled. But by the first quarter of the seventeenth century, the gap was closing

---

[5] For dearth years, see W.G. Hoskins, "Harvest Fluctuations and English Economic History, 1480–1619" and "Harvest Fluctuations and English Economic History, 1620–1759." Hoskins' account is somewhat modified by C.J. Harrison, "Grain Price Analysis and Harvest Qualities, 1465–1634."

and after 1625 a rough balance existed between the forces of life and those of death. For the century after 1625, the two series were in a form of equilibrium. The one discernible variation in the series of marriages occurred during the period of the Civil War when the machinery of parochial registration was thrust into a state of partial confusion by the conflicting wishes of the central government. The institution of civil marriage in 1653 is the factor behind the surge in marriages for that year. After the Restoration, in Terling and many other English parishes, it appears that there was a shortfall in marriage registration and it was not until 1680 that this situation was resolved.[6]

The rough outline of change suggested by these aggregated statistics can be made quite palpable only by a discussion of the calculations derived from the family reconstitution study. The more sophisticated, refined measurements yielded by this method of analysis will make it possible to distinguish the relative importance of the changing levels of nuptiality, fertility—both legitimate and premarital—, and mortality which shaped the demographic experience of Terling. Attention will be focused on providing an explanation of both the mainspring of population growth before 1625 and the stabilization that appears to have emerged toward the end of the third quarter of the seventeenth century.

In Terling the age at first marriage for both men and women was somewhat lower than that reported in most other English family reconstitution studies. For the 1550–1724 period, 112 men first married at a (mean) average age of 25.3, while 178 brides were 24.6 (see Table 3.1).

The relative precocity of marriage in Terling becomes more evident when it is compared with another village—Shepshed, Leciestershire.[7] In that Midland community during the seventeenth century, the mean age at first marriage was 29.4 for men and 28.1 for their brides. In preindustrial Shepshed more than one-quarter of all brides and more than one-third of all their grooms were over thirty when they first married. By way of contrast,

TABLE 3.1
Age at First Marriage, 1550–1724

	Number	Mean	Standard deviation	Lower quartile	Median	Upper quartile	Inter-quartile range
Men	112	25.3	4.7	22.5	24.5	27.7	5.2
Women	178	24.6	4.8	21.3	23.8	27.5	6.2

[6] E.A. Wrigley, "Clandestine Marriage in Tetbury in the late 17th century." See our discussion of nonconformist marriages in late seventeenth-century Terling (p. 168).

[7] For a fuller discussion of the demography of Shepshed, see David Levine, *Family Formation in an Age of Nascent Capitalism.*

in Terling the proportion of such late-marrying men was about one in fourteen and for women it was less than one in six. The youthfulness of the
brides and grooms is further underscored by a comparison of early marriages. In Shepshed between 1600 and 1700 just one bride in fifteen was
under twenty, whereas in Terling the comparable figure was almost one in
four. Similar differences were evident for their husbands. In early modern
Terling, one man in six married before his twentieth birthday, but at the
same time in Shepshed the figure was one in twelve.

It was possible to gain information on the first marriage ages of both
partners in twenty-seven cases. In five there was less than a one-year difference, in sixteen the groom was older, while in the other six cases the
bride was more than one year older. If we isolate the group of sixteen marriages in which the age difference was less than three years, there is no apparent pattern, although men were older than their brides more often than
not (nine out of sixteen). This finding suggests that in a small village
population of 500 or 600 the choice of partners was rather limited. At the
time that marriage became a social and economic possibility one would
have a restricted number of eligible members of the opposite sex from
whom to choose. Not surprisingly many of the young people of Terling
looked outside the village for their marriage partners. Of those who made
their choice from among the eligible group within the village, it appears
that a substantial element of randomness was obtained. It was only after
men and women passed beyond the average marriage age that it became
more common for them to marry a person who was noticeably younger.
Within the band of marriage ages that surrounded the average—say, by
one standard deviation or just under five years—there was little systematic
bias in the partners' ages at first marriage. The average age difference was
2.4 years. This figure is inflated by the fact that three men were more than
ten years older than their brides, while another five were between five and
ten years senior to their wives. On the other side, just three women were
more than three years older than their husbands. The overall impression
gained from this evidence supports the general conclusion that, although
many marriages took place among people whose ages were roughly similar,
there was still a sizable fraction of couples in which there was a marked
disparity between the ages of the partners.

Age at marriage was, perhaps, the most important variable in the preindustrial demographic regime of homeostasis.[8] By directly controlling the
onset of reproduction, Western European populations were able to more or

---

[8] The most important article on this subject has been by John Hajnal, "European Marriage
Patterns in Perspective." Daniel Scott Smith has attempted to test the hypothesis that views
the age at marriage as the key agency in the preindustrial demographic regime in his paper "A
Homeostatic Demographic Regime. Patterns in West European Family Reconstitution

less replace one generation with a successor of a similar size. Although swingeing crisis and epidemic mortality have attracted a large share of attention from both contemporary and historical demographers the effects of varying mortality have, to our mind, been grossly overstated. Of critical importance in retarding population growth in the long run was the pattern of late, postponed marriage that had the direct effect of limiting the fertile period of the female population. In conditions of low levels of premarital sex, as many as ten years were withdrawn from women's childbearing cycle. Not only was the span of years during which women bore children significantly below the physiological limit but, moreover, the prevalence of breast-feeding tended to extend the length of the postpartum amenorrhea that served to reduce the frequency of birth events during the years when women were "at risk."[9]

In Terling there was a direct relationship between age at first marriage and the ultimate number of children a woman bore. The seven women who married under twenty had an average of 6.6 live births, while the three whose first marriage occurred when they were between thirty and thirty-five had just 2.7 live births. In Table 3.2 the descriptive statistics regarding this relationship are set forth for all age groups.

Reproductive strategies coordinated the effects of late, postponed marriage with the physiological imperatives of natural fertility. The basic aim of the preindustrial demoeconomic system was quite simple: While children were desirable in themselves, as heirs, and also as a kind of hedge against old age and infirmity, an overabundance of children could be as disastrous as too few. The highest rates of fertility were attained in the initial years of marriage, after which there was usually a leveling-off until women reached the end of their childbearing years, at about age forty. Briefly stated, the reason why fertility was concentrated in these early years of marriage was

TABLE 3.2
Family Size, by Wife's Age at Marriage, 1550–1724

	Under 20	20–24	25–29	30–34	35–39	All
Number	7	10	12	3	2	34
Mean	6.6	5.1	3.8	2.7	2.0	4.6
Standard deviation	2.1	1.8	1.9	1.2	—	2.2

Studies." Roger Schofield has written perceptively on the inter-connections between nuptiality, fertility, and mortality in preindustrial populations, "The relationship between demographic structure and environment in pre-industrial western Europe."

[9] In his work on parish reconstitution material from Germany, John Knodel has considered this problem at length. ("Infant Mortality and Fertility in Three Bavarian Villages" and "Two and a Half Centuries of Demographic History in a Bavarian Village").

twofold: Among first-born children the chance of mortality was highest while the protogenesic interval (i.e., between marriage and the first birth) was always the shortest. Inasmuch as it was desirable to produce surviving heirs and given the fact that mortality under five was both severe and unpredictable, it was not feasible to "invest" in the survival of any particular child. Thus it was only when one or, better still, two children had passed through the valley of the shadow of death that a couple could be reasonably certain of having children who would reach adulthood and perhaps assist them in their adult years. For these reasons, and some others which will be discussed in passing, actual marital fertility rates deviated sharply from physiologically possible ones. It is possible to look at this phenomenon from several different perspectives, utilizing the descriptive statistics generated from the family reconstitution study.

In Table 3.3 we have presented the composite figures which describe age-specific fertility rates in early modern Terling.

The Terling figures gain added interest when they are compared with those of contemporary Colyton, Devon, and St. Méen, and eighteenth-century Breton community (see Figure 3.3).[10]

From the graphic illustration it appears that Terling's rates of age-specific marital fertility describe a flatter course than either Colyton, 1560–1629, or the French example. The closest fit appears to exist between later seventeenth-century Colyton and early modern Terling. However, it would be premature to press this comparision too far without first discussing the quite remarkable differences that existed among these four populations. When seen in a somewhat broader perspective, the uniqueness of Terling's demographic regime will be better appreciated. Elizabethan and early Stuart Colyton's population seems to have grown rather quickly due to the effects of high fertility undeterred by a later age at marriage. By the middle

TABLE 3.3
Age-Specific Fertility, 1550–1724

Age	Years at risk	Children born	Rate per 1000 years lived
Under 25	214	82	383
25–29	295	95	322
30–34	337	94	279
35–39	288	64	222
40–44	211	25	118
45–49	139	0	0

[10] Wrigley, "Family Limitation." Pierre Goubert, "Legitimate Fecundity and Infant Mortality in France during the Eighteenth Century: A Comparison."

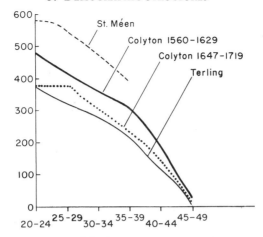

Figure 3.3   Age-specific marital fertility rates in Terling, Colyton, and St. Méen.

of the seventeenth century, a combination of even later marriage and fertility restriction within marriage produced a demographic turnaround, as the villagers were now not even replacing themselves. The Breton community was characterized by an average Western European age at marriage (slightly above twenty-five for women) and disastrously high infant mortality rates—about one child in four was dead within the first year. In these circumstances it is not surprising that there was not "the slightest trace of birth control," as the likelihood of producing surviving heirs would hardly have been compromised in that way. Such a strategy would have been self-defeating.

When viewed in this comparative perspective, the "logic" or "rationality" of the demographic regime in Terling can be better understood. In conditions of relatively low infant mortality—about half the Breton level—and a rather early age at marriage—five years below that of Colyton, 1647–1719—a low rate of fertility was sufficient for this population to achieve its major aim of producing surviving heirs.

It has already been pointed out that a population's strategy of achieving this end involved the concentration of fertility into the early years of marriage. Another set of statistics describes *duration*-specific fertility—the annual rate at which children are born in the first five years of marriage, the second five years, and so on. From these figures in Table 3.4 we can see further evidence of the way in which fertility was concentrated into the early years of marriage.

Another method of describing this phenomenon of declining fertility over the years of marriage is by a consideration of birth intervals. In Table 3.5 the information derived from our family reconstitution study that refers to this measurement is presented.

TABLE 3.4
Duration-Specific Fertility 1550–1724

Years married	Years at risk	Children born	Rate per 1000 years lived
0–4	468	176	376
5–9	366	92	251
10–14	290	61	210
15–19	194	24	124
20+	391	7	18

In Table 3.5 we can see that the (mean) average interval between births levels off after the second children were born. The spacing for the first birth was, by way of contrast, very brief. Only 14.9 months elapsed between marriage and the first child. Moreover, in a sizable minority of cases brides were pregnant at marriage and their first child was born within eight months of the celebration. For second children, the spacing was double that of the protogenesic interval but was still considerably less than all future intervals. Further births occurred at intervals of three years.

The discussion pertaining to fertility has so far considered aggregated data—the whole sample. This method literally begs the question of the influence of age at marriage on fertility. In the next section we want to present evidence that is disaggregated to allow for the effect of early and later marriage. It might be pointed out that the average age at marriage of those 105 women marrying before their twenty-fifth birthday was 20.9, while the comparable figure for the older group who married after their twenty-fifth birthday was 29.9. This nine-year age difference should be borne in mind when considering the following three sets of tables.

The information presented in the more discrete Tables 3.6, 3.7, and 3.8 not only describes that an effort was being made to have children more frequently in the early years of marriage but also suggests some telltale signs

TABLE 3.5
Birth Intervals by Birth Rank, 1550–1724

Birth interval	Number	Mean	Standard deviation	Median
0–1	94	14.9	14.7	11.0
1–2	77	29.5	16.3	26.4
2–3	61	37.0	19.5	31.8
3–4	43	38.1	19.3	33.5
5+	56	35.8	18.1	32.0

TABLE 3.6
Age-Specific Fertility, By Wife's Age at Marriage, 1550–1724

Age	Women marrying under 25			Women marrying over 25		
	Years at risk	Children born	Rate per 1000 years lived	Years at risk	Children born	Rate per 1000 years lived
Under 25	214	82	383	—	—	—
25–29	216	62	287	78	33	423
30–34	189	52	275	147	42	286
35–39	150	31	207	138	33	239
40–44	99	7	71	113	18	159
45–49	75	0	0	18	0	0

TABLE 3.7
Duration-Specific Fertility by Wife's Age at Marriage, 1550–1724

Years married	Years at risk	Children born	Rate per 1000 years lived
	Women marrying under 25		
0–4	269	103	383
5–9	210	60	286
10–14	175	48	274
15–19	130	16	123
20+	256	7	27
	Women marrying over 25		
0–4	199	73	367
5–9	156	32	205
10–14	115	13	113
15–19	64	8	125
20+	135	0	0

of family limitation. Thus, the levels of age-specific fertility of the groups of younger-marrying women aged thirty-five to forty-four were significantly lower than those of the older-marrying group. To put it another way, the age-specific fertility curve of the younger brides was concave to the upper side, while that of their older-marrying peers was convex (see Figure 3.3). In Wrigley's study of fertility regulation in Colyton it was argued that "The reason why a concavity to the upper side of a curve representing age-specific marital fertility often indicates family limitation

TABLE 3.8
Birth Intervals by Birth Rank, by Wife's Age at Marriage, 1550–1724

Birth interval	Number	Mean	Standard deviation	Median
	Women marrying under 25			
0–1	55	16.5	16.6	11.5
1–2	44	30.7	20.2	24.8
2–3	38	37.0	18.7	31.8
3–4	30	35.7	15.7	31.5
5+	45	35.1	18.8	30.9
	Women marrying over 25			
0–1	39	12.7	11.5	10.7
1–2	33	28.0	8.9	28.4
2–3	23	37.2	21.6	30.1
3–4	13	43.7	25.7	38.0
5+	11	39.0	15.1	38.0

is, of course, that most married couples want some children but not as large a number as might be borne to them without any limitation of fertility."[11]

Two further statistical measures underline the existence of this phenomenon of fertility control in early modern Terling. In the first place, women marrying under thirty were compared to those first marrying over that age. It was found that whereas the twenty-five younger brides were, on average, 38.0 years old at the birth of their last child, the six others were fully four years older, 42.0, at their last confinement. The other method of checking for the practice of family limitation is through a comparison of the mean intervals between the penultimate and last birth. In Wrigley's words:

> A marked rise in this interval is typical of a community beginning to practice family limitation. It arises in these circumstances, because even after reaching an intended final family size, additions are nevertheless occasionally made either from accident (failure of whatever system of restriction is in use), from a reversal of an earlier decision not to increase family size, of from a desire to replace a child which has died.[12]

Due to the regrettably small size of the sample it was necessary to lump both the younger and older brides together. In the sixteen cases that met the stringent requirements for inclusion, the mean penultimate interval was 39.9 months, while the last interval was, on average, 47.2 months.

So, if we can recapitulate the argument so far, the salient points would be that in early modern Terling a relatively low age at marriage was complemented by a fertility schedule whose main features were concentrated fertility in the early years of marriage and a deliberate restriction as one's family reached a desired size. Before leaving the issue of fertility, two further sets of calculations will be presented which serve to emphasize the downward pitch of the fertility curve. In Table 3.9 we show the average number of children born in each age-group, as well as a proportional distribution of these births per 1000 marriages.

High fertility in the early years of marriage was, as we have seen, achieved by a concentration of fertility. Another way of describing this phenomenon is by calculating the proportion of children born within a two-year period at each parity. In Table 3.10 we can see that, whereas 80% of all first births occurred within two years of marriage, by the third child just 10.1% of all births were less than two years apart.

The remarkable extent to which the preindustrial population of Terling was able to regulate its fertility seems to have been accomplished through the judicious usage of two measures—*coitus interruptus* and breast-feeding,

---

[11] Wrigley, "Family Limitation," p. 91.
[12] Wrigley, "Family Limitation," p. 94.

TABLE 3.9
Children Born per Age-Group, 1550-1724

Age	Frequency distribution Number	Mean
20-24	17	1.76
25-29	42	1.45
30-34	58	1.35
35-39	54	1.13
40-44	36	0.67
45-49	23	0.00

Age	Proportional distribution per 1000				
	0	1	2	3	4+
20-24	118	235	412	235	0
25-29	167	333	405	71	24
30-34	138	448	345	69	0
35-39	278	426	259	19	19
40-44	528	306	139	28	0
45-49	1000	0	0	0	0

which promoted postpartum amenorrhea and the suspension of ovulation for a period of time. In other studies it has been shown that after a child dies in infancy the succeeding child will be born after a significantly shorter interval than in other cases in which the first child lived.[13] However, the causal arrows did not point in only one direction. An infant's health was highly sensitive to its mother's condition. In Terling, for example, the mortality rate of children was affected by the pregnancy of their mothers. To compare extreme instances: for every 1000 children whose mothers conceived during the child's first three months of life, fully 417 died within a year; but for those whose mothers' next conception took place more than two years later the figure was just 57.

Infant mortality levels in Terling were comparatively low during the

TABLE 3.10
Proportion of Birth Events at Next Parity Occurring within 2 Years, 1550-1724

Birth rank	Fertile women	Next birth event within 2 years	Rate per 1000
0	35	28	800
1	35	12	343
2+	93	14	151

[13] Knodel, "Infant Mortality and Fertility" and "Two and a Half Centuries of Demographic History."

1538–1725 period. In an aggregated measurement it was found that 131 per 1000 died within the first year of life. By age fifteen, three-quarters of all children were still alive (741 per 1000). By way of contrast, the parish of Bottesford, Leicestershire, experienced an infant mortality rate of about 155 per 1000 during the seventeenth century. In that Midland village, the number of children surviving to fifteen was 715 per 1000. In the west country village of Colyton, the comparable figures were about 140 per 1000 infant deaths and something like 700 survivors per 1000 live births. In terms of the life expectation at birth, the population of early modern Terling would have lived, on average, about forty-eight years, while in Bottesford the comparable figure was forty-four and in Colyton it was forty-three.[14] (see Table 3.11).

The risk of death was not equal for all children. For boys, 127 per 1000 died in their first year, while their sisters died at a marginally greater rate, 134 per 1000. In childhood, this distinction remained, so that by age fifteen there were 745 male survivors and 738 females from each cohort of 1000 live births. This finding is somewhat noteworthy in that it reverses the usual results, which show excess male mortality in infancy and youth.

It was suggested earlier that one of the reasons why fertility was concentrated into the early years of marriage had to do with the comparatively unfavorable mortality experience of first-born children. Severe birth trauma due to maternal inexperience was probably responsible for the fact that the infant mortality rate for first-born children in Terling, 186 per 1000, was markedly higher than that for children born at the second or third parity, 136 and 125 per 1000, respectively. It was only for children born at later parities—fourth and above—that the rate rose again; for these infants, born to older women with at least three prior birth events, the mortality rate was 172 per 1000.

A similar finding, stressing the inequality of infants' life chances,

TABLE 3.11
Infant and Child Mortality Rates (MF), 1550–1724

	Reconstitution					Ledermann	
Age	At risk	Dying	Rate per 1000	Survivors	$e°$	Rate per 1000	Survivors
0	2451	320	131	1000	47.73	137	1000
1–4	1597	138	86	869		81	863
5–9	957	37	39	794		24	793
10–14	617	18	29	763		16	774
				741			762

[14] These figures for life expectation at birth were derived from the model life tables presented in Sully Ledermann, *Nouvelles Tables-Types de Mortalité*.

emerged when infant mortality rates were derived using the mother's age as an independent variable. In Table 3.12 we can see that children born to women twenty-five to thirty-four years of age were more likely to survive than those born either to more youthful or to elderly mothers. In a certain sense, this finding is to have been expected since it measures the reciprocal of the previous one in that first children were born to young mothers, while fourth and later births occurred to women aged over thirty-five.

One of our most cherished preconceptions about childbirth in pre-industrial England is that it was a bloody, gruesome affair, dangerous for child and mother alike. As we have seen, less than one child in seven died in its first year of life. For mothers in Terling, the level of mortality was also surprisingly low. Maternal mortality within three months of a birth occurred at a rate of eighteen per 1000 (fifty-eight of 3209). In just five cases per 1000 (seventeen of 3209) did both mother and child die together. In multiple birth events, however, women died more frequently: fifty-two per 1000 (3 of 57). In order to gain some kind of perspective on these rates of maternal mortality it will be useful to compare them with the chance of death experienced by the male population. For males aged twenty-five to forty-nine the annual rate of death was sixteen per 1000 (ninety-one deaths during 5551 years at risk). As can be seen from the evidence presented in Table 3.13, the heightened risk of death for women during their childbearing years had a clear effect on their life expectation at various ages.

It would be foolish to try to use this evidence to argue that life was neither nasty nor brutish in the early modern era. But the example of Terling is salutary in that it describes a village community where the levels of mortality were as low in the seventeenth century as they were in the middle of the nineteenth. Such evidence flies in the face of a conventional linear "Whig" view of human progress. It serves to remind us that Hobbes may have been a more acute political than demographic observer. To be sure, life in his time could be solitary, poor, nasty, and brutish, but it was not unduly short.

Having described the demographic parameters of early modern Terling, it is now necessary to interpret the meaning of these descriptive statistics in

TABLE 3.12
Infant Mortality by Age of Mother, 1550–1724

Mother's age	At risk	Dying	Rate per 1000
Under 25	87	17	195
25–29	104	17	163
30–34	96	13	135
35+	103	23	223

TABLE 3.13
Adult Mortality 1550–1724

Life expectation at various ages			Survivors at various ages		
Age	Men	Women	Age	Men	Women
25–29	30.5	23.9	25–29	1000	1000
30–34	26.4	21.8	30–34	966	882
35–39	23.0	19.5	35–39	905	774
40–44	19.8	17.5	40–44	835	659
45–49	17.0	15.5	45–49	740	549
50–54	14.4	14.2	50–54	634	427
55–59	12.8	11.1	55–59	495	367
				387	265

order to determine the village's natural rate of population growth. To do this it is necessary to develop a method that will allow the various elements of the demographic equation—nuptiality, fertility, and mortality—to come into play.

It should be made quite clear at the outset that the following figures are estimates. They have been derived by making a number of assumptions, some of which are quite "heroic." Nevertheless, it seems to us that it is worthwhile trying to develop some method of analyzing the total effect of the different demographic variables that are derived from a family reconstitution study.

The first priority was to create an approximation of total fertility—the average number of births per woman. For this hypothetical family we assumed that the wife married at the (mean) average age, 24.6, and had a fertility experience that corresponded to that of the whole cohort. The mean was chosen in preference to the median because it is an arithmetical rather than an ordinal measurement. The mean describes the midpoint of the area of the distribution rather than the midpoint of the cumulative frequency. This difference is important because of the skewed distribution of the marriage ages. The completed family size was derived as follows:

Age	Years married	Age-specific fertility rate	Children
0–24	0.4	383	0.15
25–29	5.0	322	1.61
30–34	5.0	279	1.40
35–39	5.0	222	1.11
40–44	5.0	118	0.59
45–49	5.0	0	0.00
			4.86

The total fertility, 4.86, is based on the assumption that both the husband and the wife live long enough for the whole of the wife's fertile period to be completed. Therefore, it needs to be revised by taking adult mortality into account. This proved to be quite a complex affair. It was impossible to make any allowance for remarriage because the available data describing the length of widowhood and widowerhood were inadequate. But, on the other hand, we have no real idea of the number of marriages that were broken for personal or socioeconomic reasons. For our present purposes we have had to assume that the incidence of remarriage was more or less balanced by the effects of marital breakdown. Bearing these caveats in mind, we began to assess the effect of parental mortality on fertility by making the assumption that the mortality experience of the husband and wife was identical. Our age-specific mortality figures relate to the combined experience of both men and women; it was decided that the creation of mortality rates with a reduced susceptibility to chance fluctuations was a higher priority than the assessment of differential effects of male and female mortality. Moreover, we also assumed that the husband and wife were exactly the same age at marriage—in this case, the wife's age. Given that this marriage was intact at 24.6, the average age at marriage, we have been able to determine the pace with which death took its toll. For the years of marriage in the 24.6–29 age-group the mortality rate was 72 per 1000 (0.072). Since the husband's likelihood of dying was assumed to have been independent of his wife's, and vice versa, the probability that their marriage would have been broken by the death of at least one of them was the product of each individual's chance of dying: $0.928 \times 0.928 = 0.861$. Thus, of every 1000 marriages intact at 24.6 there would be 861 surviving at the end of the age-period. We further assumed that these deaths were evenly distributed during the 5.4 years that this hypothetical couple was "at risk" in the age-group, so that we are interested in the midpoint marital survival. This was easily derived, as we merely added the number of intact marriages at the beginning of the age-group to the number surviving until the end and then divided this sum in two. Having established the midpoint frequency of marriages which, for each age-group, were unbroken by the death of at least one spouse, we have now to determine the implications of this set of survival rates in terms of the number of children born to each married woman.

The revised figure for legitimate marital fertility, after taking parental mortality into account, is 3.75. Next we used the illegitimacy ratio of the early modern cohort, 3.0%, to determine how many illegitimate births occurred per woman. The logic behind this procedure was that the relationship between the frequency of legitimate births and the completed family size should be proportional to the relationship between the frequency of

Age	Surviving marriages	Age-specific death rate	Survival rate	
			One partner	Both partners
24.6–29	1.000	0.072	0.928	0.861
30–34	0.861	0.093	0.907	0.823
35–39	0.709	0.105	0.895	0.801
40–44	0.567	0.114	0.886	0.785
45–49	0.445	0.144	0.856	0.733

Age	Surviving marriages	Midpoint marital survival		Potential fertility		Legitimate children
24.6–29	0.861	0.931	×	1.76	=	1.64
30–34	0.709	0.785	×	1.40	=	1.10
35–39	0.567	0.638	×	1.11	=	0.71
40–44	0.445	0.506	×	0.59	=	0.30
45–49	0.326	0.385	×	0.00	=	0.00
						3.75

both legitimate and illegitimate births and all births per woman. So, the total number of births—both legitimate and illegitimate—was derived as follows: The "typical" women had a total of 3.86 births; 0.11 before marriage and a further 3.75 afterwards.

$$(0.970/3.75) = (1.00/ \times) \therefore (\times = 3.86)$$

How many of these 3.86 children themselves survived to the average age at marriage, 24.6? By referring to the Ledermann Mortality Table, to which this cohort's infant and child mortality most closely conformed, it was found that 701 per 1000 survived to 24.6. Therefore the number of children per family surviving to the average age at marriage was: 3.86 × 0.801 = 2.71.

Of these 2.71 surviving children per family, how many actually married? Demographers have observed that in populations marrying early, marriage is practically universal but in populations where the average age at marriage is late, such as in preindustrial England, a relatively high proportion of the population never marries at all. Bearing this in mind, the incidence of marriage has been calculated on the assumption that marriage was universal at an average of 20.0 but that for every year later that it occurred there were 2% who never married (of both men and women). In early modern Terling, therefore, an average age at marriage of 24.6 suggests that its incidence was 90.8%. Of the 2.71 children surviving to the average age at marriage in our hypothetical family there were 2.71 × .908 = 2.46 who married.

If there were no difference in the sex ratio of the marrying children, then the net rate of replacement would have been: 2.46 ÷ 2 = 1.23. We divide the number of children marrying into two because we are interested in a net replacement rate (see Table 3.14).

The villagers were increasing by 23% per generation. What did this rate of generational replacement mean in terms of an annual average rate of population growth? We can find an answer to this question by using the compound interest formula: $A = P(1 + i)^n$. In our case, A means the size of the population at the end of a generation, while P is the initial size of the population, i is the rate of growth, and n is the length of a generation. We already know that the size of the initial population is 1000 and that the size of that population after one generation is 1230 but what we do not yet know is the length of a generation. To do this we started with the assumption that the length of a generation was equivalent to the mean age of childbearing. Given that the women married at 24.6 and produced 3.75 children during her marriage, how long would it take for her to have 1.875 children, the mean point of her childbearing? A mean age at childbearing was chosen in preference to a median one because of the long "tail" on the distribution of fertility. By thirty, the women had given birth to 1.64 children. Assuming that within each age-group births were distributed evenly, the mean age at childbearing was 31.1. This figure was derived by discovering the period of time that this woman would require to produce a further 0.235 children (0.235 plus 1.64, born before 30, equals 1.875). If we refer back to the earlier section in this discussion we can see that in the

TABLE 3.14
The Net Rate of Replacement, 1550–1724

Age at marriage	
GRR[a]	4.86
Revised GRR	3.86
Child survival rate	.700
Surviving children	2.71
Incidence of marriage	.908
Children marrying	2.46
NRR[b]	1.23
Generation	31.1
Annual rate of growth	0.67%
Population doubles every . . ? . . years	104.5

[a] GRR = Gross rate of replacement.
[b] NRR = Net rate of replacement.

30–34 age-group this "typical" women—after allowing for marriages broken by death—had 1.10 children, an annual average of 0.22. To produce 0.235 children at a rate of 0.22 per year would require 1.1 years. Thus the length of a generation, defined as the mean age at child-bearing, was 31.1 years. Using the formula $A = P (1 + i)^n$ makes it a relatively easy matter to determine that the annual compound rate of growth was 0.67% and that the period in which a population with a net rate of replacement of 1.23 would double would be 104.5 years.

It should be pointed out once more that no special claims are being made for the accuracy of this method of analysis. But it seems to us that it is a valuable way of measuring the overall combined effect of the different demographic variables. Moreover, it enables us to isolate each variable and test its contribution to the sum of the parts. In this way we can gain some insight into the relative importance of changes in the various components of the demographic equation.

Having developed a method with which to pierce the mystery of the reconstituted measurements, we can now provide an explanation of the causes of population growth before 1625 and of the rather more stable situation that followed. If we use an interaction formula, such as the one already proposed, then it will be possible to distinguish the social and demographic roots of these developments.

In Table 3.15 the early modern Terling cohort has been divided into two subcohorts—1550–1624 and 1625–1724—that roughly correspond to the periods of surplus baptisms and that of apparent equilibrium. After 1625 a combination of four factors—a slight rise in the age at marriage, a decline

TABLE 3.15
The Net Rate of Replacement before and after 1625

	1550–1624	1625–1724
Age at marriage	24.5	24.7
GRR[a]	5.09	4.75
Revised GRR	4.11	3.73
Child survival rate	0.701	0.692
Surviving children	2.88	2.58
Incidence of marriage	0.910	0.906
Children marrying	2.62	2.34
NRR[b]	1.31	1.17
Generation	31.9	30.8
Annual rate of growth	0.86%	0.52%
Population doubles every.?.yrs.	81.4	134.6

[a] GRR = Gross rate of replacement.

[b] NRR = Net rate of replacement.

in marital fertility (particularly at later ages), a steep decline in illegitimacy, and a small rise in mortality of infants, young children, and adults—led to a decrease in the rate or replacement.[15] In the seventy-five years before 1625 the villagers were doubling their number every 81.4 years, while in the century following 1625 the rate of population growth was significantly reduced

The nature of the sixteenth-century population explosion is something of a moot point among historians. While there is little argument that the population of Tudor England was growing—and growing quickly, at that—there has been little in the way of a convincing explanation for this phenomenon. Of course, there was a significant decline in levels of mortality from those which prevailed in the later Middle Ages but it must hastily be added that this lower death rate was in itself not the *deus ex machina* that its proponents claim. It is an axiom that in periods of demographic equilibrium the birth rate and the death rate display a tendency to fluctuate directly. And so it follows that in explaining the sixteenth-century rise in population we have to account for the failure of the birth rate to decline in conditions of falling mortality. It is at this point that our discussion of demographic change must be reintegrated with the economic developments that have already been noted. The expansion of commercial agriculture appears to have had two quite significant repercussions for the villagers of Terling. In the first place, it promoted the prosperity of a class of substantial farmers who employed wage-laborers to work their lands. And, in the second place, these wage-laborers were afforded the opportunity to marry earlier because they reached their maximum earning capacity at a relatively young age. Thus an expanding commercial agriculture with its proletarianized labor force had the effect of encouraging early-marrying groups and thereby had the result of promoting population growth. Moreover, the employment opportunity offered by wage-labor was essentially different from that of family farming.

The laborer had no need or reason to defer marriage while saving the critical sum necessary to embark on his enterprise and set up a separate household. In a very real sense the capital investment needed to set up a laborer's household was negligible in comparison to that required by even a marginal smallholder who had to have seed-corn, tools, implements, access to draft animals, and the financial wherewithal to pay an entry-fine. For these reasons the laborers—who were becoming progressively more important as the sixteenth century progressed—had no reason to postpone marriage, and, to the extent that early marriage was crucial in promoting population growth, we can see how economic differentiation created a

---

[15] See Tables 3.18, 3.19, 3.20, and 3.21.

response to a shift in the parameters of mortality that was quite contrary to what would have been expected in conditions of demographic equilibrium.

The question to which we would now like to turn our attention is that of the relative contributions made by the various components of the demographic equation—nuptiality, fertility, illegitimacy, and mortality—to the observed decline in the net rate of replacement after 1625. By simulating a state of affairs in which one variable changed while the others remained constant, it will be possible to determine the contribution made by declining fertility, plummeting illegitimacy, and rising mortality. In Table 3.16 these three counterfactual simulations are presented in the format already described.

It is clear that the most important brake on Terling's population growth was exerted by the decline in marital fertility, which was itself the product of a somewhat later age at marriage acting in concert with a pronounced fall in age-specific fertility for women over thirty-five. In contrast to the direct action taken through the "prudential" check, the role of rising mortality was small. Indeed, the decline in the level of illegitimacy can be seen to have been of more importance than rising mortality. This simulation is suggestive in that it goes no little way toward undermining belief in the efficacy of the Four Horsemen—war, famine, pestilence, and fire—during the *ancien régime*. In a community like Terling there was only one serious epidemic, in 1625. Otherwise, as can be seen in Figure 3.1, there were few other spectacular swathes made by the grim reapers. Rather, like a kind of background noise, the presence of death was always there. Family reconstitution studies—such as the Terling example being discussed here—are making it clear that mortality was not a major agent in furthering population control. In almost all studies it is being discovered that variations in age at marriage and marital fertility were the basic methods to which a population had recourse when it was trying to limit its numbers.

In Terling after 1625, the evidence for family limitation is far greater than it is for the earlier cohort. In Table 3.17 the two cohorts have been divided into two subgroups (following the logic adopted above) in order to discern the fertility experience of women by using their age at marriage as an independent variable. Not only did the younger brides in the later cohort begin to limit their fertility at an earlier age, but at every parity their rates of age-specific fertility were significantly lower.

As far as we can determine, Terling's population size remained stable for almost 150 years after 1625. In the annual totals of baptisms and burials, this stability gains an added resonance. However, the picture derived from the reconstituted data is rather different from that yielded by the aggregated statistics. As the simulation exercises make clear, there was a reduction in the net rate of replacement but not a total one. Even after 1625

TABLE 3.16
Impact of Changing Fertility, Mortality and Illegitimacy on the Net Rate of Replacement

	1550-1624	Stable mortality, declining illegitimacy, declining fertility, and later marriage	Stable fertility, stable illegitimacy, stable marriage, and rising mortality	Stable fertility, stable marriage, stable mortality, and declining illegitimacy
Age at marriage	24.5	24.7	24.5	24.5
GRR	5.09	4.75	5.11	5.11
Revised GRR	4.11	3.77	4.13	3.96
Child survival rate	0.701	0.699	0.692	0.701
Surviving children	2.88	2.64	2.86	2.78
Incidence of marriage	0.910	0.906	0.910	0.910
Children marrying	2.62	2.38	2.60	2.52
NRR	1.31	1.19	1.30	1.26
Generation	31.9	30.8	31.9	30.8
Annual rate of growth(%)	0.86	0.57	0.83	0.76
Population doubles every...?... years	81.4	122.8	84.3	92.1

TABLE 3.17
A Test for Family Limitation in Early Modern Terling

	Under 25	25–29	30–34	35–39	40–44	45–49
1550–1624						
Marrying under 25	$396(\frac{40}{101})$	$271(\frac{26}{96})$	$280(\frac{23}{82})$	$242(\frac{16}{66})$	$118(\frac{4}{34})$	$0(\frac{0}{27})$
Marrying over 25		$395(\frac{15}{38})$	$264(\frac{19}{72})$	$230(\frac{14}{61})$	$169(\frac{10}{59})$	$0(\frac{0}{39})$
Younger brides' fertility expressed as a proportion of older brides'		0.68	1.06	1.05	0.70	—
1625–1724						
Marrying under 25	$372(\frac{42}{113})$	$300(\frac{36}{120})$	$271(\frac{29}{107})$	$179(\frac{15}{64})$	$46(\frac{3}{65})$	$0(\frac{0}{48})$
Marrying over 25		$450(\frac{18}{40})$	$307(\frac{23}{75})$	$247(\frac{19}{77})$	$125(\frac{8}{64})$	$0(\frac{0}{21})$
Younger brides' fertility expressed as a proportion of older brides'		0.67	0.88	0.72	0.37	—

TABLE 3.18
Age at Marriage before and after 1625

	Number	Mean	Standard deviation	Lower quartile	Median	Upper quartile	Interquartile range
Men							
1550–1624	42	25.9	3.9	23.2	25.0	28.8	5.6
1625–1724	70	24.9	5.2	22.1	24.1	27.2	5.1
Women							
1550–1624	88	24.5	4.3	21.5	23.8	26.9	5.4
1625–1724	90	24.7	5.2	19.7	23.9	28.1	8.4

TABLE 3.19
Age-Specific Fertility before and after 1625

	Years	Children born	Rate per 1000 years lived
1550–1624			
Under 25	82	35	427
25–29	110	35	318
30–34	121	32	267
35–39	98	25	258
40–44	81	11	136
45–49	60	0	0
1625–1724			
Under 25	111	42	379
25–29	160	54	338
30–34	182	52	286
35–39	161	34	211
40–44	118	11	93
45–49	74	0	0

the villagers continued to produce sons and daughters over and above the numbers needed for simple replacement. What became of these children and young adults? Instead of viewing the seventeenth-century stabilization in simple demographic terms, it is necessary to add to it another potent factor: migration from and immigration to the village community. A great deal of recent work in historical demography has been devoted to this subject and it is becoming quite apparent that the immobile swain of days gone by has been relegated to the dustbin of history. A consensus is now developing that stresses, on the one hand, extraordinary age-specific mobility among youths and, on the other, a solid core of stable, usually substantial families.[16] By readjusting our focus it becomes possible to bring both aspects of reality into a single field of vision. Bygone historians and antiquarians were not simply wrong when they asserted the immutability of the village community. Rather, they were dyslexic. To be sure, the village notable and local worthies of the "better sort" were tied to a community by the bands of property. The proletarianized day-laborer's experience was quite different.

How can this revisionist version of population mobility help us to answer the problem defined by the conflicting suggestions of the aggregated and reconstituted measurements?

To develop an answer we must first understand the calculus employed by the local poor-law officials, the parish officers who were empowered to

---

[16] An illuminating discussion of age-specific mobility is to be found in Roger Schofield's article "Age-Specific Mobility in an Eighteenth Century Rural English Parish."

TABLE 3.20
Infant and Child Mortality (MF) before and after 1625

	Reconstitution					Ledermann	
Age	At risk	Dying	Rate per 1000	Survivors	e°	Rate per 1000	Survivors
				1550–1624			
0–1	1059	136	128	1000	46.61	137	1000
1–4	665	48	72	872		95	863
5–9	388	14	36	809		27	781
10–14	241	10	41	780		19	760
				750			746
				1625–1724			
0–1	1392	184	132	1000	46.61	137	1000
1–4	932	90	97	868		95	863
5–9	569	23	40	784		27	781
10–14	376	8	21	752		19	760
				737			746

TABLE 3.21
Adult Mortality (MF) before and after 1625

| | Life expectations | | | Survivors | |
Age	1550–1624	1625–1724	Age	1550–1624	1625–1724
25–29	29.3	28.4	25–29	1000	1000
30–34	26.1	25.9	30–34	939	926
35–39	23.2	23.4	35–39	862	841
40–44	20.7	20.8	40–44	761	763
45–49	18.4	18.2	45–49	675	682
50–54	15.9	15.3	50–54	576	590
55–59	13.5	13.6	55–59	490	447
				397	385

strike their own balance between, on the one hand, a large supply of labor, low wages, and high poor rates and, on the other, a controled supply, higher wages, and low poor rates. Excess, surplus laborers were in effect forced out. They either looked for settlement elsewhere in their native locale or else they drifted toward the urban centers, particularly London whose appetite for new recruits was insatiable.[17] When viewed in this perspective, the contradiction between the convergence of annual totals of mortality and fertility and the persistence of an albeit reduced level of reproduction above mere replacement becomes explicable. In all likelihood the community possessed an age-pyramid in which the age-groups with the highest risk of death (infants, young children, and the elderly) were over-represented, while the relatively healthy groups (adolescents and young adults) were comparatively underrepresented. In this way the annual number of births would be lower and deaths would be higher than the reconstituted evidence suggests. Social stabilization, not a demographic turnaround, explains the convergence of the annual totals of baptisms and burials in early seventeenth-century Terling. The effect of fertility limitation was to close the gap even further.

We have shown that in Terling the age at marriage and fertility, and not mortality, were the prime agents of demographic control. While the short-run implications of epidemic mortality were of real consequence, they were of little importance in the long run. The ecological parameters of life seem to have determined a range of mortality within which there was scope for considerable year-to-year variation. However, viewed in the broad context of 175 years, the positive check was of comparatively less importance. The changing strategies of family formation and marital fertility were far more pertinent in influencing the demographic pendulum. To this extent, the experience of Terling broadly conforms to the developing synthesis in early modern historical demography.

[17] E.A. Wrigley, "A Simple Model of London's Importance in Changing English Society and Economy, 1650–1750."

4
A LOCAL SOCIAL SYSTEM

On 20 November 1639 Robert Green, yeoman, lay dying. He was not an old man, probably being only some forty years of age at the time of his death. His exact age is unknown to us, for he was not baptized in Terling. His father, John Green, had arrived in Terling in the early years of the seventeenth century already married and with a young family. By the time of his death in 1626, John Green had established himself as a substantial yeoman farmer. He had served as churchwarden and as a Quarter Sessions juryman for the parish. He was literate and a man of some piety, a friend of the Puritan minister Thomas Weld and one of the village notables who had backed Weld's predecessor Thomas Rust against the ungodliness and disorder of the village alehouses. John had two sons. The elder son, Roger, married in 1614 and lived for some years in Terling, though he had left the parish by the time of his father's death, doubtless to establish himself elsewhere. At his father's death he received a legacy of cash. Robert, the younger son, inherited the lease of his father's farm in Terling together with his father's livestock and implements of husbandry. To him also fell the task of caring for his mother during the remaining years of her life. Soon after his father's death he married, though his first wife, Lydia, died in childbed in 1631. Within two years Robert had married again and his second wife, Ann, was to outlive him. They had two children, only one of whom, a daughter, was still living in 1639. During the 1630s Robert prospered. By village standards he was a fairly wealthy man. Like his father he served as churchwarden and sessions juryman. Again like his father he was literate and inclined toward Puritanism in religion. At his death, he left £200 to secure the future of his small daughter and the remainder of his goods to his wife, who was appointed his executor. Small sums were also given to his "deare friend" the Puritan vicar John Stalham and to his "love-ing cousin" Richard Tabor, a Puritan yeoman. The will was witnessed by another friend and coreligionist, John Maidstone, a gentleman farmer who had only recently moved to Terling from a parish in Suffolk. The second witness was John Abraham, a young husbandman who had arrived in Terl-ing two years before from the nearby parish of Black Notley. Robert Green died surrounded by his wife and friends and was buried three days later. His wife and child may have left Terling soon afterward, for of them we know no more.[1]

The case of Robert Green may serve to introduce some of the principal characteristics of the social structure of seventeenth-century Terling. In the history of his own family and of those of some of his friends we find il-lustrated the fluidity and unboundedness of a community constantly changing in composition as a result of geographical mobility. In his per-sonal relationships lie clues as to the nature of the ties that gave structure and stability to the community. The most fundamental of such relation-ships were those between members of the same nuclear family household.

In the household, children were reared until such time as they could be set forth independently to make their own way in the world, taking with them whatever advantages of wealth and education their parents were able to provide. Beyond the household were those ties that held together the community as an association of households; ties of kinship, of friendship, and of neighborliness. Influencing all these relationships were the over-arching structures of the distributions of wealth, status, and power among the villagers. It is with these elements of the social structure that we must now concern ourselves in order to complement our analysis of the economic and demographic structures of the village with an exploration of the relationships of the villagers both to one another and to the wider world.

THE SOCIAL AREA: EXTRAVILLAGE RELATIONSHIPS AND GEOGRAPHICAL MOBILITY

Terling had its own integrity as a social unit. The villagers lived and worked in close proximity to one another. As a unit of secular and ec-

---

[1] E. R. O. D/ACW 10/66; D/ACW 13/184; D/ACD 7, fos. 137, 137v. In this, as in other brief biographies of villagers, references are to the principal documents concerned only, in

clesiastical government the parish had a distinct identity of which its inhabitants were demonstrably aware. In the church they met together as a Christian community. Less formally, they cooperated with one another in economic activities and shared, in differing degrees, the leisure pursuits of the green and the alehouses. As a constellation of institutions focusing their interaction, as a network of ties between kin, friends, and neighbors, the village community had a special claim on their loyalties, a special place in their sense of personal identity. Yet Terling was in no way a bounded society, a social isolate. On the contrary the society of the village was deeply involved with the larger society of which it was a part. So important is this issue to our understanding of the village as a local social system that we must begin our discussion by placing the villagers within what W.M. Williams has called their "social area."[2] We must explore the geography of *extra*village relationships and establish the dimensions of the greater world within which the people of Terling lived and moved.

This objective is more easily stated than achieved. It is, of course, impossible to recover from historical records every tie that the villagers of Terling had with the inhabitants of other towns and villages. Nevertheless, sufficient evidence of such relationships does survive to enable us to form a fairly clear picture of the geographical extent of at least some extravillage relationships.

The wills of the villagers, for example, make frequent reference to kinsmen and kinswomen who were clearly not inhabitants of Terling. Unfortunately, testators commonly felt it unnecessary to specify the whereabouts of these relatives, but in some cases such detail is given and can be employed in this analysis. Again, it is evident that the marriage partners of villagers were commonly from other parishes. While the place of origin of most of these persons remains unknown to us, we do have detail of the home villages of a good number of them, since these were sometimes stated in the parish register. In addition, the parish register and the records of the ecclesiastical courts and court of Quarter Sessions can be combined to yield the places of origin of the fathers of illegitimate children begotten on Terling women and of the mothers of bastard children begotten outside the parish by Terling men. This provides further evidence of the geographical range of courtships outside the village. Recognizance bonds issued by the justices of the peace and filed among the Quarter Sessions records give evidence of Terling villagers acting as sureties in the recognizances of outsiders and of outsiders performing the same service for Terling villagers. The other records of Quarter Sessions of the assizes and of the central courts at Westminster yield the names and parishes of out-

particular to those quoted from. Supporting information is derived from both the family reconstitution study and the general name index to our files.

[2] W. M. Williams, *A West Country Village: Ashworthy: Family, Kinship, and Land,* p. 39.

siders involved in disputes with Terling people. Both wills and the mortgage indentures filed with the deeds of the parish provide information on
debt and credit relationships with outsiders. Finally, deeds and wills also
contain evidence of outsiders owning land or houses in Terling and of Terling villagers owning land or houses in other places, such land usually being
let out.

Taken together these various sources of information provide evidence of
relationships between Terling villagers and outsiders resident in London,
several towns and villages in the counties of Kent, Hertfordshire, Suffolk,
Cambridgeshire, and Norfolk, and no fewer than 108 towns and villages
within Essex. The most distant contact recorded was with a kinsman who
had emigrated to New England! Of the Essex towns and villages concerned,
fifteen lay within five miles of Terling, thirty-three from five to nine miles,
twenty-eight from ten to fourteen miles, seventeen from fifteen to nineteen
miles, and fifteen twenty or more miles from the village. Table 4.1 provides
details of the number and proportion of relationships of different kinds by
distance in miles from Terling.

As will be evident from consideration of Table 4.1, there were only two
types of relationship with outsiders—debt and credit and outsiders owning
Terling property—in which less than two-thirds of the relationships for
which we have evidence were with persons living under ten miles from
Terling. Courtships resulting in marriage or illegitimacy and recognizance
relationships were particularly concentrated within the ten-mile limit. The
geographical range of most cases of dispute involvement, kinship, and
ownership of property outside Terling was only a little greater. Nevertheless, all types of relationships examined could be and were on occasion
established with persons living over twenty miles away, sometimes much
farther than twenty miles away. The social area of Terling villagers was
largely contained within the distance of ten miles and yet, not infrequently,
it could be very much larger.

This analysis can be taken one step further if we consider the actual
shape of the social area by mapping the Essex settlements with which Terling villagers enjoyed the closest contact. Because of the scattered nature of
the evidence at our disposal, it was decided that for this purpose it was of
limited usefulness to assess closeness of involvement with Terling villagers
by simply counting the total number of relationships for which we have
evidence. Instead, we have based our estimate of the shape of the social
area upon the number of *types* of relationship that Terling villagers are
known to have had with other villages. The resulting map is presented as
Figure 4.1.

Figure 4.1 reveals that all eight types of relationship were found only
with the three neighboring parishes of Witham, Hatfield Peverel, and

TABLE 4.1
The Social Area of Terling Villagers[a]

	Distance in miles										
	Under 5		5-9		10-14		15-19		20+		Total
Type of relationship	(N)	(%)	(N)	(%)	(N)	(%)	(N)	(%)	(N)	(%)	
Kinship	15	24.2	27	43.5	5	8.1	7	11.3	8	12.9	62
Marriage partners	32	44.4	26	36.1	5	6.9	1	1.4	8	11.1	72
Illegitimacy partner	13	59.1	5	22.7	1	4.5	1	4.5	2	9.1	22
Recognisances	29	46.0	23	36.5	5	7.9	1	1.6	5	7.9	63
Disputes in courts	41	48.2	21	24.7	6	7.1	6	7.1	11	12.9	85
Debt and credit	5	29.4	4	23.5	2	11.8	2	11.8	4	23.5	17
Outsiders with land/ house in Terling	11	20.8	15	28.3	9	17.0	4	7.5	14	26.4	53
Terling villagers with house/land elsewhere	24	40.6	15	25.4	10	16.9	7	11.9	3	5.1	59

[a] Note: Subtotals have been rounded off and do not always total 100%.

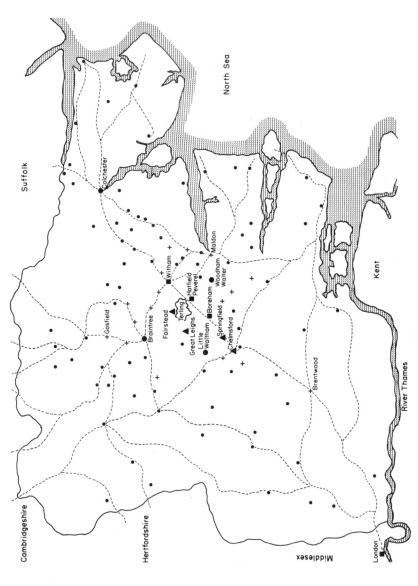

Figure 4.1 Terling's social area. Number of types of relationships: ■ = 8; ▲ = 7; ● = 6; + = 3-5; ● = 1-2; --- = principal roads.

Boreham (all lying on the main highway to London) and with London itself. Seven relationships were found with Terling's other two neighbors, Fairstead and Great Leighes, with Springfield and with Chelmsford. The last two were also road parishes, Chelmsford being both a major market and the administrative center of the county. Six relationships were found with the villages of Little Waltham and Woodham Walter, with the market town of Braintree and with the city of Colchester.

The core of Terling's social area would appear to have been a triangular area between the market towns of Braintree to the north, Witham to the east, and Chelmsford to the southwest, while close contact was also maintained with London and Colchester. A larger penumbral area, again triangular in shape, can be discerned between Gosfield, Maldon, and Brentwood, when places with which three to five relationships have been found are included. For the rest, Terling villagers had recorded contacts with villages and towns scattered all over the county, but lying for the most part in a broad corridor running from the Suffolk border toward London. This evidence would suggest that beyond its immediate neighbors the social area of Terling was shaped by the pull of those forces that were to be of such importance in the internal development of village society; the market, local administration, and the pervasive, multifaceted influence of London.

Additional strength was given to the relationships of Terling villagers with the outside world by the fact that a majority of the adult population of the village had experience of living in other communities. Attention has already been drawn to the geographical mobility of Terling's population and to the probable demographic significance of this phenomenon. We unfortunately lack for Terling such rare census-type listings as made possible the precise analysis of mobility in Clayworth, Cogenhoe, and Cardington.[3] Nevertheless the family reconstitution forms can be employed to form a picture of the nature and extent of the turnover of Terling's population.

Of all persons marrying for the first time in Terling who subsequently baptized at least one child in the parish between 1580 and 1699, only a little over a quarter of the men and a third of the women had themselves been baptized in Terling. The great majority of those marrying and settling long enough to baptize a child were not natives of the parish. This measure is not, of course, perfect since it is possible that some children born to settled families had not, for whatever reason, been baptized in Terling. In the absence of consecutive listings, however, it gives at least a disciplined estimate of the extent to which villagers had arrived in Terling as immigrants prior to marriage. Moreover it allows us to discern change over

---

[3] P. Laslett, "Clayworth and Cogenhoe," pp. 65-75; R. S. Schofield, "Age-Specific Mobility in an Eighteenth Century Rural English Parish."

considerable periods of time in a manner not usually possible when consecutive listings are analyzed. When the period studied is divided into three periods of forty years each, we find that although the proportion of women baptized in Terling remained steady at about one third for each period, the proportion of men baptized in Terling was rising over time. While some 19% of men studied had been baptized in Terling in the period 1580–1619, this proportion had risen to some 40% by 1660–1699. There may have been a significant stabilization of male immigration in the course of the seventeenth century, a finding that tallies with some recent work on trends in population mobility in preindustrial England. Where these immigrants came from we do not know, though in all probability they were drawn in from parishes within Terling's social area, either as adolescent servants or by the existence of opportunities for employment and family formation. John Rond and Agnes Dawson, for example, are first found in 1607 living as "inmates" of the miller Richard Gaymer. John was soon established as a miller himself, perhaps as Gaymer's tenant, and the couple married and began to raise their family.[4]

The arrival of young people seeking opportunities for settlement and marriage was only one aspect of immigration into Terling; couples who married in Terling were, in themselves, a minority of all those who baptized children in the parish in this period. Over the years 1580 to 1699 only a little over one-third of new couples baptizing children in Terling had actually been themselves married in Terling. A number of these families were headed by men born to Terling families who had married outside but who had brought their wives back and settled in the village. The vast majority, however, simply appear in the parish register already married. An example is provided by Robert Johnson and his wife. They were questioned in 1607 by the authorities since there was doubt as to the validity of their marriage. Both had formerly lived in Upminster, more than twenty miles from Terling. Mary Johnson had lived there for some ten years until the death of her first husband. Robert had been a laborer and had cohabited there for a year with one Elizabeth Whitland by whom he had had a child, "but was not marryed unto her . . . but would have marryed her if the inhabitants would have suffered him and therefore he left her and her child there and went to London." Some time later he met his future wife at Aveley market, proposed marriage to her, and they went together to London and were married. What brought them to Terling we shall never know, but they had arrived by 1603 when they baptized a daughter there. At the time of their examination in 1607 Robert was a laborer.[5] This extraordinary story

[4] E. R. O. D/ACA 30, fo.179.
[5] E. R. O. Q/SR 181/97.

throws a beam of light into the darkness that shrouds the existence and life experience of the laboring poor. But for their examination there would be nothing to distinguish this couple from the scores of others who made their brief appearance in the parish registers. They were not vagrants but rather the flotsam and jetsam of rural society in the period. Having achieved a settlement, the Johnsons stayed. Their daughter, Frances, married a laborer in 1625 and bore him seven children. Three died in infancy, two disappeared from the records, presumably moving elsewhere, while two married in Terling and carried the family line on into the eighteenth century.

Not all couples establishing themselves in Terling necessarily stayed there, however. The arrival of immigrants was balanced by the departure not only of unmarried adolescents but also of whole families. An indication of this mobility is provided by the fact that of all couples beginning to baptize their children in Terling between 1580 and 1699 only about half the men and half the women were ultimately buried in Terling. Some moved on, like Anthony Clay, his wife, and four children who were returned to Terling from Witham under the Law of Settlement in 1683. After this unsuccessful attempt to seek better times elsewhere both were ultimately buried in Terling.[6] Indeed, this case prompts the reflection that the law of settlement and the greater sensitivity of parish authorities to the mobility of the poor may have been partly responsible, in concert with the general demographic deceleration, for the evident stabilization of mobility that took place over the course of the seventeenth century. Some evidence of this has been presented here. Equally relevant is the fact that while in 1580 to 1619 some 40% of both men and women who baptized their children in Terling were buried there, by 1660 to 1699 this proportion had risen to over 60% of both men and women.

The population of Terling was thus highly geographically mobile, though the rate of the turnover of population was diminishing over time. However, this mobility, while experienced by all social groups, was not equally shared by all. An examination of the evidence for population turnover, which takes note of the relative social position of the families concerned, reveals that over the whole period of study persons in Category I, the gentlemen and great farmers of the parish, were the most fluid element in village society. The husbandmen and craftsmen of Category III were the most stable element. The experience of the yeomen of Category II lay somewhere between. In the case of the laboring poor of Category IV, however, we find that members of this group were subject to very rapid turnover prior to 1620, but that their rate of turnover stabilized gradually

---

[6] E. R. O. Q/SO 2, fo.223.

in the period 1620 to 1660. By the later decades of the seventeenth century, the laborers of Terling were almost as stable as the husbandmen and craftsmen of the village. The overall stabilization of population mobility in seventeenth-century Terling, then, was produced above all by the checking of the mobility of the poor after 1620. The more stable situation that had come into being by 1671 is illustrated by the figures presented in Table 4.2. As can be seen, only in the case of the householders in Category III were less than 50% of householders first generation villagers. The turnover of population had stabilized in Terling, but it was still very considerable.

Village society in Terling was thus very far from being bounded by the horizons of the parish. Important as was the unit of the parish in the lives of the villagers, their society was essentially fluid. It was perhaps this very fluidity that led contemporaries to place such stress upon the relationships that bound village society together, on kinship and neighborliness, on the hierarchical social order with its attendant privileges and obligations, which gave enduring structure and stability to their fluid social world. How important were kinship and neighborliness to the internal cohesion of village society in Terling? How pervasive were the distinctions of wealth, status, and power in the life of the community? The remainder of this chapter will be concerned with these questions.

THE NETWORK OF KINSHIP IN TERLING

It is now some years since Professor Williams argued that "It does seem as if the general structure of English kinship is now clearly established." Reviewing the findings of a number of social scientists, he pointed to the general predominance of the nuclear family in household structure; the bilateral tracing of descent which gives a unique set of kin to every individual; a "recognition" of kin that is both shallow in depth and narrow in

TABLE 4.2
Population Mobility: Terling Householders 1671

Social category of householders	Number of generations settled in Terling			
	First generation	Second generation	Third or more generation	Total
I	6 (60.0%)	4 (40.0%)	0 (0.0%)	10 (100%)
II	18 (62.1%)	7 (24.0%)	4 (13.8%)	29 (100%)
III	10 (47.6%)	5 (23.8%)	6 (28.6%)	21 (100%)
IV	35 (56.5%)	15 (24.2%)	12 (19.3%)	62 (100%)

range. He emphasized that modern English kinship is "a flexible permissive system" having few strong obligations or rules of behavior between kin. Kin sentiments are rarely sufficiently strong to overcome geographical or social distance, while kinship is in general functionally unimportant as compared with ties of neighborliness. In sum, kinship should be seen as merely one of several networks of connection within communities from which individuals might select one another for various purposes.[7]

Historians probing the distant past might well expect to discover a very different situation. Those concerned with the sixteenth and seventeenth centuries have long been aware of the preoccupation with lineage and of the effective importance of kin ties among the ruling class of the period.[8] Of realities lower in the social scale, however, little is known, though recent work suggests that expectations based on the experience of aristocrats and gentlemen should not be too readily generalized for the mass of the population. In particular, the last decade has seen two major advances in the discussion of English kinship in the past. Peter Laslett's work on census-type listings has transformed our knowledge of kinship links *within* households. He has revealed the overwhelming predominance of nuclear-family households in rural England as early as the sixteenth century and has demonstrated that the complexity of household structure diminished sharply as the social scale was descended.[9] Alan Macfarlane's careful analysis of the diary of the Essex clergyman Ralph Josselin for the mid- and later-seventeenth century has displayed Josselin's lack of interest in lineage and his very restricted recognition of kin. While stressing the closeness of ties within his nuclear family and the probable early importance to him of relationships with his uncles, Macfarlane shows firmly that "apart from the nuclear family there was no effective kin 'group' in Josselin's world." Josselin's key relationships beyond his own nuclear family were with personal friends and neighbors.[10]

These findings prompt further research into issues that the nature of their evidence has not permitted these scholars to explore. Laslett, for example, is less able to examine kinship links *between* households on the basis of listings alone. Nor is he able to explore the nature and quality of kinship relations either within or between households, though ultimately these

---

[7] W. M. Williams, *A West Country Village: Ashworthy*, pp. 183–184 and Chapter 6.

[8] L. Stone, *The Crisis of the Aristocracy, 1558–1641* (abridged edition) pp. 269–271; A. M. Everitt, *Change in the Provinces: The Seventeenth Century*, pp. 26–29; M. E. James, *Family, Lineage and Civil Society. A Study of Society, Politics, and Mentality in the Durham Region, 1500–1640*, pp. 25–27; L. Stone, "The rise of the nuclear family in England," pp. 13–14.

[9] P. Laslett and R. Wall ed., *Household and family in past time*, Chapter 4.

[10] A. Macfarlane, *The Family Life of Ralph Josselin. A seventeenth-century clergyman. An essay in historical anthropology*, pp. 82, 149 and Chapters 7 to 10.

issues may prove of more significance in the process of social change than the preliminary problem of household structure. Macfarlane's analysis faces problems of typicality. Josselin was a clergyman, an immigrant to his parish, geographically isolated from kinsmen; was his experience therefore unusual?

These are issues that we will attempt to explore more fully in the case of Terling. We will begin by reconstructing and analyzing the network of kinship links between households in Terling in 1671. Next, wills will be examined to provide information on kinship recognition and on relations between close kin over the period 1550 to 1700. Finally, a variety of sources will be used to assess the relative importance of kin and neighbors for a variety of practical purposes. Throughout, the analysis will be comprehensive, dealing with as large a section of the population as is possible. Most importantly, the results reported will be comparable to results that may be provided in the future for any other village for which the same basic sources are available. Our first questions, then, concern the extent to which households in Terling were linked by kinship, the nature of those links, and the extent to which they varied with age, sex, and social position.

Terling, like most English villages, has no census-type listing of the inhabitants for any date in the sixteenth and seventeenth centuries. What it does have, again like many other villages, is a series of Hearth Tax listings, the most comprehensive of which, that of 1671, has already been described. In an attempt to reconstruct the network of kin in Terling, the kin of each householder on this list have been traced using both the family reconstitution forms and a name index based on every other record of the village available to us for the period 1524 to 1700. All evidence of connection between individuals has been recorded in this index. Wherever possible the kin of each householder were traced back for two generations and forward to the date of the listing. Uncles, aunts, cousins and second cousins, siblings, nephews, and nieces were included where possible. If the householder was or had been married, affines were also traced in the same fashion. In effect, the kin of each married couple were traced.

Despite every effort to be thorough, the information available was often incomplete. This incompleteness was usually a genuine reflection of population mobility and lack of local kin ties. Nevertheless, the kin links established must necessarily be regarded as a minimum estimate since some links may be concealed. For comparison, a maximum estimate of kin links has also been provided that includes suspected or simply possible links based, for example, on identical surnames. Some of these additional links are strongly suspected; others are very long shots, based on slight evidence. Comparison of the minimum and maximum estimates thus provides a range of error, the truth doubtless lying somewhere between the two. The results of this analysis are given below:

	Minimum		Maximum	
Total householders	122	(100%)	122	(100%)
Related to other householders	48	(39.3%)	64	(52.5%)
Unrelated to other householders	74	(60.7%)	58	(47.5%)

To say that some 50 to 60% of householders were unrelated to other householders, even very distantly, is not, of course, to say that they had no kin in Terling. Most of them were married and had children. It is to say rather that their *households* (which in the English context we can confidently expect to have been predominantly nuclear-family households) were isolated within the village in terms of kinship, unlinked to other households by either blood or marriage. Many, of course, had kin in other villages, as we have seen.

Figures of this kind, whatever their intrinsic interest and value in qualifying the assumption that the inhabitants of seventeenth-century villages were densely interrelated, are of little further use unless placed in some sort of comparative context. Do they indicate a relatively high or relatively low degree of kin linkage? Comparative material is unfortunately very hard to come by. Compared to Professor Williams' study of Gosforth in the 1950s, the extent of kin linkage in Terling was low, whichever estimate we use.[11] Williams found that 80% of occupiers and their wives in Gosforth were closely related to at least one other household. This comparison, while a salutary warning to those who would assume a greater degree of kin linkage in the past than in the twentieth century, is nevertheless vitiated by the great disparity between the economies of the two villages, let alone their different historical contexts. However, a better comparison can be made with the three eighteenth-century French villages examined in an important thesis by Emmanuel Todd. Each of these villages had an economy based on large-scale commercial farming, like that of Terling.[12]

Comparison with the villages studied by Todd necessitates the use of "first-order" kin links only (i.e., those links between households established

[11] W. M. Williams, *The Sociology of an English Village: Gosforth,* pp. 69–85.
[12] E. Todd, "Seven Peasant Communities in Pre-Industrial Europe. A comparative study of French, Italian and Swedish rural parishes," p. 31 and chapters 4 and 5. We would like to thank Dr. Todd for permission to refer to his unpublished dissertation.

through parents and children or through siblings).[13] Reworking the Terling material in this way means using only proven links and dropping more distant kin links. For the sake of comparability Todd's minimum estimates of linkage are used. The results of this comparison are presented in Table 4.3, together with the comparable figures for Gosforth.

As Table 4.3 indicates, a lower proportion of Terling households were linked to other households by first-order kinship links than in any of the French villages. Terling's experience was closer to that of modern Gosforth, though even here the difference is more striking than the similarity. Two further comparative measurements can be made. The first of these, *absolute kinship density*, is a measure of the absolute number of kin links of the average householder or conjugal family unit in the respective villages. It has the advantage of going beyond the simple categories of "related" and "unrelated" and of allowing for the fact that some householders had links to several others. The second measurement, *relative kinship density*, represents the proportion of kin links observed of the total number of *possible* kin links in the respective villages. Again, first-order links only are employed.[14] The results are presented in Table 4.4.

Once more we find that in comparison with the French villages, the kinship network of Terling was very loose indeed. Furthermore, this would continue to be the case even if the Terling figures were corrected up

TABLE 4.3
First-Order Kinship Links between Householders–Conjugal Family Units[a]

	Terling 1671	Gosforth 1950–1953	Wisques 1778	Longuenesse 1778	Hallines 1776
Total number of HH–CFUs	122		23	42	50
Unrelated to others	67%	50%	43%	26%	18%
Related to 1	26%		39%	36%	30%
Related to 2	7%		14%	19%	22%
Related to 3+	0%		4%	19%	30%
Total % related	33%	50%	57%	74%	82%

[a] Householders in the case of Terling; Conjugal Family Units in the case of the French villagers. See Footnote 13.

[13] The links established by Todd were between conjugal family units (CFUs) rather than between householders. His results are, however, comparable to those obtained for Terling since the vast majority of households in these French villages were, in fact, nuclear-family households, while in the case of Terling the kin of householders' spouses have also been reconstructed.

[14] A very clear exposition of the method of calculation is to be found in E. Todd, "Seven Peasant Communities," pp. 218–220, 232–234.

TABLE 4.4
The Density of Kinship Networks (First-Order Links)

	Terling 1671	Wisques 1778	Longuenesse 1778	Hallines 1776
Total number of HH–CFUs	122	23	42	50
Absolute kinship density	0.39	0.77	1.36	1.73
Relative kinship density	0.3%	3.5%	3.3%	3.5%

substantially from the minimum estimate of kinship linkage on which these calculations are based.

Comparison with Todd's French villages, while useful in setting the Terling findings in context, has necessarily been based only on the closest kin links. Returning to Terling alone, consideration can now be given to *all* kin links and maximum and minimum estimates can be reintroduced in Table 4.5.

These results indicate yet again the relative looseness of the network of kinship in Terling. Whichever estimate is used it is clear that even those householders who had kin among other householders usually had only one such link. Fairly extensive kinship networks certainly existed, but they were few and untypical. Whether these findings are characteristic of all English villages, of certain types of community—for example, lowland parishes involved in a tenant farming system—or are the results of circumstances peculiar to Terling, it is as yet impossible to say. One would surely expect to find considerable variation in England as in France. What will be of ultimate significance when comparative material becomes available will be the question of the range of variation and the factors in-

TABLE 4.5
Kinship Links in Terling (All Links)

	Minimum	Maximum
Total number of householders	122 (100%)	122 (100%)
Unrelated to others	74 (60.7%)	58 (47.5%)
Related to 1	32 (26.2%)	39 (32.0%)
Related to 2	10 (8.2%)	16 (13.1%)
Related to 3	4 (3.3%)	6 (4.9%)
Related to 4	2 (1.6%)	3 (2.5%)
Total related	48 (39.3%)	64 (52.5%)
Absolute kinship density	0.59	0.83
Relative kinship density	0.5%	0.7%

fluencing it—economic system, social structure, age structure, or demographic rates.

While comparison between parishes with different economies and demographic rates must await further research, some progress can be made in investigating the influence of age and social position on the network of kin in Terling.

Analysis by age carries us on to rather dangerous ground. The family reconstitution forms yield the exact baptismal date of only forty-one householders. In other cases, age can only be roughly estimated on the basis of marriage dates, and in still other cases, no reasonable estimate can be attempted. The resulting figures need not be repeated. Suffice it to say that the distribution of householders with at least one kin link by age approximated closely, on both maximum and minimum estimates, to the distribution by age of all householders. The calculation of kinship densities for particular age-groups showed little variation save that the kinship densities of the groups aged 60–69 and 70+ were somewhat lower than those of younger groups. Most householders with kinship links, single or multiple, were aged between thirty and fifty, as indeed were most householders in the population. Presumably this is a simple reflection of the fact that persons of this age were most likely to have adult brothers, affines, and even parents and parents-in-law still alive and heading their own households.

Turning to the question of the influence of wealth and social position, we step on to much firmer ground. Comparisons between particular social levels were made on the basis of the analysis of the 1671 list which has already been presented in Chapter 2.[15]

It can be said immediately that relative wealth seems to have had very little influence on the likelihood of a householder having kin among other householders in 1671. On both minimum and maximum estimates, the distribution of householders with at least one kin link by social category was very close to the distribution of householders by social category in the whole population. To this extent the experience of the householders was homogeneous. This general statement, however, must be modified when consideration is given to multiple links, the density of linkage, and the type of links concerned.

Householders with multiple kin links to other householders were, as we

---

[15] In this and in subsequent analyses by social position we have found ourselves obliged to refer to villagers as belonging to "Category I," "Category IV," etc. The stylistic effects of adopting this convention are sometimes unfortunate. We have, however, maintained this usage in order to be clear about whom we are talking. Adoption of such terms as "craftsman," for example, can hide large distinctions between villagers who would share that designation and we have found our four wealth-categories a better guide to the stratification of the community. It is to be hoped that as readers become accustomed to this convention it will be found less jarring.

have seen, rather few. These householders were, however, concentrated in Categories II and IV. As a result, variations in kinship density emerge between social categories, as can be seen in Table 4.6. The significance, if any, of these differences is difficult to assess. In the final analysis, what is abundantly clear is that the kinship network was extremely loose for *all* social ranks.

In turning to the types of links involved, we must restrict the analysis once more to proven links. There were seventy-four such links, linking forty-eight householders. Of these, 68% were first-order links, viewed as links to householder and spouse. More precisely, and from the point of view of the householder alone, 30% were between householder and closest affines (i.e., parents and siblings of spouse). Twenty-four percent were parent–child links between householders. Sixteen percent were distant affinal links (e.g., wife's second cousin). Fourteen percent were between brothers, 11% between second cousins, and 5% between aunt and nephew/niece, or between first cousins. Most links were thus very close links by blood or marriage. Reassembling the material in order to determine whether links were between or within generations, it emerged that 60% of links were between generations and 40% within generations. This difference, like the very low kinship density of the village, most probably relates to the geographical mobility of children leaving the parish to enter service and/or marrying and settling elsewhere.

Summarizing the discussion so far, we have established that the kinship network in Terling was loose. Variations by age in the likelihood of having kin among other householders were as might be expected given the age structure of the householders. Social position had little influence on the likelihood of having kin available in the village. Such kin links as existed were generally close and were rather more likely to be between than within generations. One final question can be asked before leaving the network of kin. Did kinship links cross the social scale or were they contained within particular social categories?

Some 54% of proven kinship links in Terling were in fact between individuals in different social categories.[16] Having said so much, however, one must go on to ask the nature of these links and to determine which sections of village society were linked by them.

Close analysis of interlinking very rapidly becomes exceedingly complex and somewhat opaque. However, a number of general points stand out

---

[16] That kinship links might extend far across the social scale of a village has been noted in a number of other studies, for example, W. G. Hoskins, *The Midland Peasant*, p. 199; M. Spufford, *Contrasting Communities*, p. 111; D. G. Hey, *An English Rural Community. Myddle under the Tudors and Stuarts*, p. 204. The nature and the typicality of such linkage, however, has been little discussed.

TABLE 4.6
Kinship Densities by Social Categories

	Category							
	I		II		III		IV	
	(Min.)	(Max.)	(Min.)	(Max.)	(Min.)	(Max.)	(Min.)	(Max.)
Absolute kinship density	0.02	0.04	0.16	0.20	0.08	0.13	0.34	0.46
Relative kinship density	0.02%	0.03%	0.13%	0.16%	0.07%	0.11%	0.28%	0.38%

clearly. First, although an overall majority of kin links were vertical socially, the proportion of vertical as against horizontal links varied between social categories. All the links of householders in Category I were vertical, as were over 80% of those householders in both Category II and Category III. Only 31% of the links of householders in Category IV were vertical. Category IV was thus the only social category closely internally linked by kinship. Second, the examination of links by social category reveals certain patterns of linkage. Householders in Category I were linked only to Category II save for a single link to Category IV. Two-thirds of householders with links in Category II were linked either upward to Category I, downward to Category III, or internally, rather than down, to Category IV. Nevertheless linkage between Categories II and IV was actually more common than linkage between Categories III and IV. The links of householders in Category III were overwhelmingly upward or internal. In short, links between the more substantial householders and those at the bottom of the social scale were evident, but were very much the exception rather than the rule. This was despite the fact that Category IV contained 50% of all householders.

What circumstances lay behind those links that crossed the social scale? There is a little evidence of social mobility, either permanent or related to the life cycle. Upward social mobility, in particular, probably required geographical mobility. There is some evidence of differentiation between brothers, perhaps as a result of unequal inheritances or varying marital fortunes. The great majority of close links that crossed the social scale, however, were produced by marriages between the daughters or sisters of men in Category II and husbands drawn from Category III and occasionally Category IV. Some of these brides were young and may have expected to rise again in the social scale in the course of their lives as their husbands accumulated or inherited property. Others were undoubtedly downwardly socially mobile. Of the more distant links that crossed the social scale less can be said save that they were produced by the same variety of circumstances operating in earlier generations.

In conclusion, it can be said that the loose network of kinship in Terling extended across the social scale of a community highly differentiated in terms of wealth and social position. Such extension, however, was largely among the middling ranks of village society and was very limited in form. The laboring poor participated little in this: Unlike their wealthier neighbors, most of their kinship links were to one another.

THE RECOGNITION OF KIN

Analysis of the network of kinship reveals much about the relatively insignificant place of extended kinship ties in the social structure of the village, but can be no more than a prolegomenon to the question of the quality of relations between kin, about which it tells us nothing. Without further evidence and in particular evidence of a more subjective cast, it is impossible to assess the full significance of kinship in the lives of these villagers. A valuable form of further evidence is that provided by the references to kin in the wills of the villagers. Such references yield evidence of the range of kinsmen recognized by testators. It must be said immediately, however, that such references are not good evidence of the full range of kin of whom testators were aware. Those mentioned in wills can be assumed to have been only those to whom the testators felt strong ties of sentiment or obligation. Presumably they were also aware of others. For this reason the evidence to be presented cannot be regarded as fully comparable to that derived by Macfarlane from the diary of Ralph Josselin. [17] Nevertheless, wills alone can provide evidence of the kin held closest at a critical point in the lives of individual testators.

One hundred and ninety-two wills were examined for the period 1550–1699.[18] The analysis was based upon all references to kin in these wills and not simply to kin who were beneficiaries of the will. The nature of the relationship concerned was usually clear from the internal evidence of the will. On occasion some relationships were clarified by reference to the family reconstitution forms and other evidence. Finally, concern here is not with the actual number of kin mentioned by testators but only with the geneological range and depth of their recognition of kin.

Over the whole period mention of kin beyond children (140 wills) and spouse (116 wills) was rare. Next in order after the testator's own nuclear family came grandchildren, brothers, nephews and nieces, sons-in-law, and sisters of the testator (all mentioned in between twenty and thirty-five wills); brothers-in-law (seventeen wills) followed a little behind. Cousins, "kinsmen," and a scattering of other relatives were only occasionally mentioned. Testators thus concentrated their attention heavily on their own nuclear families, on those of their married children, and on their own or their spouses' nuclear families of origin. The comparative frequency with which brothers and brothers-in-law were mentioned, commonly as supervisors or executors of a will, suggests that from the point of view of the testator's children, relationships with uncles may well have been of some significance in early life. Overall, the range of kin mentioned was both narrow and shallow.

---

[17] Comparison of the range of kin mentioned in Josselin's diary with those mentioned in his will serves to underline this point. A. Macfarlane, *The Family Life of Ralph Josselin*, p. 158 cf. Appendix C.

[18] Numbers of wills for fifty-year sub-periods were as follows: 1550–1599, 63; 1600–1649, 65; 1650–1699, 64.

Looking at the evidence by fifty-year periods, very little change is observable over time. Only two changes are worthy of note. First, godchildren were not infrequently mentioned in the very early wills. Such references disappeared in the seventeenth century. Second, illegitimate children or grandchildren were occasionally mentioned at the very end of the sixteenth century at the time when the illegitimacy ratio was peculiarly high in Terling. Such references were absent after 1600.

These results are fully compatible with the interpretation of Josselin's kinship recognition put forward by Macfarlane, even to the probable significance of uncles, especially paternal uncles. They also tally with the near-comparable study of eighteenth-century wills by Johnston for the parish of Powick, Worcestershire.[19]

Did the range of kin mentioned by Terling testators vary with social position, sex, and stage in the life cycle? Taking the question of social position first, testators were placed in four categories approximating as closely as possible to the four categories used elsewhere in this book. Most testators fell into Categories I to III.[20] Between these categories no variation of any significance in kinship recognition can be reported. The sample of wills from Category IV was small (seven in all) but consistent in showing that testators in this category had the narrowest recognition of all; a single testator mentioned one kinsman beyond wife and children. The search for variation by sex proved equally fruitless. Women did not vary from men in their recognition of kin on the basis of sex alone.

In order to examine the issue of life-cycle variations, the testators were separated into four groups on the basis of both internal evidence and evidence from the family reconstitution forms. These are: those whose children were all married; those whose children were in part married and in part unmarried; those whose children were all unmarried; those with no children. Some obvious variations emerged. Testators whose children were all unmarried or who had no children obviously had no grandchildren, sons-in-law, or daughters-in-law to mention. Otherwise the same concentration on very close kin, in particular the testator's nuclear family, was evident throughout. There were only two exceptions. One of these was that mention of siblings or of spouse's siblings was most common among testators who either had no children or whose children were all young and unmarried. This was for two reasons. On the one hand, testators without

---

[19] A. Macfarlane, *The Family Life of Ralph Josselin*, p. 157ff.; J. A. Johnston, "The Probate Inventories and Wills of Worcestershire Parish, 1676–1775," p. 32. Johnston's study is not fully comparable since his attention was confined to legatees alone.

[20] In this respect Terling testators were unlike those of Willingham, described in M. Spufford, "Peasant inheritance customs and land distribution in Cambridgeshire from the sixteenth to the eighteenth centuries," pp. 169–171.

direct heirs turned to their nearest kin. On the other hand, testators with very young children sometimes brought in their brothers or brothers-in-law as executors or overseers of their wills who could be trusted to look to the childrens' best interests. The other exception was that more distant kin, from nephews and nieces to unspecified "kinsmen" and even godchildren were most often mentioned by men without children or by widows and unmarried women. The reasons for this are sufficiently obvious as to require no further comment.

To summarize, kinship recognition as evidenced in wills, showed a heavy concentration on very close kin. It varied little with social position or sex and only in ways that might be anticipated when consideration is given to the life-cycle stage of the testator. Testators seem to have been little concerned with their broader range of kin, kin who were commonly geographically distant from them. Their interest and concern was focused, rather, upon their own nuclear families and it is to relations within the nuclear family that we must now turn.

RELATIONS WITHIN THE NUCLEAR FAMILY: INHERITANCE

The most intimate of human relationships leave few records to the historian of the common people of England. While we may know in some detail the crops that a man grew or the contents of his wife's kitchen and wardrobe, the quality of their relationships with one another or with their children is almost invariably beyond us. Valuable as the village study method may be as a means of exploring many aspects of popular life in the past, it has provided us with little direct evidence on this issue, and it is as well to declare the fact. In the absence of surviving diaries, we have few sources that allow us to step beyond the cottage door other than to take an inventory of goods. Marital offences and scandal left their mark in the Act Books of the church courts and will be considered in their place. Of more normal domestic affairs we know little. The nearest we can approach harmonious marital relations is by noting the conventionalized designations "my beloved wife," "My loveing wife" which became common form in wills of the later seventeenth century, expressing the contemporary ideal of conjugal harmony. On occasion a testator stands out as somewhat unusual, the standard formula giving way to something more personal. Robert Green in 1639 refers in passing to "my loveing deare wife"; Jane Salter in 1568 asks to be buried "by my late husbande."[21] The rest is largely silence.

---

[21] E. R. O. D/ACA 13/184; D/ACR 6/190.

Some wills again cast a little light on the aspirations of parents for their children. Some such references concerned education and will be dealt with in a later chapter. Others expressed more general concerns. The yeoman Francis Allman, who died in 1584, desired his children to be "orderly kept"; the carpenter John Aldridge, who died in 1602, wished his children to be "well and carefully brought up."[22] Other testators left hints of family conflict in their arrangements. Provision might be made for goods to be divided between widow and children if it proved impossible for them to live together peacefully. Christopher Chandler went so far in 1649 as to appoint three mediators "to cease and pacifye" any such disputes as might arise.[23] Conflict might also be anticipated between siblings, as in 1569 when Richard French laid down that his eldest son should enter a bond to pay his younger brothers their inheritance. More drastically, Thomas Brokes in 1673 had to insist that his principal heir should allow his sister and mother access to the family house for a stated period to remove their legacies.[24] Sibling conflict could be bitter indeed, as when William Rochester accused his brother Richard of tampering with the will of John Rochester their elder brother. This touched off a feud that led to violence, cases in the church courts, Quarter Sessions, Assizes and the Star Chamber, and eventually to the childless Richard's disinheriting of his surviving brothers.[25] More common, however, was the trust reposed in brothers charged with caring for the interests of their nephews and nieces as overseers of wills.

Such references as these can be placed in broader perspective only by the evidence provided by wills of the inheritance customs of the village. These alone allow a more firm and systematic examination of marital and parent–child relationships and yield us clues to the nature of conventional aspirations and common practice.

In dealing with inheritance, it must first be emphasized that there was no rigidity in the inheritance customs of Terling villagers. On first examination their wills give the impresssion of a bewildering variety of inheritance strategies that might be adopted by individual testators. On closer analysis a number of regularities emerge within a range of options which appears to have been governed by three factors: the types and amount of property to be disposed by will; the family-cycle stage of the testator; the demographic fortunes of the testator's primary family.

---

[22] E. R. O. D/ACR 7/313; D/ACW 4/128.
[23] E. R. O. D/ACW 15/175. Other examples can be found in D/ACW 5/51 and D/ACW 6/87.
[24] E. R. O. D/ACR 6/297; D/ACR 9/133.
[25] E. R. O. D/ACW 3/94; D/ACW 6/163; D/ACC 3, fos, 12–149v, D/ACD 2 fos, 88v–93v. P. R. O. STAC 5 A7/30, A8/1,13, A19/9, A27/35, A33/20,39, A39/18, A54/13, A55/23, A57/6.

In the absence of inventories, the exact wealth of testators cannot be established. Nevertheless the types of property involved could be significant. Over the whole period 38% of testators bequeathed land, 39% bequeathed houses, 11% stock, 78% cash sums, and 83% household goods. Turning to the issue of the family cycle, 22% of testators had no children, 25% had only married children, 22% had some children married and some unmarried and 31% had only unmarried children. They were thus fairly evenly divided between those who were still wholly or partly responsible for providing for their children and those who had no such responsibility. Clearly the marriage of children and especially of sons was *not* dependent upon inheritance.[26] Indeed, where the dates of childrens' marriages can be recovered from the family reconstitution forms it emerges that in the case of testators whose children were all married, their marriages had commonly taken place between five and twenty years before the date of the will. Where children were all unmarried they rarely married soon after inheritance and their marriages fell anything up to twenty-five years after the deaths of their fathers. Inheritance would appear to have had *immediate* significance for marriage only when a family was already in the process of dissolution. Where this was the case, children commonly married within five years before or after the parental death. Clearly family property could be broken up and distributed to children over very long periods of time: There was no single point of dissolution.

Demographic fortunes varied very widely indeed. Over the whole period, only 11% of male testators were faced with an unproblematic inheritance in that they had only a single son or a single daughter. A further 22% had no children. For the rest, a distribution of property among their children was necessary and this could sometimes be a very complicated matter indeed.

Consideration of these factors casts some light upon the question of why some villagers chose to make wills while others did not. Testators from Categories I and II, with substantial property to leave, seem always to have been inclined to make wills regardless of their demographic fortunes or of their stage in the family cycle. Testators in Category III were likely to make wills in the sixteenth century only when they had unmarried children to be provided for. Over time, however, as their prosperity improved, will making became more common for testators in this category even where they did not face such problems of providing for young children. As has already been indicated, there were very few testators from Category IV at any time. This being so, it is perhaps significant that all of them had young, un-

---

[26] Cf. D. G. Hey, *An English Rural Community Myddle*, pp. 204–205; C. Howell, "Peasant inheritance customs in the Midlands, 1200–1700," p. 145.

married children to provide for. It was probably this which persuaded them to take the highly unusual step for persons of their social position of making formal wills distributing their small stocks of goods.[27]

The whole complex of economic, demographic, and family-cycle circumstances must be taken into consideration in examining the actual decisions made by testators and recorded in their wills. No single variable is in itself sufficient to explain their behavior. Analysis by wealth alone, for example, does little to clarify the situation. Indeed wealth seems to have been of less overall significance than family-cycle and demography, save for the fact that the very poor rarely made wills. Where wealth *was* important was in broadening the options open to the testator by providing more and more varied types of property for transmission. It does not seem to have influenced a man's aspirations for his widow or children. These can now be examined.

Male testators clearly felt a strong sense of obligation to provide as far as possible an independent home and living for their widows. The possibility of the remarriage of their widows does not seem to have been something that disturbed them and there are few examples of conditions in the event of remarriage being placed on bequests. Where there were no children of the marriage, widows most commonly received the entire inheritance if it was in personal property alone. Where house and lands were involved, they received a life interest, the property passing subsequently to more distant kin. Where all children were married, widows usually received a life interest in a house and/or land, if these were available. If not, a share of personal property was allocated to secure their future. In a handful of cases, very precise maintenance of annuity arrangements were laid down for widows. Some of these suggest that the widow might go to dwell with a married child, but such arrangements were clearly viewed with suspicion. Alternatives were always provided for in the event of such cohabitation proving fragile or disagreeable. In cases where only some children were married, widows received an interest in house and lands either for life or until their childrens' majority, or alternatively were allocated portions of cash and goods. It is clear in such wills that while married children were to receive their part of the inheritance promptly, the portions allocated to unmarried children were to be managed by the widow until their majority or marriage. Where all children were unmarried, the widow was similarly left in control of house, land, and personal property. Allocations of property to particular children might be made, but were to take effect only at a future date. Very clearly the principal legacy of the widow was the duty of

---

[27] Cf. M. Spufford, "Peasant inheritance customs and land distribution in Cambridgeshire," p. 171.

completing the upbringing and "putting forth" of the children. Testators laid down the guidelines for the task and provided the wherewithal to see it through, together with provision for the widow's future thereafter. No change was observable over time in either aspiration or practice.

Coming to provision for children, it should be clear from the preceding discussion that in many cases (about half) bequests to children were not expected to be of immediate effect. They were mediated through the widow. Frequently the ultimate outcome would be rather different from that laid down by the testator as a result of the early deaths of some of the children. This point deserves to be stressed since it was something of which testators were very aware. They commonly made explicit provision for the redistribution of portions in the event of a child's death, a point to which we shall return.

Where a testator had only a single child, inheritance was unproblematic. The child (or, if a married daughter, sometimes the son-in-law) usually received all save the portion reserved for the widow. In cases where there was only one son, but also a daughter or daughters, land and house usually went to the son. Wealthy testators might leave an additional house or houses to their daughters. Cash and goods were divided among children in a manner that does not appear to have been grossly unequal, though the valuation of goods is clearly difficult in the absence of inventories. Where there were two or more sons, with or without daughters, several arrangements were possible. If house and land were involved, these usually went to the eldest son. The other children received cash or goods, sometimes in more or less equal portions, sometimes not. If the eldest son was already married and independently established, however, house and land might go to a younger child. Among the very wealthy it was sometimes possible for several children, or even every child, to be provided with a house and sometimes land too. It is clear, however, that this did not involve the subdivision of a family's main landholding. Extra accumulations of land, very commonly geographically distant and sublet, were hived off. In those cases where all children were already married, real property was very rarely involved. This finding may be fortuitous, but more probably indicates that children had been set up earlier. Where some children were married and some not, the eldest son receiving land was often required to pay out cash legacies to his younger siblings over a period of years. This practice may have had the effect of equalizing what appear to be unequal inheritances at first sight.[28] In those wills where no real property was involved there was usually either a fairly equal division of cash and

---

[28] Cf. C. Howell, "Peasant inheritance customs in the Midlands," p. 145; M. Spufford, "Peasant inheritance customs and land distribution in Cambridgeshire," p. 157.

goods among entirely married or entirely unmarried children, or else tokens were left to married children and larger sums left to the unmarried. Finally, where a testator had no sons but two or more daughters, house and land usually went to the eldest girl, cash and goods to the others. If cash and goods only were involved, there was generally a fairly equal division among entirely married or entirely unmarried daughters.

Clearly these inheritance practices show a bias in the direction of male primogeniture, but to classify them as constituting a "primogeniture system" would seem to us crude and erroneous. If there was a single concern running through the varieties of behavior observed, then it was that of maximizing the opportunities of as many children as possible to set up their own family units in due course. The distribution of houses and essential household goods, the specifications that minors were to receive their portions at marriage or at their age of majority all reinforce this interpretation. The primogeniture bias might indeed be interpreted as in part a preparing of the way for the child who would first face the world independently. As we have shown, testators were very aware of their childrens' mortality and must often have realized that the ultimate portions received by younger children might be larger and more equal than those specified in the will, as some died and their portions were reallocated to the survivors. Again, land left to the eldest might be the most valuable and prestigious inheritance, but it was not infrequently burdened with the need to provide for siblings. Most of the children of Terling's villagers had ultimately to go out into the world literally alone. While some children were undoubtedly advantaged by the primogeniture bias, most notably where real property was involved, the inheritance strategies of many fathers may have operated in such a way as to set their children forth fairly equally into a competitive world where they would be expected to stand on their own feet. The extent to which they stood alone or could call upon support from kin or others must be our next concern.

KIN AND NEIGHBORS

A number of types of documents permit us to examine the extent to which individuals drew upon kin for services of various kinds. This evidence will enable us to attempt some estimate of the relative importance of kin and neighbors in the lives of the villagers.

The first relationship to be considered is that between testators and the chosen executors of their wills. Over the whole period, 192 testators chose 222 executors. Of these, 87% were kin and only 13% nonkin. Of the kin selected, 95% were first-order kin, 78% being the wives or children of the testators. If nonkin were selected they were often designated in terms indicating close personal relationships such as "my welbeloved friende." Over time there was no marked change in the relative proportions of kin employed as against others. Clearly there was an overwhelming bias towards the closest kin in the handling of family property.

In addition to executors, testators sometimes appointed overseers and supervisors of their wills—a custom that was dying in the seventeenth century. Of the seventy-one overseers or supervisors named, 45% were kin. The kin chosen were most commonly drawn from the nuclear family of origin of either the testator or his wife—brothers and brothers-in-law predominating. In addition, some more distant kin were selected, especially cousins. Nonkin were again distinguished in such terms as "my welbeloved neighbors and friends." Again we have a strong tendency to draw upon kin, many of them not residents of Terling, in a matter involving family property. The implication is that in such affairs it was kin who were most deeply trusted, despite the fact that they were relatively unavailable locally.

In contrast, the witnesses of wills were, as might be expected, overwhelmingly neighbors. Only 5% are known to have been kin. For this simple, though potentially important service, testators drew upon their neighbors. Some of these neighbors were a very personal choice and were referred to elsewhere in wills or were designated friends. Others appear to have been particularly prestigious neighbors and recur in many wills. Still others were the scribes who wrote numerous wills. The evidence suggests that given the looseness of the kinship network within the village and the suddenness with which a man might find himself at death's door, the tendency was to seek immediate aid within the neighborhood. Other evidence would support the picture of the neighborhood as the source of further forms of aid and support.

References to debt, for example, are frequent in wills. Unfortunately they are for the most part unspecific, but it has proved possible to collect information on seventy specific debt and credit relationships from wills alone. Of these, 17% were between kin, 67% were between neighbors, and 16% were between Terling villagers and unrelated outsiders. Clearly financial aid of this kind was most commonly sought and found among neighbors.

The debts concerned were generally small; 38% were for less than £1, only 16% for more than £20. Interest was certainly known but was probably not charged on the smaller debts. Explicit references to interest were made only in the case of larger sums. Formal bonds and mortgages were likewise mentioned only for sums of £5 and above. The local credit market probably functioned partly by charging interest and partly by the advancing of small sums interest free in return for reciprocal aid from neighbors at other times. Relationships of debt and credit thus helped to bind together the village community. Of those mentioned in wills, some 56% were horizontal relationships between villagers of similar social position, while 44% crossed the social scale. Even the poor were involved in the lending of small sums and widows in particular stood out in this respect. Doubtless, involvement in neighborly reciprocity of this kind could be a valuable form of insurance against hard times when they came.[29]

Two further forms of support for which evidence survives are those of acting as compurgator for a person in the church courts (i.e., swearing to his or her innocence) and acting as surety for a person in a recognizance issued by the justices of the peace.

Seven Terling men brought in a total of twenty-four named compurgators to the ecclesiastical courts in our period. Of these, five brought in neighbors only, one brought kin only, and one brought a single kinsman and five neighbors. This might suggest that the compurgators were recruited from a pool of contacts that included kin only if they were near at hand and had a close personal relationship to the individual involved. The more extensive evidence of recognizance sureties strengthens this hypothesis.

Eighty-four recognizances have been examined for the period 1578 to 1693, most of them falling in the years 1600 to 1630. In most cases the principal in the recognizance provided two sureties. In 6% of cases the principal found kin only to act for him. In 18% one kinsman and one other acted. In 76% only nonkin acted as sureties. Where kin were involved they were most commonly the fathers, brothers, or brothers-in-law of the principal. Of the nonkin involved, some were outsiders from other towns and villages. Those who were neighbors from Terling can be examined more closely in order to discern the factors that influenced their recruitment.

Occupational solidarity had some influence. Craftsmen tended to draw upon fellow craftsmen, while yeomen and husbandmen who held land of the same manor were prone to stand by one another. Personal friendship is also evident, being indicated by the fact that some men linked by recognizance relationships were also linked in other contexts, for example in wills. There was also a degree of group solidarity among the elite of parish notables who acted as churchwardens, sessions jurymen, and so forth. Being party to the dispute that had resulted in judicial proceedings was another factor that led men to give their support. Finally there is clear evidence of the influence of patronage and clientage within the village community. Village notables, husbandmen, and craftsmen showed a good deal of solidarity in standing surety for one another and in Categories II and III

---

[29] Cf. B. A. Holderness, "Credit in a Rural Community, 1660–1800."

the recognizance links are almost wholly horizontal socially. Laborers, however, were almost completely dependent on recruiting support from above where they found prestigious patrons to assist them.

The examination of the recognizances of men who were bound in this way on several occasions shows that some of the connections revealed to kin or neighbors were enduring and recur twice or more. Other supporters were recruited on an ad hoc basis. Overall it is clear that the assistance of kin as against neighbors was not simply a function of the relative availability of kin and neighbors in the village. Of the recognizance where no kin were used, almost half were cases in which the principals involved can be shown to have had adult kinsmen available in the village. They either chose not to use them or found themselves unable to gain their support.

The findings of this and the preceding sections can now be usefully summarized. Evidence has been presented that the network of kinship in Terling was loose. Households were either isolated or relatively isolated in the village in kin terms. It has been suggested that this phenomenon was a product of the high degree of geographical mobility and the geographically exogamous marriage which characterized the villagers. The recognition of kin appears to have been restricted, on the evidence of wills. Inheritance customs were flexible and varied with the particular circumstances of the testator. They indicate strong internal ties within the relatively isolated nuclear families of the villagers and a general desire to set children into the world independently. Experience and behavior in these respects varied little with social position, but were influenced by the developmental cycle of the nuclear family and by demographic fortune. No change in behavior of any significance could be discerned over the period studied.

In practical matters, the assistance of kin was clearly preferred in the handling of family property. Even here however, kin beyond the nuclear family and the nuclear families of origin of the testator and his wife were of little significance. In other forms of aid and support, kin of any kind seem to have been of little functional importance as compared with neighbors. In part this was because they were less available locally, but even where adult kin were available, they were called upon selectively. The historical evidence suggests the existence of a flexible and permissive kinship system remarkably similar to that described by some modern students of English society. The nuclear family was very important indeed. Beyond it, there is little evidence that kinship was an important independent element in the structuring of social relations. In Terling, neighbors and personal friends selected from among them seem to have played the supporting role that in other societies might be played by the wider kin group. Neighborliness in its turn was structured by shared social position and shared roles in local institutions, by a degree of occupational solidarity, by patronage and client-

age. The structure of neighborly interaction can be said to have been influenced to a large degree by the distributions of wealth, status, and power
in village society. These factors must now be considered before we draw
together the various elements of the local social system that gave order and
regularity to the social relations of the fluid population of Terling.

WEALTH, STATUS, AND POWER

The distribution of wealth in Terling has already been dealt with at some
length. What most concerns us here is the extent to which the distribution
of wealth overlapped with that of the other two elements in social
stratification: status and power.

As has been indicated in Chapter 2, the conventional early modern status
designations of the gentleman, yeoman, husbandman, craftsman, and
laborer did indeed tally for the most part with the hierarchy of wealth in
Terling. The discussion can be carried further only by the use of independent indicators of social standing. These we have found in (a) those
villagers who were repeatedly called on to act as sureties in recognizances
(acting as sureties between two and eleven times); and (b) those villagers
called on to witness several wills (ranging between two and six wills each).
The scribes of wills who appear repeatedly have been excluded.

Of the twenty-two men who acted repeatedly as recognizance sureties,
sixteen (73%) were drawn from Category II, six (27%) from Category III,
and one each from Categories I and IV. Wealthier villagers predominated,
though the very wealthiest were little involved. In addition to their wealth,
fourteen (64%) of the men held parish offices, sometimes on several occasions, while ten (45%) served on manorial juries. These men were very active participants in parish affairs.

The forty-five men who witnessed two or more wills included three (7%)
from Category I, twenty-eight (62%) from Category II, eleven (24%) from
Category III, and three whose relative wealth could not be satisfactorily
determined. Thirty-two (71%) held at least one parish office, while fifteen
(33%) were active in manorial institutions. Status as measured by selection
as a recognizance surety, or will witness, clearly overlapped very largely
with wealth and service in local institutions. Most of those involved were
yeomen, though rarely the largest farmers. Of the craftsmen and tradesmen
involved, blacksmiths, carpenters, and innkeepers were very prominent,
perhaps because of their central role in village life. For the most part, then,
status, wealth, and power ran together.

Will-witnessing and standing as surety indicated prominence in community life, centrality in the network of neighborly interaction. Parish of-

fice not only indicated status but also conferred real power. Only the landlords of the village controlled greater power than did the village officers. Throughout our period, there were landowning-gentry families resident in Terling, though the greatest of them, the Mildmays, were permanently resident only from the 1620s. Nevertheless, the evidence makes it clear that the gentlemen of the parish chose, for the most part, to participate little in parochial institutions before the late seventeenth century. Their field of activity was wider, encompassing county affairs. How restricted or open was access to power at the parish level and how broad a section of village society participated in parish government?

Information survives on participation in the whole range of parish offices from sidesman to membership of the "Towne meeting" or parish vestry, which emerged after 1660. The chronological coverage of the evidence is not consistent, however. Full information for all years is available only for the churchwardens and for the men who represented Terling on the presentment juries of the half-hundred of Witham at Quarter Sessions. Nevertheless, enough exists to allow us to examine the social position of a good number of men known to have held other offices over substantial periods. The results of the analysis are presented in Table 4.7.

Table 4.7 demonstrates strikingly how far parish office and participation in local institutions was restricted to the wealthier sections of village society. It also indicates how hierarchy could be observed even in parish office. The most prestigious posts, such as churchwarden, sessions juryman, vestryman, and overseer, went overwhelmingly to the yeomanry and wealthier tradesmen. The humbler offices of constable and sidesman, which were also controlled by the more important officers, went most frequently to husbandmen and craftsmen. The laboring poor were almost totally excluded. This situation was relatively fixed, there being few signs of change over time. Two points of change that deserve note are first that the participation of gentlemen and of the greater farmers increased in the later seventeenth century. While such participation did not usually go beyond attending vestry meetings, it did sometimes involve service as overseer and churchwarden, while all constables of this social rank served after 1670. The other element of change was that husbandmen and craftsmen served more often as churchwardens after 1660. This may have been partly a result of the fact that by this period many of the yeomen of the village were noncomformists. It may also have owed something to the fact that the formal emergence of the vestry rather devalued the status of the office of churchwarden.

Information on participation in manorial institutions for the occasional years when we have such information is also presented in Table 4.7 for comparison. As can be seen, participation in manorial affairs was only a

TABLE 4.7
Participation in Parish Offices and Institutions

Office	Social Category											
	I		II		III		IV		?		Total	
	(N)	(%)	(N)	(%)	(N)	(%)	(N)	(%)	(N)	(%)	(N)	(%)
Churchwardens												
1590–1699	9	9.7	52	55.9	19	20.4	1	1.0	12	13.0	93	100
Sessions jurymen												
1590–1689	9	8.3	60	55.0	26	23.9	1	0.9	13	11.9	109	100
Constables												
1630–1699	4	11.8	13	38.2	17	50.0	0	0.0	0	0.0	34	100
Sidesmen												
1596–1612	0	0.0	5	33.3	9	60.0	0	0.0	1	6.7	15	100
Overseers of the poor												
1660–1699	6	23.1	15	57.7	4	15.4	0	0.0	1	3.8	26	100
Vestrymen												
1670–1699	14	35.9	20	51.3	5	12.8	0	0.0	0	0.0	39	100
Manorial jurors												
1601–1701	1	1.9	26	50.0	19	36.5	3	5.8	3	5.8	52	100

little broader socially. The manor courts of Terling were nothing more than registries of land transactions by the seventeenth century, meeting very irregularly. Though they clearly retained some significance and might help to focus the interaction of part of the population, they too lay very much in the control of the wealthier villagers.

Power, in the sense of participation in office and control of institutions, was thus concentrated high in the social scale of Terling. It was in fact even more concentrated than the figures presented in Table 4.7 would indicate, for some men served in several offices and served repeatedly. Examining the men who acted as churchwardens and sessions jurymen (the two key offices for much of our period) by five-year periods a picture of oligarchy emerges. For most five-year periods between ten and fifteen men dominated these offices. In the later seventeenth century, when information on a fuller range of offices is available, we find between twenty and thirty men controlling parish affairs in any given quinquennium. Even within these oligarchic groupings, four or five key figures usually stand out. Between 1590 and 1599, for example, Thomas Hewes was twice a sessions juryman and no fewer than ten times a churchwarden! In the years 1600 to 1614 Robert Tabor was seven times churchwarden and four times sessions juryman. Andrew Page, a key figure of the Restoration period, served twice as sessions jurymen, thrice as churchwarden and also one term as overseer of the poor and one term as a vestryman between 1670 and 1679.

The overlap of wealth, status, and power, the common participation in parish affairs, and the myriad other services performed for one another by the more substantial villagers of Terling surely justifies our regarding these men as a distinct group in village society. They formed a local ruling group that possessed a distinct social identity. Whether any other group within village society (save the poor on relief or the nonconformists of the later seventeenth century) had a comparable collective identity is open to question. No doubt the ruling group was not without its internal distinctions, between the mere yeoman and the great farmer bordering on gentility. Perhaps its identity was one peculiar to the specific social context of Terling and implying no sense of class identity beyond the parish border. But *within* the parish it was clear enough and by the later seventeenth century had its institutional expression in the vestry meeting. It was nonetheless a group that was relatively open, into which newcomers might be readily incorporated. For them the key was wealth.

Most of those whom we find emerging among the ranks of the parish ruling group in the course of the seventeenth century were true newcomers, first-generation residents of the parish. The very extent of population mobility in Terling makes it exceedingly difficult to deal firmly with the whole issue of social mobility. We have already seen how few householders in Terling in 1671 could trace their families back in the parish to more than one earlier generation. Social mobility was part and parcel of geographical mobility, and evidence of internal social mobility is sparse. Yet the whole issue of social mobility in this society is sufficiently important to deserve some comment.

The fortunes of fourteen Terling families have been traced from the later sixteenth century through to 1671. No suggestion can be made that their experience was typical or that it necessarily represents the overall experience of the parish. It may, however, highlight some of the factors involved in social mobility in rural Essex. Of the fourteen families, five maintained their social position, be it high or low, throughout the period. Five more declined from Categories II and III to Category IV. Three rose from Category III to Categories II and I. One fluctuated, first falling and then regaining its former yeoman status.

Of principal interest to us here are the factors involved in social mobility. Upward social mobility depended primarily on the slow accumulation of wealth and in particular of land over two or three generations. This process might be assisted by diversifying economic activities as craftsman, trader, and farmer and by direct involvement in the food market. It could also be helped along by good marriages and by the good fortune not to have too many children. The Fincham family provides an example. Christopher Fincham first appeared in Terling in 1599 as an apprentice cooper. In due course he filled his master's shoes and became established in the early years of the seventeenth century as a cooper and carpenter. Perhaps he prospered in the building boom of the time, but certainly he prospered and by the second decade of the new century he held land. At his death in 1639 he left his son a house, land, and his tools. Thomas Fincham, the son, pursued an industrious life as the village's principal carpenter and gradually bought more land. He also achieved recognition by being selected as a sessions juryman. His own eldest son Thomas inherited part of his father's land and ultimately bought up the land left to a younger brother. He continued as a carpenter and figured prominently among the rulers of the parish as churchwarden, overseer, constable, and vestryman.[30]

The slow and modest success of the Finchams can be contrasted with the fortunes of those whose social position declined. Decline usually meant the loss of the family land and reduction to laboring for a living. This might in turn be the result of chronic indebtedness (perhaps after bad harvests), personal failings such as drunkenness, or simply the misfortune of too many

---

[30] E. R. O. Q/SR 146/22; D/ACW 13/172; D/ACR 9/10.

children to be provided for. The Norrell Family provide an illustration. In the later sixteenth century, John Norrell was a yeoman of modest prosperity. He lived to a great age and in his declining years seems to have retired and handed over his land to his son Augustine. Augustine was one of the leading figures in parish affairs in the second decade of the seventeenth century, one we shall meet again. At his death in 1626 he was faced with the problem of providing for five sons and three daughters. His land was left to the eldest son, William, but was heavily burdened with the payment of cash sums to the other children. Of William we hear no more. Presumably he established himself elsewhere. One son only, John, stayed on in Terling, but his inheritance of £7 was insufficient to set him up at the social level of his yeoman father. He spent his life as a laborer and was in receipt of parish relief in his old age. His son, another John, was also a laborer and like his father was excused from payment of the Hearth Tax on the grounds of poverty.[31]

If any more general points can be made from the evidence of internal social mobility they are these. It was undoubtedly more easy to fall than to rise. Decline could be very rapid. Ascent was slow and painful. No family rose from the ranks of the laborers, though several declined to join them. More generally, it should be emphasized that the study of social mobility within the confines of one village is altogether unrealistic. Those families that stayed on in Terling generation after generation were the exception. Opportunity for the young existed and was sought over a very much broader area than that of the parish. In dealing with social mobility, the appropriate unit would be Terling's full social area rather than the parish itself. Finally, the case histories traced have a common factor that may be of general significance. Decline and loss of land, when it occurred, seems usually to have taken place between 1590 and 1620. This period may have been one of peculiar difficulty for the small man, perhaps partly as a legacy of the disastrous harvests of the later 1590s, perhaps partly as a result of inability to pay the market rents demanded for leasehold land. Despite this possibility, however, the evidence of upward mobility balances that of downward mobility, and it would seem probable that the changes in the profile of social stratification in Terling that were set out in Chapter 1 derived principally from the imbalance between an expanding population and available opportunities. Men came and went in the upper reaches of village society in a kaleidescope of shifting fortunes. At the same time, the parish filled up at the bottom.

We may now draw together the various strands of this discussion of the social structure of Terling and of the village community as a local social system linked to the larger society of Essex. What were the characteristics

---

[31] E. R. O. D/ACW 10/61; Q/R Th5.

of village society? Above all it was fluid. It was little structured by ties of kinship. Its most functionally important social bond was that of neighborliness. The neighborhood itself was highly stratified in terms of wealth, status, and power and was headed by a local ruling group with considerable social power by virtue of its control of land, employment, poor relief, and the institutions of social regulation. Newcomers were rapidly assimilated into the local hierarchy of rank and wealth. Neighborly reciprocity between villagers of similar social standing, patronage and clientage between those occupying different places in the social hierarchy, gave further structure and a degree of stability to this essentially fluid society. Opportunities for the young to get a living, for family formation, and settlement existed in Terling. Men died, some without heirs at all, some leaving only heiresses. Men moved out. Yet the opening of opportunities could not be guaranteed to synchronize with the coming to adulthood of young people seeking opportunity. Consequently they went out also into the larger society beyond the village, as servants, as laborers, as men looking for land, seeking the chances that occurred elsewhere just as they did in Terling. Their parents, when they died, attempted to fit them as well as they could to survive in the competitive environment that they entered young and little cushioned by kin.

Ideally such a system might have operated over a sufficiently large area in such a way as to produce "dynamic equilibrium," a rough balancing of available opportunity and of mobile young people seeking a place in settled society. Perhaps it sometimes did. But such an equilibrium could be upset by several factors. One might be structural economic change, working to either restrict or to expand opportunity. Another might be simple demographic pressure, an expansion of numbers beyond the capacity of the system to absorb them. There was little sign of structural change in either the economy of Terling or indeed that of Essex within this period, as we have seen. But there is abundant evidence of demographic pressure. The fertility of the later sixteenth century thus threatened the life chances of the young adults of the early seventeenth century. As the curve of demographic expansion peaked between 1600 and 1620 immense strains may have been placed upon the social system that we have described. It was flexible enough, as the demographic response to the trauma of the early seventeenth century indicates. It emerged into the calmer waters of the later seventeenth century with its essential structures intact. Yet it was also significantly modified. Most obviously it carried a greater burden of poverty. But what of subtler changes? Might not the strain of the early seventeenth century have produced a social adjustment to accompany that in demographic behavior? Might it not have promoted shifts in the quality of the crucially important neighborly relations within the parish, new forms of conflict, and novel means of control?

5

CONFLICT AND CONTROL: THE VILLAGERS AND THE COURTS

In the fluid society of sixteenth- and seventeenth-century Terling, neighborliness was a crucial social bond. Good neighborliness was a critically important social virtue. But to imagine the tone of village life as an idyll of rustic harmony would be to err grievously. The village was riddled with petty conflicts. Not all neighbors were "good." Some, indeed, were downright disorderly. John Clark, for example, was in the opinion of his neighbors "a raskally knave." To his superiors, he was "a common disturber of the peace." Born in 1580, John had rapidly taken the downward path and as early as 1598 was objected to as "of small credit" when he was produced as a compurgator in the church courts. His mother, who was a woman of some piety to judge by her will, was doubtless disappointed in him and left him only a shilling. John, however, continued his course undeterred. In 1604, he was complained of by the wife of a St. Osyth husbandman for showing her "discurtissie in takeing up her coates." He also "swore by the lords blood" that "if it were not for shame" he would kill her husband. This would appear to have been the only occasion upon which shame restrained him. A year later he was presented at Quarter Sessions as a disturber of the peace, the presenting jurymen throwing in for good measure that he had not attended holy communion for two years. Soon afterward, he was bound over to keep the peace to another laborer. Two years later he was presented as a drunkard and "alehousehaunter" and was named as having taken part in a spectacular drinking bout in Thomas Holman's inn. He next appears in the ecclesiastical courts in 1611, presented by the churchwardens for adultery with Robert Allen's wife. For his contempt in this case he was excommunicated. In the same year he was bound over to keep the peace again. Our final glimpse of him comes in February 1619, sitting drinking with John Harris and Richard Birchall in Toby Tweed's alehouse in time of divine service.[1] This was a case of like meet like. Richard Birchall was at this time in the process of undermining the modest prosperity that he owed to inheriting the trade of his father-in-law, a wheelwright. Birchall had already appeared in the church courts for fathering a bastard on his wife's younger sister, had been excommunicated, and was to continue to chalk up a considerable record of prosecutions for drunkennes and for neglect of church attendance. In 1619 he escaped a sudden end to his career when he was acquitted at the Assizes on a charge of horse stealing.[2] John Harris, a tailor, was also frequently in his cups and commonly neglected his religious duties. He also received (and ate) the animals stolen by Robert Richardson, a thief and poacher who boasted that he "had a dogg that he would not take forty shillings for." On one occasion he stood off the privy watch who were searching for two stolen geese, while his wife plucked them and Richardson made off to hide himself in Terling Park.[3]

This brief excursion through the darker streets of the village, pausing to glance in at the windows of the alehouses and of the cottages of the poor, can serve as an introduction to both the commoner disorders of village life and to the principal means by which conflict was handled in the community and social regulation enforced. In John Clark's minimal sense of shame, we have a glancing reference to the internalized customary norms of social behavior instilled in the young by precept and example. These overlapped at many points with the more highly articulated prescriptions of secular magistrates and religious moralists, though they were at other points vaguer and more flexible than the letter of canon or statute law. For the rest we have the spectrum of sanctions that might be invoked against offenders. The most powerful of these, though those that have left least trace to the historian, were the informal sanctions of gossip, bad reputation, and low credit in the eyes of the neighborhood in general and of powerful neighbors in particular. If these failed, then there might be an appeal to the formal intitutions of conflict resolution and social control: the courts.

Unlike some other villages in this period, Terling had no courts of its

---

[1] E. R. O. D/ACW 5/178; Q/SR 167/28, 169/70, 176/17, 181/72, 194/61; D/ACA 22 fo. 339, 32 fo. 261, 40 fo. 130.

[2] E. R. O. D/ACW 7/251; D/ACA 37 fo. 38; Assize Calendar 35/61/T/48.

[3] E. R. O. Q/S Ba 2/4.

own to which disputes might be taken or offenders presented. The courts of
the various manors, whatever their powers might have been in medieval
times, had ceased by the turn of the sixteenth century to have any function
other than the registration of land transactions. This fact may perhaps have
been a matter of some significance, encouraging the villagers to take their
disputes to the local institutions of ecclesiastical and royal justice. Victims
of theft, assault, or other crimes might bring an indictment against the person responsible before the justices of the peace at Quarter Sessions or (if the
crime was serious) before the Assize justices at their twice-yearly visitations. Both these courts usually met at nearby Chelmsford. Villagers
threatened by others might have a recongnizance of the peace issued by a
justice against whoever sought to do them ill. In addition to these privately
initiated actions, representatives of the village sat on the presentment juries
of the half-hundred of Witham, charged with reporting to the justices at
Quarter Sessions the minor misdemeanours of their neighbors. Moral or
religious offences were similarly presented by the churchwardens to the
twice-yearly visitations of the Archdeacon of Colchester or to the occasional visitations of the Bishop of London. A few cases were also taken to
the court of the Bishop of London's commissary in Essex and Hertfordshire.
On occasion, particularly bitter or difficult disputes might be carried
beyond the local courts to the central institutions meeting in the capital: to
the Star Chamber, the Court of Requests, or the Bishop of London's consistory court, for example. From the early 1630s this constellation of legal
institutions was further supplemented by regular monthly meetings or
"petty sessions" of the justices for the division of Essex within which Terling lay. These sessions were primarily concerned with minor misdemeanours and with the administrations of the Poor Laws.[4]

The various courts could bring to bear a hierarchy of sanctions. The ec-

---

[4] The survival of court records for Essex is remarkably good. Quarter Sessions and Assize
records survive very fully for the period 1560 to 1699, though files for a number of sessions are
missing. Missing files are, however, fairly evenly distributed in time. Unfortunately there are
no surviving files of civil cases at Assizes. Again, there are no detailed reports of business
transacted in Petty Sessions from the 1630s onwards. The records of the court of the Archdeacon of Colchester are virtually complete from 1570 onwards. Equally good are the records
of visitations by the Bishop of London, though a number of books are not yet available to the
public for research. The court books of the Commissary in Essex and Hertfordshire survive
from 1621 but contain very few Terling cases. This chapter is based upon the above records, as
listed in the bibliography. Cases between parties in the church courts are little referred to,
since the surviving records provide insufficient detail of their nature. The occasional Terling
cases heard before the Central courts in Westminister are also excluded from the general
analysis, though they too are occasionally introduced in order to clarify local disputes. This
chapter is therefore concerned with the relationships of the villagers with the local courts of
church and state, the legal institutions with which they were most closely involved.

clesiastical courts might simply admonish an offender or order the payment of a small fine. Alternatively, they might order the person convicted to undergo formal penitential rituals with greater or smaller degrees of publicity. The justices might simply bind over a disorderly villager or might order fines, whipping, or imprisonment in the house of correction. Assize judges controlled the ultimate sanction of death—a fate not uncommon in a time when a man might be "hanged for a shilling," in Cromwell's phrase. Probably three Terling villagers were strangled on the gallows at Chelmsford in our period.

By contemporary standards Essex was a particularly closely governed county within what has been seen as an increasingly closely governed England. The machinery of the law was abundantly available to the villagers if they chose to use it—and use it they did. Over the years between 1560 and 1699 just over 300 cases originating in Terling are known to have been brought to the attention of the justices of the peace and assize judges. These "cases" include not only formal prosecutions by bill of indictment and public presentment but also disputes that resulted in no more than the issue by a justice of recognizances to keep the peace, to be of good behavior, or to answer the complaint of a neighbor. Between 1570 and 1641 the ecclesiastical courts dealt with over 400 presentments of Terling villagers, while from 1663 to 1690 the revived church courts handled another 100 such cases. In any given decade between twenty and 100 Terling villagers appeared before one or other of the local courts.

The degree of involvement of the villagers with the courts was thus considerable. More significantly, it was not evenly spread over time. While there was an average of just over two cases per annum in Quarter Sessions and Assizes for the whole period, in fact there were no fewer than forty-seven years that witnessed no known cases. In the remaining years, business in these courts was particularly concentrated in the years 1603 (eight cases), 1607–1612 (an average of 7.5 cases per annum), 1617–1619 (eighteen cases), 1630 (fifteen cases), 1670–1672 (sixteen cases) and 1684 (eleven cases). These fifteen years accounted for over one-third of the total of known Terling cases. Overall, Terling business in Quarter Sessions and Assizes started at a low level, showed a significant increase during the 1590s, rose to a peak between 1607 and 1620, and settled back to its pre-1590s level only after 1660.

The ecclesiastical courts were generally busier than the secular courts. From 1570 to 1640 they handled an annual average of 5.6 Terling cases, the vast majority of these cases being heard before the correction courts of the Archdeacon of Colchester at Kelvedon. In the whole of this period there were only five years when no Terling cases came before the church courts, all of these years falling before 1583. Peak years existed, such as 1604 (thirteen cases) and 1620 (twenty-two cases). Overall, however, the church courts witnessed a much steadier and sustained increase in business from Terling than did the secular courts. The number of presentments rose steadily from the mid-1580s, reached a peak in the 1620s and then fell somewhat in the 1630s up to the point at which the courts collapsed with the outbreak of the Civil War. After 1660 the courts were revived but dealt with comparatively little disciplinary business. Regular presentments seem to have lapsed and after the 1660s separate records were no longer kept for the correction courts. Over half the post-1660 cases, in fact, came from a purge of nonconformists conducted in the single year 1679.

When all due allowance is made for occasional gaps in the records, it seems quite clear that both the secular and the ecclesiastical courts shared a broadly similar experience. In both cases, business from Terling rose steadily at the close of the sixteenth century, peaked in the reign of James I, and then steadily declined. Had the records of petty sessions survived for the years after 1630, this picture of declining business might need some modification. Nevertheless it was real enough. Entries in the accountbooks of the churchwardens and overseers of the poor for visits to the justices do not suggest a brisk trade in the later seventeenth century. Moreover, by the final decade of the seventeenth century the system of hundredal presentment juries, which brought most Terling business to court, had lapsed in Essex. If the decline in court business was real enough, so too was the dramatic upsurge of earlier years. Record survival is very good for the years before 1630 and there can be no doubting the reality of the phenomenon. Again, it cannot be explained simply in terms of a rising population. Both the numbers of cases and the numbers of persons prosecuted rose much faster than did the population of the village. Something was happening in Terling.

In this experience Terling was not alone. Mr. Walker and Professor Samaha, in their studies of felony prosecutions in Essex, have both noted significant rises in the level of prosecution in the last years of Elizabeth. Professor Cockburn has argued that these trends were national, assize prosecutions being high between 1590 and 1630 and reaching an absolute peak in the first decade of James I's reign. For the ecclesiastical courts of Essex, Dr. Emmison has noted the general rise in business from the 1580s onwards.[5]

---

[5] J. C. M. Walker, "Crime and Capital Punishment in Elizabethan Essex," pp. 13–16; (We would like to thank Mr. Walker for permission to refer to his unpublished dissertation.) J. Samaha, *Law and Order in Historical Perspective. The Case of Elizabethan Essex*, p. 19; J. S. Cockburn, *A History of English Assizes, 1558–1714*, p. 101 (see also his recent "The Nature and Incidence of Crime in England, 1559–1625: A Preliminary Survey," p. 53); F. G. Emmison, *Elizabethan Life: Morals and The Church Courts*, p. x.

The complementary evidence of prosecution statistics drawn from various levels is tantalizing and suggests a number of exciting interpretative possibilities. But it would be dangerous to spring too readily to the conclusion that rural England was experiencing some kind of crime wave or explosion of delinquency across the board at the turn of the sixteenth century. As legal historians have repeatedly urged, the recoverable statistics of criminal prosecutions, even where record survival is excellent, must be understood less as a measure of the actual incidence of crime than as an index of the willingness of villagers to take one another to court. The crucial point is that, in the absence of a professional police force, the vast majority of criminal prosecutions in this period depended above all on the ability and preparedness of the victims of crime to initiate prosecution privately, meeting its costs largely from their own pockets. At the same time, minor offences were presented to the justices and church courts by unpaid, amateur, temporary village officers (petty constables, churchwardens, presentment jurymen). They often lacked a taste for their duties and were sometimes scandalously negligent from the point of view of the authorities. Their ambivalent position is admirably summed up in the song attributed to James Gryffon, constable of Albury in 1626:

> *The Justices will set us by the heels*
> *If we do not as we should*
> *Which if we perform, the townsmen will storm*
> *Some of them hang's if they could.*[6]

These very facts, while frustrating to the historical criminologist, may nevertheless be turned to advantage by the social historian. For the very nature of prosecution in the early modern period suggests that the shifting pattern of prosecutions may provide the basis of a study of changing social relationships reflected in a greater readiness to prosecute in the courts.

What can have underlain such changes? Part of the answer must lie in increasing pressure from above. Both the royal and ecclesiastical authorities, as we have seen, were anxious to establish greater order and higher standards of obedience and conformity in the localities in this period. Directives flowed out from Westminister; local courts became better organized, more closely overlooked, busier. All of these tendencies were at work in the case of Essex. From the 1580s the court of the Archdeacon of Colchester can be seen establishing more regular presentment by churchwardens and better record-keeping. The justices of the peace of Essex were also making new efforts from the 1590s. Detailed "charges" began to be put to the hundredal jurymen of the half-hundred of Witham, for example, to inform

---

[6] Quoted in F. Aydelotte, *Elizabethan rogues and vagabonds*, p. 489.

them of their duties and stimulate their efficiency. Bland presentments of "All well" became less common. Yet pressure from above can explain only the broad trends of court activity in this period. It cannot adequately illuminate the varying chronology of change in individual villages. It is this intimately *local* chronology that must be investigated if we are to understand the local response to authoritative pressure, to see the blending of national policy with indigenous local change. Without a grasp of the little dynamic of change in the villages, we cannot fully appreciate the course and consequences of the greater dynamic of national history.

In the case of Terling, it can be said quite positively that pressure from above evoked a response only when the village notables who mediated between the courts and the village community became persuaded that local interests were best served by cooperation with the authorities. It should be emphasized that the overwhelming majority of court cases from Terling were freely brought in from below by either private prosecutors or village officers. In the church courts no purges initiated from above and swiftly carried out by the churchwardens are to be found before the later seventeenth century. On the contrary, the archdeacon could have severe difficulty in breaking the reluctance of churchwardens to prosecute where they felt local interests to be at variance with official demands, as during the enforcement of Laudian liturgical changes in the 1630s. In Quarter Sessions and Assizes there were only two occasions (in 1630 and 1644) when the county justices showed aggressiveness in insisting upon the returns of the village constables to specific articles of enquiry. This unusual (and highly effective) rigor was occasioned in 1630 by the tightening of administrative control in a year of harvest failure that had witnessed outbreaks of rioting and in 1644 by a county-wide purge of alehouses instigated at the suggestion of the Puritan ministers of Essex.[7] For the rest, the villagers brought some of their quarrels to the courts for adjudication, took action against some neglecters of communal obligations, and sought, through their officers, the punishment of individuals guilty of moral offences or of threatening by their disorders the precarious harmony of village life.

With what, exactly, were the villagers concerned? Cases brought before Quarter Sessions and Assizes can be divided up into four broad categories. First there were cases of homicide. Only two such cases are in fact known, both occurring during the Civil War years. One of these concerned the murder of her illegitimate child by Elizabeth Codwell, a woman who was undoubtedly mentally ill, and has been discussed elsewhere. The other, of

---

[7] The situation of 1630/31 is fully described in J. Walter and K. Wrightson, "Dearth and the social order in early-modern England," p. 35 ff. Records of the purge of 1644 are in E. R. O. Q/S Ba 6.

which less is known, concerned the murder of an old man. Both persons accused were sentenced to hang, and in one case we can be certain that the sentence was carried out.[8] The second and much larger category is that of interpersonal disputes. This category of privately brought cases involved cases of theft, assault, forcible entry and disseizin, poaching, and the issue of recognizances to keep the peace or to answer complaints.[9] Cases of obligation enforcement involved the public presentment of individuals who failed to repair roads and bridges or to scour ditches, those who defaulted on their obligations to perform labor on the highways, and those who failed to perform their duties as constables or watchmen. Regulative prosecutions, almost invariably publicly brought, included the prosecution of alehousekeepers and their disorderly customers, of those who failed to attend church, of persons who erected cottages without four acres of land, and a variety of other occasional offences against the penal laws, such as swearing, taking inmates or lodgers, or keeping greyhounds for hunting. The usefulness of employing broad categories of this type is that they allow one to cut through the confusing mass of business brought before the courts and to establish the essential broad patterns of the use of the courts by the villagers.

Over the whole period, regulative prosecutions predominated, accounting for 56.2% of all business, while interpersonal disputes came second with 33.7% of business. Obligation enforcement and homicide followed far behind. As can be seen from Table 5.1, however, both the absolute numbers and relative proportions of cases in different categories varied markedly over time. The number of interpersonal disputes brought to these courts rose sharply in the 1590s and continued to be high through to the 1610s before declining. The relative rominence of regulative prosecutions, on the other hand, expanded over the period, their absolute incidence being highest in the first and second decades of the seventeenth century. The use of these courts by Terling villagers thus varied substantially over time and showed a marked increase in prosecutions stemming from interpersonal disputes at the turn of the sixteenth century, followed by a sharp rise in the incidence of regulative prosecutions. The peak period of activity of both kinds fell between 1600 and 1619.

---

[8] Elizabeth Codwell's case is fully discussed in K. Wrightson, "Infanticide in earlier seventeenth century England," pp. 13–14. Of the second homicide there is no record of a trial, probably because of record loss or the emergencies of the war and temporary suspension of the courts. However, we do know from a parish register entry that one George Smith was actually hanged for the killing.

[9] Recognizances to keep the peace or to answer an accusation have been counted as separate "cases" only when they were not issued in the course of the preparation of another known case. In some cases the use of these recognizances helps to repair the occasional loss of indictments when files are missing.

TABLE 5.1
Pattern of Terling Prosecutions: Quarter Sessions and Assizes, 1560–1699

	Homicides	Interpersonal disputes	Obligation enforcement	Regulative prosecution	Row totals
1560–1579	—	3 (11.5%)	10 (38.5%)	13 (50.0%)	26 (100%)
1580–1599[a]	—	20 (69.0%)	1 (3.4%)	8 (27.6%)	29 (100%)
1600–1619	—	40 (42.1%)	3 (3.2%)	52 (54.7%)	95 (100%)
1620–1639	—	10 (20.0%)	6 (12.0%)	34 (68.0%)	50 (100%)
1640–1659	2 (4.4%)	18 (40.0%)	4 (8.9%)	21 (46.7%)	45 (100%)
1660–1679	—	8 (22.9%)	6 (14.3%)	22 (62.8%)	35 (100%)
1680–1699	—	4 (15.4%)	0 (—)	22 (84.6%)	26 (100%)
1560–1699	2 (0.6%)	103 (33.7%)	29 (9.5%)	172 (56.2%)	306 (100%)

[a] These 20-years totals mask the fact that most business was concentrated in the 1590s.

These figures can be complemented by an analysis of business in the church courts over the period 1570 to 1639. In Table 5.2, business has been broken down into cases involving the fabric and furniture of the church, prosecution of failings on the part of minister and churchwardens, religious offences (usually neglect of church attendance or failure to take communion), cases involving sexual and marital regulation, and, finally, cases involving the regulation of other forms of personal behavior (e.g., drunkenness).

Table 5.2 illustrates both the general increases in church court prosecution and the components of that increase. Over the whole period these courts were primarily concerned with the enforcement of religious conformity, with sexual behavior and with other aspects of personal comportment. The 1580s saw an increased concern with religious offences which was maintained thereafter. Prosecutions for sexual offences rose considerably at the turn of the sixteenth century, declining only in the 1630s. Other forms of personal behavior received regular attention mainly in the second and third decades of the seventeenth century, the same decades which witnessed the overall peak of church court prosecution for the villagers of Terling.

Taken together, as they surely must be, the patterns of prosecutions originating in Terling indicate that the overall increase in court business at the close of the sixteenth and opening of the seventeenth centuries is to be accounted for by a number of overlapping phenomena. First, there was a sharp increase in the number of interpersonal conflicts brought to the courts. Next, there was a heavier concentration on sexual offences. Finally, there was an initiative in prosecutions aimed at the closer regulation of the personal behavior of the villagers in other spheres. Throughout, there was a steady enforcement of religious duties of a kind unknown before the later

TABLE 5.2
Pattern of Terling Prosecutions: Ecclesiastical Courts, 1570–1639

	Church fabric and furniture	Minister and churchwardens	Religious offences	Sexual and marital	Other personal behavior	Row totals
1570–1579	0	0	12	4	2	18
1580–1589	0	1	21	10	3	35
1590–1599	2	7	22	24	6	61
1600–1609	10	2	17	34	1	64
1610–1619	3	6	34	21	13	77
1620–1629	7	1	20	21	32	81
1630–1639	8	8	25	10	8	59
	30	25	151	124	65	395

years of Elizabeth's reign. The question of religious offences can be put on one side for consideration in the next chapter. The significance of the other shifts in the nature of the relationships of Terling villagers and the courts can be further explored by the closer analysis of particularly prominent types of offence. From this we can hope to discern the degree to which these prosecutions followed significant patterns.

The three most prominent categories of interpersonal dispute were prosecutions for theft, cases in which individuals were bound to keep the peace to other persons, and cases of assault. The twenty-four cases of theft involving Terling villagers were spread over the whole of our period. Some tendency toward bunching can, however, be observed. Seven of the cases come from the years 1597–1603, the only period at which theft was a regular component of court business. These years embraced the height of the harvest disasters of the late 1590s, together with the early years of recovery. It seems possible that we have an example of a phenomenon familiar to students of crime in this period: the increased incidence of theft cases in years of peculiar economic hardship. This would also appear to be the case when we consider two further petty thefts in the winter of 1630–1631 and two more in the winter of 1649–1650. Both years witnessed dearth and extreme suffering in Essex.

Of the total of twenty-four theft cases, three involved the theft of a Terling man's property by individuals from other villages, while seven involving Terling people allegedly stealing from outsiders; in the remaining fourteen cases both accused and accuser were from Terling. In all, twenty-eight Terling villagers were accused of theft, while eighteen villagers were victims. None of those accused was prosecuted for theft more than once. As might be expected in the light of existing studies, the accused thieves were drawn for the most part from the lower ranks of village society. Twenty were of Category IV, while an additional five were of Category III. In contrast, their victims were drawn from Categories III (eight), II (seven), and I (three). Accused thieves were also less likely to have been natives of Terling than their victims and left much less evidence of interpersonal contacts in the records of the village than did the more prominent villagers from whom they stole. One might hypothesize from this evidence that the accused thieves were persons in a marginal position in village society, a position perhaps in which prosecution was less likely to have been inhibited by the complex filter of personal relationships that could interpose between the committing of an offence and its prosecution.

Additional evidence would tend to support such a suggestion. In 1600, for example, Grace, the daughter of William Payne, was publicly accused in church by Elizabeth, the wife of Thomas Belsted, of stealing gloves, an apron, and a handkerchief from her. The Paynes were a family of low social status, William Payne being a shoemaker and laborer. They were also given to petty delinquency of various kinds. William Payne, the father, was prosecuted for drunkenness; Grace, herself, later bore an illegitimate child. Other members of the family found themselves in trouble for such offences as prenuptial fornication, failure to attend church, or failure to pay the parish rate. They were, however, well established in the community and were related by marriage to some of the more substantial parishioners. Elizabeth Belsted, the accuser, was the wife of a blacksmith and also a member of an established family. She was, however, a woman of "suspected life and character," prosecuted as such in the church courts, as well as for her lewd and scandalous behavior at a dancing on the village green. At other times she was accused of abusing the sacrament of baptism and of stirring up contention among her neighbors. These circumstances may have helped to defuse her accusation of Grace Payne, for there is no evidence of a case having been brought in either Quarter Sessions or Assizes. Instead the churchwardens, Joseph Cavell and John Burchard, both of whom left evidence of their personal connections to the Payne family, prosecuted Elizabeth Belsted in the church courts for "brabbling" and causing a disturbance in church. This action, perhaps, preempted a possible court case.[10]

Rather different was the case of Robert Whitehead, a poor husbandman prosecuted for stealing a sheep in the winter of 1623–1624. His confession, which has already been quoted, reveals that he was driven to theft by hunger and the needs of his wife and seven children. The sheep was stolen from Hugh Tabor, a very substantial parishioner, who swiftly initiated a prosecution. Further evidence reveals that Whitehead was a newcomer to the village, a subtenant of one of the leading yeomen. In 1623 he had been prosecuted and excommunicated for his failure to attend church and he was indeed still excommunicate at the time of his offence. He left little evidence of personal connections among the villagers. Hugh Tabor, in contrast, was a member of a leading family, long established in the village, who enjoyed a galaxy of known connections both personally and through his brothers. In this case there were few cross-currents that might keep the case from the courts. Whitehead, however, was lucky and the case seems not to have been pressed to a conclusion. No actual indictment was entered in the Quarter Sessions and his recognizance to appear was relaxed. Perhaps Tabor was willing to relent because of the circumstances. Robert

---

[10] E. R. O. D/ACA 25 fos. 103, 112, 115v, 165; D/ACA 37 fo. 132; D/ACA 40 fo. 111; Greater London Record Office DL/C/324.

Whitehead was still living in Terling six years later and was never again in trouble of any kind.[11]

Theft prosecutions, then, were primarily initiated by more substantial, established villagers against their poorer, less established, and more marginal neighbors. The evidence would suggest that they provide less a record of the incidence of crime than of occasions upon which an offence gave rise to a prosecution uninhibited by intervening considerations or mediating action. That such occasions were rather more numerous in years of economic stringency, such as 1630–1631 and 1649–1650 and in the period from 1597 to 1603, may reflect some of the strain put upon social relations in a period when even some of the middling rank of villagers may have been struggling to keep their heads above water.

Further evidence of such strain may be observed when we turn to the second category of interpersonal disputes—those that resulted in the issue of recognizances to keep the peace. Twenty-three such cases are known, of which fifteen resulted from disputes between neighbors, six concerned a Terling villager and an outsider, and two involved a general binding of a man to keep the peace, no threatened victim of violence being named. These cases were very much bunched in time; sixteen of them belong to the years 1599 to 1612. Of the forty persons involved in these conflicts, eleven were from Category II and twenty-two from Category III. The persons concerned were evenly split as to whether they were natives of the village or newcomers but most were firmly enough rooted to judge by the surviving evidence of their personal connections. While the precise nature of the original quarrels that resulted in these bindings to keep the peace remain for the most part hidden from us, they would certainly appear to suggest the existence of a high degree of conflict among villagers of middling status in the first decade of the seventeenth century—conflict bitter enough to result in threats of violence and consequent preemptive bindings to keep the peace.

This suggestion is strengthened by an examination of prosecutions for assault. Though more evenly spread in time than recognizances to keep the peace, the nineteen cases of assault were nonetheless bunched to a degree in 1595, 1604–1610 and the year 1655–1656. These years accounted for two-thirds of the known cases. Of the nineteen cases, thirteen arose from disputes within the village, six from disputes between villagers and outsiders. Of the forty-three Terling villagers involved, five were drawn from Category I, thirteen from Category II, nine from Category III and fifteen from Category IV. Of the latter, however, thirteen were involved as the auxiliaries of men of higher social status, as in a case of 1571 when John

---

[11] E. R. O. Q/SR 243/61; Q/S Ba 2/7.

Rochester, Esq. assaulted a husbandman and his wife with the aid of five laborers.[12] Assault was very much an offence of the more prominent and wealthy villagers. Laborers do not appear as principals in assault cases before the mid-seventeenth century though it is, of course, possible that brawls between laborers may have been kept out of court by the expenses of prosecution. The flurry of cases at the end of the sixteenth and beginning of the seventeenth centuries nevertheless points once more to a period of unusual tension among the villagers of middling and superior wealth and standing.

We have a clearer idea of the actual nature of the disputes involved in certain of these cases. In 1595, for example, Richard Rochester, a man on the borderline between yeoman and gentle status, distrained sheep for rents owed to him by his brother William Rochester, John Price, and William Burton. The distraint was made at Michaelmas in a bad harvest year and may have been a severe blow to the men involved, quite apart from breaking the obligations of neighborliness and restraint on the part of landlords in a time of economic stringency. Richard Rochester was unlikely to care, for his relationships with both his brother and Price had irretrievably broken down. For two years Richard and William had been engaged in a dispute over the inheritance of the lands of a dead elder brother that was extremely bitter and was to end in the Star Chamber. Price had openly sided with William Rochester in this case. A further element in the situation was that both William Rochester and Price were indebted and William was soon to die in a state of chronic indebtedness. Richard Rochester's action may have rubbed salt in their wounds, even threatened their livelihood. Two assault and two disseizin cases resulted from his action and further fuel was heaped on the fire of the ongoing feud between the brothers which ended only with William's death.[13]

Possibly of a similar nature was the case of William Hare's assault upon the wife of John Biggen in 1607. Hare's will of 1608 shows him to have been deeply in debt, all his goods being ordered to be sold to cover his obligations to his creditors. John Biggen was related by marriage to John Aldridge. Biggen was also a "wellbeloved frende" and supervisor of Aldridge's will. Aldridge, who died in 1602, had left money in the care of his executors and supervisors to be "putt forthe. . . . to their their best commoditie and encrease" until the majority of his sons John, Thomas, and William. William Aldridge happened to be one of William Hare's principal creditors.[14]

---

[12] E. R. O. Q/SR 37/31.

[13] E. R. O. Q/SR 131/24, 25, 30, 132/40; D/ACW 3/198, 4/79; P. R. O. STAC 5 A7/30, A8/1, 13, A19/9, A27/35, A33/20, 39, A39/18, A54/13, A55/23, A57/6.

[14] E. R. O. Assize Calendar 35/49H/32; D/ACW 4/128, 4/324.

The case between Thomas Holman and Richard Rochester in 1610 was of a rather different nature, though like the case of 1595 it was an incident in a long-standing feud. Rochester had been instrumental in having Holman, an innkeeper, presented in 1607 for drunkenness and keeping a disorderly house. Holman swore revenge against Rochester, claiming that "ware yt not for ye Law he would have the bood of the said Rochester." Instead he tried to saw down the pales of one of Rochester's closes and later stole the plough irons and pulled up the pales of both Rochester and the two yeomen who had supported him in presenting Holman. They then got up a set of articles of complaint against Holman. Meanwhile, Rochester had to be bound over to keep the peace to Thomas Holman's wife, while in 1609 Holman was bound to keep the peace to William James, an ally of Rochester. Finally, in 1610 Holman was prosecuted and fined for an assault on Rochester, one of Rochester's witnesses being William James.[15]

Feuding of this nature could clearly thoroughly disrupt the peace of the village, involving ever larger numbers of villagers as the principals drew upon their networks of friends and kin to support them against their opponents. It was another such feud that lay behind the rash of cases of assault in 1655–1656. It is almost certainly for this reason that the recognizance of the peace, essentially a preventive instrument, was so commonly used to stabilize conflicts that were approaching critical mass. Private mediation might be the first step, as in 1614 when Geoffrey Richard struck John Baker "and brock his head and shed bloud in the Churchyeard." The churchwardens presented the case to the Archdeacon, and when Richard appeared he explained "that all partyes are agreed and satisfyed and therefore craveth to be dismissed." This case, like some other affrays to which we have incidental references, never reached the Quarter Sessions. Failing such informal settlement, a recognizance of the peace could (and usually did) halt matters. More than one regonizance was soon relaxed with the brief note explaining "They are agreed."[16] Thomas Holman was something of an exceptional case. He was an outsider who had entered the village when he married John Aldridge's widow in 1603. He was a fairly prosperous man. For both reasons he may have been less amenable than some villagers to informal pressure. Even more to the point, he was a peculiarly violent man in both word and deed, given to "great threats and words tending to danger" and not above taking up a sword in the course of a drunken quarrel. In the early stages of his feud with Rochester he was admonished by some of his neighbors "to keepe the peace and also to remember that he was bound to his good behavior." He

---

[15] E. R. O. Q/SR 181/36, 72, 182/43, 188/71, 192/64.

[16] E. R. O. D/ACA 37 fo. 5. For examples of recognisances of the type quoted, see E. R. O. Q/SR 404/55, 476/40.

demonstrated his contempt for such counsel by "castinge upp his legge and layeing his hand on his tayle makeinge a mouth in very contempious sorte."[17]

Holman's contempt was, however, almost unique. For the most part, the public peace was kept. As for the conflict that threatened it so much in the first decade of the seventeenth century, it seems possible that it derived largely from the economic strains of the period. In view of what historians have discovered of the difficulties experienced by small to middling husbandmen in the decades after 1595 as they battled against the indebtness inherited from the catastrophic harvests of the 1590s, it seems possible that such strains exacerbated conflict among the middle groups in village society. Such conflict was certainly responsible for a good deal of court business from Terling in the years up to 1612. It has been commented earlier that some of the larger yeomen and smaller gentry of Terling seem to have consolidated their position in the early decades of the seventeenth century, while some husbandmen and yeomen sold land and declined. Whether such elements of economic tension lay behind a period of sharp interpersonal conflict must remain an open question in the absence of more detailed evidence, but it is at least a reasonable possibility.[18]

If this was so, such conflict was less common after 1612. From that date the courts handled business of this type infrequently. Prosecutions thereafter became predominantly regulative and public in Quarter Sessions and Assizes. At the same time the nature of the cases presented began to overlap to a large degree with that of the cases brought to the ecclesiastical courts. Before pursuing these developments in the various courts, however, we may pause to examine a matter that was almost exclusively the concern of the church courts; the regulation of sexual and marital behavior. By doing so we may add a further dimension to our understanding of the difficult years at the turn of the sixteenth century—years that provide the immediate background to the regulative initiative which was to come.

In the years 1570 to 1641 the ecclesiastical courts handled well over 100 sexual and marital prosecutions originating in Terling. Thereafter their authority in these matters effectively lapsed and the revived courts handled only four such cases after 1662. These cases were almost invariably brought to court by the presentments of the churchwardens to the Arch-

---

[17] E. R. O. Q/SR 182/43.

[18] The kind of situation in which even substantial villagers could find themselves is illustrated by Thomas Uprichards alias Hewes. A court of requests case reveals that Hewes, one of the more wealthy yeomen of the parish, fell deeply in debt at the turn of the century, for reasons unknown to us. His creditors threatened to prosecute him. On 2 May 1607, while the case continued, a parish register entry reveals that Hewes hanged himself in his own barn. P. R. O. Req. 2/404/2.

deacon's visitations. In the period of their power prior to 1641, bastardy was by far the commonest offence prosecuted by the churchwardens, followed by prosecutions for incontinency and adultery which did not involve pregnancy, by cases of prenuptial pregnancy or fornication, and by a scattering of prosecutions for lewd behavior of various kinds. Cases were brought on mere suspicion, on rumor of "common fame," but above all when a "great bellie" betrayed the indiscretions of the villagers. All sexual activity unsanctified by marriage was a matter for public concern and seems to have been a matter of public knowledge, though not all sexual lapses were greeted with the same degree of hostility.

Cases of simple incontinency or of adultery were fairly well spread over time up to 1640, as were cases in which Terling men had begotten illegitimate children outside the village. After 1640 we know little of such matters since they are revealed to the historian only by the court books of the Archdeacon, or by the occasional Quarter-Sessions case. Prosecutions concerning illigitimate children born within the village, however, and cases involving prenuptial offences were surprisingly bunched in time. Some two-fifths of the bastardy prosecutions, for example, came in the ten years following 1597, while there was a further flurry of such cases in 1613–1616. Prosecutions for prenuptial offences were grouped in 1598 to 1603 and in the years 1625 to 1640.

In dealing with offences of this kind we have the opportunity at last to test the efficiency of the village officers in prosecuting offences, since the parish registers provide an independent source of information on the real incidence of illegitimacy and bridal pregnancy. In the case of illegitimacy, their efficiency was very high indeed. For the period 1570 to 1640 we know of seventy-one cases of bastardy; sixty-three of them are recorded in the parish register, fifty-six in the church court books, and five among the Quarter-Sessions files. Of known illegitimacy cases, 79% were thus brought before the ecclesiastical magistrates, while a further 4% came before the justices of the peace, though not before the Archdeacon. Altogether over 80% of known cases led to prosecutions. Bridal pregnancy presents a rather different picture. Between 1570 and 1640 the parish register provides thirty-nine cases of brides whose first child was baptized less than 8½ months after marriage, most of whom were probably pregnant at the time of their marriage—many of them heavily so. Of these, only ten cases were prosecuted in the church courts. The church courts do, however, provide a further ten cases not apparent in the parish register, since either the marriage or the subsequent baptism was not celebrated in Terling. Just over 40% of all known cases of bridal pregnancy can therefore be said to have led to prosecution in the courts. Over the whole period the churchwardens were clearly far less concerned with punishing prenuptial sexual relations that with dealing with bastardy. This situation, however, was not unchanging. Whereas only 35% of known cases of bridal pregnancy reached the courts in 1580–1599 and only 28% in 1600–1619, the figure for 1620–1639 was 73%. Concern with this offence clearly grew over time to match the constant concern with illegitimacy.

That the village officers should always have been efficient in bringing the parents of illegitimate children before the courts is scarcely surprising. Bastardy was not only an offence against Christian sexual morality but it also struck against the fertility-restraining marriage pattern with its implicit insistence that only those capable of sustaining an economically independent household had the right to marry and have children. Moreover, bastardy was a potential source of conflict if the paternity of the child were in doubt and of expense to the community should the parents be unable to maintain the child. Despite this hostility we should, of course, expect to discover occasional cases of illegitimacy in the records. For most of the period studied bastardy was indeed occasional: six cases in the 1570s, four in the 1580s, four in the 1630s and so on. What is much more problematic is that there was also what can only be described as an explosion of illegitimacy at the turn of the sixteenth century. Of the eighty-two cases of illegitimacy known from all sources for the period 1570 to 1699, twenty-seven cases (32.9%) relate to bastards conceived in the years 1597 to 1607, while there was a smaller flurry of cases in the years 1613–1616. Thereafter bastardy became sporadic once more and increasingly rare after 1630.

Terling was not alone in experiencing such a dramatic upswing of illegitimacy. As the research of Peter Laslett and Karla Oosterveen has shown, the peak of illegitimacy at the turn of the sixteenth century was a national phenomenon.[19] To what extent does the case of Terling provide clues as to the causes of this astonishing and, until recently, unsuspected aspect of the history of the period?

Over the whole period studied, sixty-nine Terling women bore illegitimate children. Of these sixty-one bore only a single base child, while eight bore more than one bastard. One of them had as many as four illegitimate children. Eighteen of the sixty-three known fathers were outsiders. Of the Terling men involved, forty-two fathered only one bastard, while three offended more than once.

Establishing the social position of those involved in the bastardy cases is somewhat problematic. About a third of the women and a quarter of the

---

[19] P. Laslett and K. Oosterveen, "Long-term Trends in Bastardy in England, 1561–1960," p. 256.

men involved were extremely obscure individuals, sometimes appearing only in the parish register when the child was baptized and in the court records when their case was presented. No social status can be given them with any certainty but it is unlikely that they were people of any wealth or standing in the community. Their very obscurity suggests rather that they were poor and that they were only temporarily resident in Terling. Probably they were servants, though we cannot be sure. What is known of the social position of the parents of bastards is set out in Table 5.3.

As Table 5.3 shows, both overall and for particular subperiods a higher proportion of fathers than of mothers was drawn from the upper social categories. Despite the presence of some members of families of leading or middling rank, however, it is clear that bastardy was very much an offence of the poor and the obscure. Indeed, comparision of the three periods shows that not only were the poor and obscure disproportionately involved in bastardy but they were increasingly so as time advanced. In dealing with illegitimacy we appear to be dealing with not one but two phenomena. First, the explosion of illegitimate births at the turn of the century and the subsequent decline in the incidence of bastardy; second, the gradual decline in the involvement of villagers of some substance and the confinement of bastardy to the poor and obscure.

A surprising amount of information can be recovered concerning the circumstances of many of these cases. Indeed, enough is available to indicate that bastardy was very much a compound phenomenon and far from being a simple product of rustic licentiousness. Over the whole period twenty-six cases (31.7%) can be grouped as being the product of fairly unambiguous sexual delinquency. These include cases of adulterous liaisons between married men and village girls, the sexual exploitation of servant girls by their masters, a case of technical incest between a man and his dead wife's sister, and cases involving persons who are known to have committed sexual offences at other times. However, a further thirty (36.6%) can be grouped as cases that relate less to simple delinquency than to problems and delays in the process of marriage entry. These are cases where marriage was intended by the parents and/or was actually achieved after the birth of the child. Such a case was that of Catherine Jackson, When she was presented for carrying Richard Chapman's child in 1599, her father came to court and explained that "god willing she and the sayd Richard Chapman intend to solemnize matrimony and lyve like man and wyf together." They married in 1602. Similarly, in 1601 Bridget Rogers and William Hulke, both servants, explained "that they are contracted and the bannes asked betwene them." When Grace Burles appeared before the court in 1602 it was pointed out that "Edward Shipman was the father therof who myndeth shortlye to marye her" but that he "was prest for a soldier in the last

TABLE 5.3
Parents of Illegitimate Children: Social Position[a]

	Social category					Row totals
	I	II	III	IV	?	
1570–1609						
Mothers	—	4 (10.3%)	7 (17.9%)	17 (43.6%)	11 (28.2%)	39
Fathers	1 (4.0%)	4 (16.0%)	5 (20.0%)	9 (36.0%)	6 (24.0%)	25
Both	1 (1.6%)	8 (12.5%)	12 (18.75%)	26 (40.6%)	17 (26.6%)	64
1610–1649						
Mothers	—	1 (4.3%)	2 (8.7%)	8 (34.8%)	12 (52.2%)	23
Fathers	—	1 (6.2%)	3 (18.8%)	6 (37.5%)	6 (37.5%)	16
Both	—	2 (5.1%)	5 (12.8%)	14 (35.9%)	18 (46.2%)	39
1650–1699						
Mothers	—	—	—	6 (75.0%)	2 (25.0%)	8
Fathers	—	1 (20.0%)	1 (20.0%)	3 (60.0%)	— (0.00%)	5
Both	—	1 (7.7%)	1 (7.7%)	9 (69.2%)	2 (15.4%)	13
1570–1699						
Mothers	—	5 (7.2%)	9 (13.0%)	31 (44.9%)	35 (34.8%)	69
Fathers	1 (2.2%)	6 (13.3%)	8 (17.8%)	18 (40.0%)	12 (26.7%)	45
Both	1 (0.9%)	11 (9.6%)	17 (14.9%)	49 (43.0%)	36 (31.6%)	114

[a]Fathers of illegitimate children who were not Terling inhabitants have been excluded. One man and one woman recur in two of the periods.

presse." Edward escaped the perils of war, came home, and married her six months after the birth of the child.[20] In other cases incautious or irresponsible activity on the local marriage market can be inferred since one of the parents did shortly marry, though to another person. Margery Bishop bore a bastard in July 1611 (father unknown) and married Thomas Thornton in October the same year. Mary Griggs was not long widowed when she bore a base child in 1615. She was very possibly seeking a new husband. She did remarry less than two years later and was seven months pregnant at the altar. When her second husband died she again quickly remarried (being only three months pregnant this time). Again, three cases relate to a stable, though illicit, relationship between John Strange and Agnes Turner. They had three children over a period of years; neither offended with any other person, yet for whatever reason they never married. Finally, there are twenty-six bastardy cases (31.7%) in which the circumstances are wholly unknown and cannot be reconstructed. As might be expected, these involved most of the parents of bastards who remain obscure in the records.

The simple registration of a base baptism or the entry of a case in the court books could thus cover a multitude of circumstances. It is our misfortune that too often the offenders stood silent before their judges rather than seeking to explain themselves. Looking at the circumstances of cases over time, we find that the same variety can be found across the whole of our period; there was, however, some variation in the *proportions* of cases of different type. The proportion of cases where nothing is known remained fairly constant at 30 to 40% over the three periods used for the analysis of the parents of bastards in Table 5.3. The proportion of cases involving marital delays and frustrations, however, fell from 45% in the first period to 10% in the final period. That of cases of clear delinquency rose from 25% to 50%. We have a third aspect of the history of bastardy. Its incidence declined, it became more confined to the poor, and it came to involve much clearer and less ambiguous delinquency.

To what extent can these characteristics of bastardy in Terling help to explain the peak of cases at the turn of the century? In the first place they help to reveal the complexity of the problem. Bastardy clearly involved much more than the activities of the sexually delinquent. Indeed, at its height its causation was more complex and those involved more broadly spread through village society than was to be the case later in the seventeenth century. Terling, like any village, had its share of sexual delinquents, its whores and its irresponsible men, its repetitive offenders. Yet the peak of cases between 1597 and 1607 cannot be explained simply in terms of their activities. Even when cases involving known sexual delinquents and

---

[20] E. R. O. D/ACA 25, fos. 32v, 171, 198v.

repetitive offenders are excluded from consideration, the peak of cases remains at the beginning of the seventeenth century, though the flurry of cases in 1613–1616 is smoothed down to more normal proportions. What must be explained is the question of why so many additional cases occurred over and above the expected trickle of cases produced by delinquent villagers.

Our suggestion is that the answer lies in the legally ambivalent behavior of the villagers during courtship. Society in Terling was fluid, particularly so among the young, unmarried servants, and laborers who passed through the village. Those of them who were of an age to do so, who had a partner in mind and could find regular employment, a cottage, and settlement in the village, might marry and stay on. Others passed on their way. Courtship among the pool of eligibles that existed in Terling and its neighboring villagers must frequently have been informal and relatively unsupervised. It revolved around the dancings on the green, the gatherings of servants and neighbors in the alehouses, rather than the formally arranged match. Kin can have had only limited sway over the choices of the young, since they were frequently geographically distant. Parental influence was mitigated in part by the simple facts of mortality. Of those marrying in Terling between 1520 and 1699. for whom we know the date of their father's death, 58% of bridegrooms and 42% of brides had already lost their fathers. The comparable figures for loss of mothers were 52% and 50%. Even where parents survived, the influence of patriarchal authority was unlikely to be decisive on those children who had already left home—even less so if they had little or nothing to inherit. Partner selection among the majority seems most likely to have been based upon personal compatibility, even upon romantic love. "Protestations of love" were a common enough feature of Essex courtships in this period, to judge by the detailed bastardy depositions among the Quarter-Sessions files. Once marriage was within sight it is clear enough that sexual relations began in earnest in many cases, especially in the later sixteenth century. One-third of all brides traceable to the baptism of their first child in Terling between 1550 and 1599 were pregnant when they married. The church might frown upon such actions but custom permitted them and the churchwardens for the most part turned a blind eye.

All this was very well so long as expectations of housing, a settlement, land, or employment were met and marriage ensued. Where such expectations were frustrated and plans dislocated, a pregnant bride-to-be might find herself the mother of a bastard, as we have seen. There must always have been a number of girls who either mistook their man or who were victims of circumstances beyond their control. But might not such cases have been more common at particular periods? When marriage opportunities were unusually good, one might expect to have few bastardy cases of this type. When opportunities were particularly bad, one might expect young villagers to have had sufficient sense to exercise restraint, with the result that again there would be few bastardy cases. But what if they found themselves in a period of transition between the two, a period of peculiarly unstable opportunity?

Something of the kind may have been the case in Terling. In the later sixteenth century, marriage opportunities seem to have been good. The village was expanding and immigrants were readily enough absorbed. Into this situation came the disastrous harvests of the 1590s. Vagrants died in the fields and barns. Husbandmen fell into debt. What was the effect upon the marital expectations of the young? One effect was that the later 1590s saw a dip in the annual average of marriages in Terling. There was a brief flurry of bastardy cases, some certainly involving delayed marriage plans. As the crisis passed over recovery began. There was a minor marriage boom in the early years of the seventeenth century—but also a boom of illegitimate births. Of the twenty-two bastardy cases between 1600 and 1607, eleven can be classified as marriage-related and three as involving simple delinquency, while eight remain a mystery. Our hypothesis would be that in the aftermath of the crisis the marriage chances of the young appeared good but were, in fact, sufficiently insecure to produce a crop of bastard births temporarily superimposed upon the normal trickle of cases produced by simple delinquency. Not only the poor were involved; some daughters of more substantial householders found themselves bearing their first child unwed.

As the seventeenth century advanced, the courtships of the children of the more substantial villagers regained their former security. The behavior of the poor may have adjusted to the changed climate of opportunity. A period of demographic deceleration was beginning that depended on the recognition of their situation by the villagers and was certainly reflected in restrained marital fertility, as we have seen. Such an adjustment in the direction of sexual caution may also have lain behind the declining incidence of bastardy. Illegitimacy was gradually confined to a small minority of the very poor, the sexually exploited, and the delinquent.

Bridal pregnancy provides supporting evidence for such a subtle change in popular sexual behavior. In the later sixteenth century, a third of all brides traceable to a first birth in Terling were pregnant at marriage. In the first half of the seventeenth century this figure was reduced to some 20% and in the second half of the century to 11%. Moreover bridal pregnancy, which had been a phenomenon found at all social levels, became increasingly confined to couples from Categories IV and III. This trend in behavior was reinforced by the tougher attitude toward bridal pregnancy taken by the churchwardens in the 1620s and 1630s, which has already been remarked upon. Not only was a much larger proportion of offences brought before the courts, but a change took place in the nature of the prosecutions. Prior to the 1620s prenuptial pregnancy was almost never prosecuted if marriage had already taken place. Persons presented were those who had been observed to be pregnant but whose marriage was not yet accomplished and was perhaps uncertain in the eyes of the churchwardens. One may surmise that the essential point of the prosecutions was to hasten the solemnization and avoid adding further to the wave of illegitimacy in the village. After 1620 couples were prosecuted even when long married—some had been married more than eight months when their child was born—someone was keeping a careful count. The churchwardens seem to have discovered an interest in defending the principle that there should be *no* premarital sexual relations. They had turned their faces against what had customarily been tolerated.

In other cases, too, the village leaders used their authority and power in ways that must have contributed to the reinforcement of the process of demographic stabilization. A number of cohabiting immigrant couples were examined as to their marital status. Prosecutions in Quarter Sessions for taking in inmates and lodgers or for maintaining cottages without four acres of land and allowing the poor to inhabit them indicate a concern with stabilizing the fluidity of the population.[21] Finally, in 1617, we have an indication of an informal control of the marriages of the poor when a laborer presented in the courts for incontinency protested:

> that he is contracted in matrimonie . . . and that the banes of matrimonie were asked betwene them in Terling Churche . . . and *the parishe would not suffer them to marry* else they had bin marryed ere now and he confesseth they have lyved togither a yeare[22] [emphasis added]

In these changed circumstances it is unlikely that the breakdown of the period 1597 to 1607 could have repeated itself. Nor did it.

For the rest, the churchwardens continued to bring before the courts the occasional cases of adultery and sexual incontinency of other kinds that came to their notice until the expiry of the church courts in 1641. After

---

[21] E. R. O. D/ACA 30 fos. 167, 179; Q/SR 181/97, 199/113, 227/24, 256/43; Assize Calendar 35/68/H/35, 35/71/H/90, 35/71/H/92.

[22] G. L. R. O. DL/C/324 fo. 51v. our italics. Such informal inhibition of the marriages of the poor was far from unknown in rural England of the period. For a similar case involving another Terling Villager, see our account of Robert Johnson, pp. 80–81. By "the parishe" and "the inhabitants," we may be sure that these laborers meant the notables of the parishes concerned, in particular the ministers and parish officers. The use of the term in this sense is of some significance.

1660 they showed little interest in such powers. Perhaps by that time too many of them had ideological objections to the ecclesiastical courts; perhaps they no longer needed them. The courts had already played their part in reinforcing an adjustment of behavior that was essentially accomplished.

If the church courts were used by the village officers to redraw the boundaries of conventionally permitted sexual behavior, they were also used in concert with the secular courts to establish stricter regulative control over other aspects of village life. For the early seventeenth century saw the buildup in Quarter Sessions and Assizes of a new pattern of regulative activity that was complemented and continued in the ecclesiastical courts up to 1640.

This regulative activity, this growing willingness of village officers to make public presentments of misdemeanors, was directed principally against the village alehouses. Between 1560 and 1649 seventy-three prosecutions in the secular courts (60% of regulative prosecutions and one-third of all prosecutions) directly concerned the alehouses and the prescribed activities which they harbored. Most of these cases were brought between 1607 and 1625.

The most prominent category of alehouse offence in Quarter Sessions and Assizes was that of selling ale without a licence, accounting for twenty-eight cases over the entire period studied. These cases were largely grouped between 1609 and 1619 (fifteen cases), there being only occasional cases thereafter up to the 1650s. The twenty-eight cases involved only nineteen persons, several of whom offended repeatedly. Eleven were drawn from Category IV, five from Category III, and three from Category II. Fourteen were first-generation villagers, while five belonged to established families. The earlier prosecutions show the parish officers dealing with a fairly widespread offence, fourteen of the persons prosecuted being presented to the courts before 1619. Thereafter the jurymen and constables were largely concerned with creaming off a number of repetitive offenders. Control over unlicensed aleselling would appear to have been effectively established by the early 1620s—and indeed it was reported to enquiries of the justices of the peace in 1624–1625 and in 1630 that the village had no such offenders.[23] After the brief collapse of alehouse licensing during the Civil War, control was reestablished in 1644 after a petition of Essex ministers that included among its signatories John Stalham, minister of Terling.[24]

This pattern of activity fits what is known of the regulation of unlicensed

---

[23] E. R. O. Q/SR 245/32, 272/25.

[24] E. R. O. Q/SBa 2/48, Q/SBa 6/8/9. A further report of 1670 stated that in that year the parish had only two licensed and no unlicensed ale-sellers. E. R. O. Q/SR 423/40.

ale-selling in this period. Occasional participation in the ale trade was one of the longest established employments of the poor in English society, observable as far back as the thirteenth century.[25] The Terling alesellers were indeed commonly poor. The participation of some villagers of middling status is to be accounted for partly by the prosecution of keepers of the village inn who had been temporarily denied licences for allowing disorder, yet continued to sell ale. Again, small husbandmen and craftsmen may have become involved in an attempt to supplement their incomes in a time of economic adversity or at particularly difficult stages of the family cycle. Some were aged; some had large families to support. Control of the numbers involved in the ale trade was an increasing preoccupation of both central and local government in the century after the passing of the Licensing Act of 1552, concerned as they were to limit the quantities of barley diverted into the ale trade and to combat petty disorders. Their principal problem in achieving such control was that of establishing respect for the law's definition of an offence among both potential offenders and the local officers charged with their prosecution. Such respect appears to have been established in Terling in the course of the second decade of the seventeenth century by the sustained activity of the village officers. A widespread customary economic activity had become locally established as an offence and brought under control.

Control of the numbers involved in ale-selling was complemented by regulation of the activities of licensed alehousekeepers and their customers. The need for such an initiative was another major theme of contemporary writing on the subject of public order and was particularly prominent in the work of moralistic writers and preachers advocating a reformation of popular manners. These public moralists castigated the alehouses as promoters of drunkenness, debauchers of servants and children, harbors of all disorder, enemies of church attendance, and a major cause of secondary poverty occasioned by excessive drinking. Such attitudes may have found an echo in Terling, since there were thirty-three prosecutions in Quarter Sessions, Assizes, and the church courts of alehousekeepers who allowed disorders in their houses. The various courts also saw sixty prosecutions for drunkenness, "alehousehaunting" and sitting "tippling" for more than an hour. In addition, men were prosecuted for gaming in alehouses, for swearing in alehouses, and for suspected sexual incontinency in alehouses, while three alehousekeepers were presented for charging excessive prices for their beer.

To take only the two major categories of offence, there were only very

---

[25] A full discussion of the alehouse and its place in village society in the period is given in K. Wrightson, "Alehouses, order and reformation in rural England, 1590–1660."

occasional prosecutions for disorders in alehouses or for drunkenness before 1607. In 1607–1608 the innkeeper Thomas Holman was presented for disorder and there was a burst of drunkenness cases. A lull followed while the parish officers turned their attention to unlicensed alehouses. Then, from 1616 on, a major attack was launched on the alehouses and their customers. Disorderly alehouses were the subject of a burst of Quarter Sessions and Assize prosecutions in 1616 1618 and of seven church court presentments in 1619–1621. Thereafter alehouse disorders were presented with regularity up to 1650. In concert with this attack, drinking offences were the subject of nineteen prosecutions in the various courts between 1616 and 1621, this initiative being followed through with regular prosecutions of drunkards and tipplers through to 1647.

Against whom was this initiative directed? The eighteen persons prosecuted for keeping disorderly houses were predominantly of low social status, small craftsmen, and laborers, and were usually first-generation villagers. As with unlicensed ale-selling, the prosecutions took the form of an initial attack upon widely tolerated practices, such as drinking in service time, reveling, dancing, and gaming in alehouses. After 1630 their object was rather the harassment of a repetitive offender—the inkeeper John Aldridge—who was, incidentally, the stepson of the notorious Thomas Holman.

Individuals prosecuted for drunkenness, tippling, or alehouse-haunting were rather more spread across the social scale. Almost two-thirds were drawn from the laboring population, but a quarter came from the village yeomanry. They were fairly evenly divided between newcomers to the village and members of established families.

The initiative against alehouse and drinking disorders can be said to have been directed by the parish officers against the lower ranks of village society and against a number of their fellow offenders, promoters, and defenders among the more substantial yeomen and craftsmen. The initiative was in line with contemporary insistence upon the need to control the alehouses, both as an end in itself and as the first step in the establishment of a more disciplined social order. The moralist Samuel Hammond called it the very "foundation of reformation."[26] Indeed, the village officers of Terling explicitly subscribed to such views. In a petition of 1620, at the height of the assault upon the alehouses, they clearly aligned themselves with the moralistic position. They complained that Terling had "gotten to itselfe an evil report amongst other places" as a result of the activities of its alehousekeepers. Drunkenness, disorder, and other abuses "shameful to be spoken of" were alleged to abound "whereby the name of god is highly

---

[26] S. Hammond, *Gods Judgements upon Drunkards etc.* To the Justices of Peace.

dishonoured, idlenes maintained and our parishe of itselfe poor enough impoverished and decayed."[27] Indeed, their complaints were justified. A compilation of the known offences of the persons known to have sold ale with or without a license in Terling over our period reveals that few are known to the records only as sellers of ale. The great majority provide a catalogue of disorders both as alehousekeepers and individuals. They tolerated "disorders" in their houses on Sundays and holy days, allowing gaming, tippling, drunkenness, fighting, swearing, music, and dancing. They sold their ale too dear, harbored suspected thieves, sheltered sexual offenders, and abused the constables. As individuals, they were prosecuted for failure to attend church, neglecting to take holy communion, standing excommunicate. They were involved in a variety of sexual and marital offences ranging from lewd words to bigamy and were accused at various times of theft, assault, drunkenness, damaging the churchyard wall, and appropriating a spit belonging to the parish.

The list of offences attributed to alehousekeepers is an impressive monument to their centrality in village life. Equally striking is the nature of the offences that alarmed and outraged the village officers. With some significant exceptions they were mostly petty, "crimes without victims," even "normal disorders." They were essentially part of the ebb and flow of normal village life, especially among the "poorer sort" of the village, for whom the alehouse appears to have been the focal point of neighborly interaction in leisure hours. The demonstrably novel urge to put down such petty disorders is a matter of some significance, for it was initiated and sustained in the face of considerable difficulties. The drive for greater "order" could in itself arouse novel forms of conflict in the village.

The consequences of Richard Rochester's prosecution of Thomas Holman in 1607 have already been seen. In the same Quarter sessions, Rochester, together with John Wood and Augustine Norrell, two yeomen, also presented Thomas Baker and three other villagers for drunkenness and alehouse-haunting. This presentment provoked a petition to the justices in Thomas Baker's defence, signed by the minister, two gentlemen farmers, and several substantial yeomen. They urged the justices "to have compassion upon this poore man" and suggested that he had been prosecuted "rather of meere mallice, then of any just cause of defect on his behalfe."[28] Again, in 1627 the Puritan minister of Terling, Thomas Weld, attempted to prevent the renewal of the alehouse license of William Holmes, intending "reformation of disorder which is in his house." He found himself opposed by the lord of the manor of Terling, Robert Mildmay, and by five other

---

[27] We must thank the Honorable C. R. Strutt for bringing this petition to our attention, together with other materials in his collection of evidence on the history of the parish.
[28] E. R. O. Q/SR 182/36.

petitioners drawn from among the most substantial villagers. They took the view that Holmes was "a person of honest lyfe and conversacon," a man "fitt to keepe an Alehouse in respect he is aged and cannot worke and besides hath not wherewithall to mayntayne him selfe and his charge and soe is lykely to become chargeable to our parish yf he should not be lycensed."[29]

Such responses to prosecution were possible only when the person presented to the courts was able to activate networks of personal connections which included some of the "better sort" of the parish and thereby secure their intervention. Thomas Baker, for example, was a blacksmith from a long-established family and was probably well known among his neighbors. With the exception of his prosecution for drunkenness he was never charged with any offence. His fund of goodwill in the village may have been considerable. The case, however, was more complex. His ten defenders were men interconnected by various ties. Above all they had a shared social position as leading villagers and included several men who served as churchwardens and sessions jurymen. Rochester, Norrell, and Wood were not at this time among the ruling group of the village. They had prosecuted the village alehouse-haunters on their own private initiative. The parish officers probably resented this and chose to disregard the prosecution as unnecessary and malicious. Moreover, there was a further element in their action. The central figures among the petitioners appear to have been George Cannon, Thomas Jackson, Andrew Pelsett, and John Fletcher. These men left evidence elsewhere of close personal connections to either Thomas Holman, Robert Melford, or John Clark, all three of whom were prosecuted by Rochester, Norrell, and Wood at the same time as Thomas Baker. Holman, Melford, and Clark had considerable histories of disorder, unlike Thomas Baker. It seems very possible that their friends were disposed to support the less culpable Baker partly as a means of discrediting the prosecutors in their attack on Holman and the others.

A simple presentment of disorderly behavior could thus activate several levels of conflict in the village. The case of William Holmes was somewhat similar. Mr. Weld, who was a quarrelsome man, had perhaps acted too precipitately in attacking Holmes. Holmes had never been accused of disorder before, though he was later to be presented for allowing gaming and for over-charging his customers. He was, like Baker, a member of a long-established family and he had many recorded relationships with more prominent villagers. In particular, he was an old servant of Sir Thomas Mildmay, former lord of the manor of Terling and a kinsman of the present

---

[29] E. R. O. Q/SR 257/76.

lord. He was also connected to George Cannon, Mildmay's bailiff and a surety for Holmes' alehouse license as long ago as 1606. Holmes must have called on one or both of these powerful friends and they proceeded to recruit a group of other village notables. This combination was sufficient to defeat Mr. Weld, especially since the patron of his own living was against him. Mildmay even went so far as to send a private letter to the justices, though as a Puritan he was sufficiently unsure of the rectitude of his support of Holmes against the vicar to say that if there should be any future disorder in Holmes's house he would willingly join with Weld to see Holmes suppressed.[30]

It was the possibility of activating networks of personal connection of this kind and of touching off a small explosion of conflict within the village that made prosecution of any but the most notorious of offenders so dangerous to local harmony. This factor, above all, made the presentment jurymen and petty constables of the period so notoriously unwilling to prosecute petty offences. A too-rigorous village officer could threaten to create more problems than he solved by prosecuting. He might also dislocate his own personal relationships. For example, George Cannon, whom we have seen supporting Thomas Baker in 1608 and William Holmes in 1627, was faced with such problems. In 1613, when serving as churchwarden, he was himself in trouble for *failing* to present certain offenders whose misdeeds had come to the ears of the Archdeacon.[31] Cannon was a man of central importance in the village; he left behind him evidence of a constellation of close personal connections to other villagers at all social levels. He acted on occasion as a surety for both Richard Rochester and Thomas Holman. He was the brother-in-law and a regular surety of the notoriously disorderly cowleech John Clark and fellow-petitioner with the sternly Puritan squire Robert Mildmay. Cannon was a mediating figure if ever there was one in village society. Conscientious performance of his duties as a village officer would threaten to plunge him into a morass of conflicting loyalties and obligations. Though he served as a presentment juryman eight times, he was almost never responsible for actually presenting a case to the justices.

Cannon was not alone in his attitude. For similar reasons, other village officers greatly preferred admonition and private mediation to prosecution. Prosecution was commonly resorted to only when local patience had been exhausted, as when Robert Wakeling was prosecuted for keeping a disorderly house "after warninge given hym," and another alehousekeeper for refusing to forbear unlicensed selling "upon frequent warning."[32]

---

[30] E. R. O. Q/SR 257/77.
[31] E. R. O. D/ACA 34 fo. 148v; G. L. R. O. DL/C/323 fo. 109.
[32] E. R. O. Q/SBa 6/8/9.

Despite this situation, the parish officers of Terling did develop a will to prosecute, sufficient indeed to promote a regulative initiative in the second and third decades of the seventeenth century which established a new quality in the relationships of the villagers with the courts. At the simplest level one might argue that the burgeoning importance of regulative prosecutions must have derived from a greater desire for the suppression of previously tolerated behavior on the part of officers of middling and high social standing. They directed their attention increasingly at offenders among the poorer villagers and at their supporters among persons of higher status. The sporadic interpersonal conflict of earlier years was giving way to a pattern of hostility between the ruling group of villagers and the village poor. To speak simply of a greater demand for order is to use a blunt instrument to examine this highly complex phenomenon. The concept of order was certainly ubiquitous in this period but it was far from monolithic. Order in the passive sense of maintaining local harmony might be as well served by a failure to prosecute offences as by an active enforcement of the stacks of penal statutes placed on the backs of local officers in Tudor and early Stuart England. It would be more satisfactory to place the development of a greater desire to modify and control popular behavior within the context of an adjustment of attitudes and social relationships within Terling of a more complex nature. It is clear enough that the village was to a considerable degree economically polarized in this period, and there is good reason to believe that the early seventeenth century saw the process of polarization at its height. The existence of economic and social inequality in Terling, however, was no novelty. More significant would seem to be the likelihood that in the early decades of the seventeenth century—a period of intense strain in this community—this polarization became more complex; that the economic differentiation of the parish elite from the laborers and poorer craftsmen was accompanied by a significant differentiation of attitudes and behavior.

The villagers of Terling can be said to have made use of the local institutions of church and state in in two essentially different ways. On the one hand they used them defensively, seeking to preserve their property, the public peace, the conventional norms of sexual behavior. On the other hand, the courts could be used offensively to promote new standards, new conceptions of order. For almost fifty years from the beginning of our period, the sessions jurymen of Terling appeared before the high constable, were sworn in, perhaps listened to a detailed charge informing them of what offences should be presented, yet commonly sat as mute as fishes. By 1620 their successors were prepared to remind His Majesty's justices of Assize "that the magistrate beareth not the sword for naught, but is ordained by God to take punishment on them that do evil." In doing so they were no doubt secure in the knowledge that they themselves had been play-ing their part in the divine plan with unprecedented enthusiasm. In both word and deed they showed that custom was on the retreat in Terling before changes in social attitudes which were to play a significant part in remolding the pattern of social relationships in the village.

6

CHANGING CULTURAL HORIZONS: EDUCATION AND RELIGION

In 1630 when the justices of Essex, spurred on by the Privy Council, ordered a rigorous enquiry into the state of public order in the parishes, the task of answering their formidable questionnaire for Terling fell to Mathew Warren. He was not found wanting. A man of many parts; tailor, grocer, one-time alehousekeeper, Mathew was well equipped to make the village report. Moreover, he could do it himself, for he was literate. His lengthy reply to the justices' articles of enquiry with its careful penmanship, wayward phonetic spelling, and proud signature stands as a monument to his endeavor, to the pain it cost him, and to his sense of achievement. Point by point he answered the articles. There had been no "quarrilles affrayes or bludsheded" in Terling, no "soweres sedechon betwen naybores." The watch was "duely set" and "hewancryes spedeley sent forthe wethe owte aney stay." There were no unlicensed alehouses, though the licensed houses had their faults. John Aldridge had allowed one youth to get drunk and permitted strangers to play "shovilbord," while he and two other alehousekeepers were overcharging for their beer. For the rest, the village was a model of godly order. "For swarers," Mathew proudly claimed, "ower town is well reformed "; "proffaners of the Saboth or Lordes daye not aney." "For popish reqeusantes brownestes or sectaries or aney parsones absentinge them sellves from the parryshe churche wee have not aney thar fore noo penalltes have bin leved or be stowed on the pore." And,

142

finally, lest his efforts go unremarked, "Written and Answard bey mee Mathew Warren."[1]

Of course, not all of this was strictly true. We can allow Mathew a bit of local pride and the shrewd good sense to tell his superiors what they wanted to hear. Only three months earlier Warren's fellow constable, John Humphrey, had been obliged to "humbly intreate a reformation" from the justices against the disorderly alehousekeeper Thomas Maye and one Roger Stepkin, who had sworn "by God" three times in his presence.[2] Nevertheless, it was true enough for the most part. We have other evidence to show that Terling in 1630 was a village free from serious violence, one in which real efforts had been made and were to continue to be made to reform the "common country disorders." The church *was* generally full. The disorderly and ungodly *were* on the defensive. Both constables and their fellows among the village officers were literate and showed a peculiar fascination with that key word of the early seventeenth century: "reformation."

Several of the elements of this situation were relatively new. For Terling in 1630 was witnessing a period of consolidation in a process of cultural change that had begun in the last years of the sixteenth century, gathered momentum in the 1610s and 1620s, and was to enter a new phase in the 1630s and 1640s. We have already seen the evidence for shifts in social attitudes reflected in presentments to the courts. We may now take up other elements of change in popular education and in religious affairs, which together promoted a significant expansion of the cultural horizons of the villagers—or some of them.

The transmission of any culture is a complex phenomenon. It involves, in addition to the passing on of the material elements of the culture, the descent through time of the skills of a given technology, of social roles, of conventional forms of behavior and received ideas, mentalities, goals, and aspirations.[3] The tracing of cultural change necessarily involves us in the difficult task of establishing the interrelationship of the myriad different elements of the cultural compound.

That the broad structures of the material and social environment of the villagers of Terling persisted relatively unchanged in our period has already been established. That there were nevertheless significant developments in the relatively prosperity, life-chances, and economic expectations of the villagers is equally clear. Within the context of the perdurance of the princi-

---

[1] E. R. O. 272/25.

[2] E. R. O. 271/35.

[3] J. Goody and I. Watt, "The Consequences of Literacy," p. 28ff. The discussion that follows is greatly influenced by the suggestions of Goody and Watt and by those of R. S. Schofield in his "The Measurement of Literacy in Pre-Industrial England."

ple structural characteristics of village society, change also occurred in social attitudes, expectations, and behavior and in the villagers' mental apprehension of the world. To say that such a cultural dynamic could exist within a relatively stable socioeconomic environment is not to claim that it was independent of that environment. Far from it. As we shall see, the process of change was intimately affected, shaped, and channeled by the social-structural context in which it took place. But it is to say that the broad, established structures of village society were sufficiently flexible to accommodate change and to ride out the conflicts to which it gave rise. In the processes that we can trace we see the maturing of an old society rather than a transition to new social forms. That was to come, but not yet. Change was still containable. Its explosive elements could be dampened, defused, overlain, smothered. Be that as it may, it was not reversed and it gave a new richness to the texture of village life.

In the history of the slow course of cultural change in the village, educational advance—and, in particular, progress in the matter of basic literacy—was of major importance for two connected reasons. In the first place, the achievement of basic literacy opened up the prospect of independent access to the flourishing literate culture of early-modern England. Men or women who could read plain English could amuse themselves with penny ballad sheets, tease their curiosity with almanacs, follow the course of political controversy in newsletters and pamphlets, or probe the mysteries of salvation with Bible and printed sermon. Some did so, some did not. The point is that, given the skill, they *could* if occasion arose. A new world stood before them that they could enter at their will, freed from reliance on the intermediary priest or potentate. Literacy could enrich and expand the traditional orally transmitted culture. It might also transform it. For literacy could bring about a subtle modification of the relationship of the individual to his cultural world in a second sense. Ability to comprehend the written word, access to records of thought and deed fixed in time by virtue of their committal to paper, could revolutionize the relationships of men to both past and present social reality. The ability to read written records could give a new purchase on both past and present quite distinct from that of an illiterate awareness of "immemorial custom." Custom, beneath its cloak of antiquity, was patently redefinable to serve the needs of each new generation. Literacy could strip customary practice of its authority by comparison with the fixed word. It could give a new awareness of the past, a new perception of the present. Moreover, it allowed comparison not only of the known past with the present, but of the real with the ideal.

In making these points we must, of course, avoid the error of asserting too rigid a distinction between the literate and the oral cultures of the period. Some literates doubtless used their skill only instrumentally, while continuing to draw their attitudes and perceptions from the traditional oral culture. Again, in a partially literate population, the illiterate might well have opportunities to hear and be influenced by the products of a literate culture in which they could not themselves participate directly. Yet the potential effects of a broader popular literacy were nonetheless great as the people of the period were quite well aware. It was with precisely these issues that contemporary religious moralists were concerned when they urged the contrast between blind adherence to profane custom and the liberating knowledge of divine law, juxtaposing biblical precept and popular example. The point has relevance beyond the sphere of religion and manners which most concerned them. Access to the literate culture could, as they knew, transform the individual's perception of his world. Individual literacy gave the possibility of direct personal access. Widespread popular literacy not only meant that many individuals had such access but also that there were more intermediaries available for those who remained themselves unlettered.

Improvements in popular education thus contained the potential of momentous change. Whether that potential was realized depended on many circumstances. In Terling it was to be partially realized. Before pursuing this issue, however, we must establish the extent of popular literacy in our period, both in village society and in rural Essex as a whole.

Levels of literacy in Terling were influenced as much by educational provision and achievement in other villages as in Terling itself. The simple facts of population mobility make this clear. Many of Terling's literates acquired the skill as children in other settlements. Terling's experience was thus a compound of both indigenous and external developments. For the county of Essex as a whole we are fortunate in being able to draw on the results of David Cressy's researches into the impact of educational change in sixteenth- and seventeenth-century England. Essex shared fully the expansion of facilities for popular education that was so marked a feature of social change in provincial England at this period. The last decades of the sixteenth century saw a steep rise in both the numbers of schoolmasters licensed to teach in rural Essex (not least in the half-hundred of Witham) and in the educational qualifications of those licensed. Though this growth in the availability of education was arrested—indeed, reversed—in the later seventeenth century, it led to a decline in the level of popular illiteracy that was permanent. This in itself must certainly have meant that, even when the numbers of schoolmasters active in the county declined, a sufficiently literate populace existed to allow the informal transmission of basic literacy to continue—from parent to child, neighbor to neighbor.[4] Cressy's analysis of subscription to the various oaths taken by villagers as a result of governmental insistence in the seventeenth century provides a measure of the total achievement of the period. Though the level of adult male illiteracy varied considerably from parish to parish within Essex, it is probable that by the 1640s Essex men were 60 to 70% illiterate. By the 1690s they were 50 to 55% illiterate.

This overall picture of declining male illiteracy must, however, be qualified when consideration is given to variations in achievement between different social levels and between the sexes. The fact that not all villagers could afford either the time or the money to have their children educated is vividly demonstrated by the hierarchical nature of socially specific illiteracy. Using ecclesiastical court depositions that provide information on social status Cressy found that, while illiteracy was almost totally eradicated among men of gentry status, it remained overwhelmingly strong among laborers and servants in husbandry. Women again remained largely illiterate. While yeoman illiteracy had been reduced to some 30% by 1640, husbandmen remained around 70% illiterate. The achievement of tradesmen and craftsmen was good overall (under 40% illiterate by 1640) but varied between trades. Textile and clothing workers, for example, were relatively literate; workers in the building trade were relatively illiterate.[5] The first onslaught on popular illiteracy was thus so shaped by variations in the need felt by different social groups to acquire the skill and by their ability to pay for schooling as to open up marked educational differentials among the rural population.

The experience of the villagers of Terling broadly conformed to this pattern. Though the village had no school as such before the nineteenth century, schoolmasters, commonly unlicensed, were active in the village from the late 1580s through to the Civil War period.[6] Teaching took place in the church in the 1630s when John Gibson found himself in trouble in the church courts "for teaching of schollars in the church."[7] Doubtless this had been the case from the start. It is of interest that Gibson was prosecuted as a result of information brought privately to the Archdeacon rather than by a public presentment of the churchwardens. The Laudian church

[4] D. Cressy, "Education and Literacy in London and East Anglia, 1580–1700," pp. 87, 103–114, 138, 148. For the possible significance of informal teaching see T. Laqueur, "The Cultural Origins of Popular Literacy in England, 1500–1850," p. 257ff.

[5] D. Cressy, "Education and Literacy in London and East Anglia," pp. 238, 286, 291ff, 310–335.

[6] E. R. O. D/ACA 18 fos. 109v, 213, 22 fo. 107, 27 fos. 133, 172, 52 fos. 226v, 253v; G. L. R. O. DL/C/325 fo. 39, DL/C/624 fo. 205.

[7] E. R. O. D/ACA 52 fo. 253v.

authorities of the 1630s disapproved of such use of the church. The church-wardens and other village officers doubtless felt that it was appropriate enough. Teaching in the church probably reflected the main content of the education of the village children beyond basic literacy. While the earliest schoolmaster was a man too fond of the ale-bench and the card table[8] (common occupational hazards for schoolmasters in the period), his successors were more disciplined men. At least two of them were graduates—and Puritans to boot. For the years after the Civil War we have no evidence of the presence of a schoolmaster, through probably teaching was available either in Terling or in nearby townships.

Evidence of the decline of illiteracy in the village is abundant. Though we have no surviving list of signatures to any of the oaths of the period that would enable us to take stock of the situation at any single point in time, the various records consulted provide examples of the signatures or marks of 330 men and thirty-six women in the period 1580 to 1699. Some of these persons provided only a single surviving example of their ability or inability to sign their names (the generally accepted criterion of ability to read, since writing was taught only after a tolerable level of reading ability had been achieved).[9] Many provide several examples, some as many as ten or more.

The evidence used is drawn from all the sources available to us. It includes persons signing or marking their own wills or the wills of others, jurymen signing or marking their presentments to Quarter Sessions, signatures on deeds and bonds, signatures to depositions in the courts, and other miscellaneous examples. There are a number of problems in the use of this evidence. In some wills or deeds, for example, what appear to be signatures have clearly been written in by the scribe rather than by the individual witness. Such examples have been excluded. Again, the evidence is not always consistent in the case of individuals. Augustine Norrel, for example, signed a petition, a Quarter-Sessions presentment, and three separate wills, yet made a mark at the foot of his own will. Andrew Page signed three sessions presentments and one set of churchwardens' accounts, yet put a mark on another set of accounts and on a deed which he witnessed. Various explanations underlie such inconsistency. Some literate testators were too weak from illness to sign wills dictated on their deathbeds. Some literate men might on occasion make a mark or write initials only as a form of shorthand. Still others very possibly learned to sign their names only in adult life. Robert French, for example, made a mark

---

[8] E. R. O. Q/SR 112/70.

[9] These issues are fully discussed in R. S. Schofield, "The Measurement of Literacy in Pre-Industrial England."

when acting as a will witness in the 1580s, yet left six examples of his signature on wills made in later years. In the face of such contradictory evidence we have counted as literate any person who was able on any occasion to sign, subject to our being confident that the signature is genuine and that we are dealing with the same person. A further convention adopted is that of dating. Though a number of persons provided examples of signatures or marks from more than one of the periods which we have adopted, they have been counted in the sample for the period when they first appear. The results are presented in Table 6.1.

TABLE 6.1
Levels of Illiteracy in Terling, 1580–1699

	Number and percentage illiterate[a]			
	Men		Women	
1580–1609	44 of 86	53%	11 of 13	85%
1610–1639	38 of 98	39%	7 of 8	88%
1640–1669	19 of 70	27%	8 of 8	100%
1670–1699	22 of 76	29%	5 of 7	71%

[a]Illiterate is defined as being unable to sign name.

The figures in Table 6.1 indicate a steady decline in male illiteracy, which was, however, arrested at the close of the seventeenth century. Female illiteracy seems always to have been high, though perhaps declining at the end of the seventeenth century, but the sample of women is so small as to be of little value beyond indicating that female illiteracy was generally much more widespread than that of men.

This evidence may provide us with a guide to general trends but must not be assumed to reflect accurately the real incidence of illiteracy among men and women, for the simple reason that the sample is extremely biased towards the upper half of village society. It was the more substantial villagers who were most likely to make or witness wills, appear as sessions jurymen, and the like. For this reason the material has been reworked and broken down according to social position. In many cases the actual document providing the example of a signature or mark also gives the social status or occupation of the person concerned. In other cases it has proved easy to establish the relative social position of the person involved from other evidence. Where this could not easily be done, the person concerned has been excluded from the sample. Those remaining have been grouped according to our by-now-familiar social categories. This has been done since we feel that to do so brings out most accurately the hierarchy of illiteracy in the village. To group a rich tradesman with a poor craftsman under "crafts and trades," for example, would obscure real differences. Moreover, by using these categories we can attempt to estimate overall male illiteracy for each of the periods involved. This has been done by assuming that the number of men in each category was similar to the number of male householders in each category in 1671. This assumption is less plausible for the first period when the population was still growing, of course, and must mean that the estimated male illiteracy for our first period is likely to be rather high. Nevertheless, the exercise is useful as one way of overcoming the bias of our sample. The estimates provided are intended as no more than reasonable approximations, though their closeness to Cressy's independent estimates suggests their broad plausibility.

The message of Table 6.2 is clear enough. Male illiteracy was substantially reduced in early seventeenth-century Terling. In the late seventeenth century, levels of illiteracy stablized. The first major period of advance in popular education was over. Further progress probably came only in the nineteenth century.[10] Equally striking is the social bias in the achievement of the seventeenth century. Gentlemen and large farmers were wholly literate by the end of the sixteenth century. The illiteracy of yeomen and wealthy craftsmen declined to the later seventeenth century, when it stablized at 15 to 20%. Husbandmen and moderately prosperous craftsmen followed a generation behind the yeomanry, again stablizing in the later seventeenth century. The laboring poor were almost a century behind the husbandmen and craftsmen. Their overwhelming illiteracy began to be eroded only at the end of the seventeenth century. It seems probable that in the earlier part of our period they had simply been unable to afford schooling for their children. At the close of the seventeenth century, rising real incomes may have led some to put their children in school, however briefly. Alternatively (or additionally) the fact that a significant advance in basic literacy had been achieved higher in the social scale may have promoted more informal learning—more of what Professor Plumb has called "cultural seepage."[11]

Where families can be traced over time it becomes clear that the major period of advance in Terling itself came among persons educated in the village at the end of the sixteenth century and coming to adulthood somewhat later. The Belsteds, the Booseys, the Finchams, and the Norrells all acquired literate members of the family in these years and remained literate thereafter. Some families, of course, never acquired a literate member. Every member of the Baker family for whom we have evidence

---

[10] For the history of illiteracy after 1750, see R. S. Schofield, "Dimensions of Illiteracy, 1750–1850."

[11] J. H. Plumb, *The Commercialisation of Leisure in Eighteenth-century England*, p. 4.

TABLE 6.2
Socially Specific Illiteracy of Terling Men, 1580–1699

Social category	Number and percentage of illiterate[a]				
	1580–1609	1610–1639	1640–1669	1670–1699	
I (Gentry, large farmers)	0 of 11 0%	0 of 11 0%	0 of 6 0%	0 of 10 0%	
II (Yeoman, wealthy craftsmen)	15 of 27 56%	9 of 29 31%	4 of 27 15%	3 of 18 17%	
III (Husbandmen, craftsmen)	21 of 28 75%	16 of 30 53%	4 of 14 29%	6 of 19 32%	
IV (Laborers, poor craftsmen)	5 of 5 100%	6 of 6 100%	8 of 10 80%	7 of 11 64%	
Estimated overall male illiteracy	84%	74%	56%	49%	

[a] Illiterate is defined as being unable to sign name.

was illiterate throughout the whole period. The Hares might have expected to join the ranks of the literate but the economic collapse of William Hare in the early seventeenth century seems to have prevented them from following other yeoman and husbandman families. Once established, literacy could persist in some families despite declining fortunes. Though the only representative of the Cannon family left by the 1690s was a laborer, he could write. On the other hand, downward social mobility could rob a family of its hard-won gains. The Gaymers were literate in the early seventeenth century. Their late seventeenth-century representative, a younger son who had stayed on as a laborer, was illiterate. It seems probable that the persistence of literacy in a family depended (the question of being able to afford schooling apart) on whether or not individuals had a use for the skill in their work or equally in their recreational and devotional life.

What were the uses of literacy in a seventeenth-century village? Clearly the skill had some direct practical applications. Teaching a child to read and write was increasingly seen as beneficial for its future occupations. Many a yeoman and husbandman had his "writings and evidences," his deeds and bonds, and must have appreciated the ability to make and read such vital documents. Some were increasingly involved in marketing which involved written agreements and contracts, a further practical application of literacy. The disadvantaged position of the illiterate in such dealings is amply demonstrated by an account of the making of a bond by one of the villagers in 1598. James Noble, a petty chapman "being a very simple man altogether unlitterated and not knowing whether the contents were such as they were read to him" was extremely unwilling to put his hand to the document, the more so when one of the bystanders told him to "take heede what he sealed unto." Matters were delayed while he obtained a copy to show to his literate friends.[12] Tradesmen and craftsmen gradually developed a new sophistication in their dealings in the course of the seventeenth century. By the 1690s most put in written bills to the churchwardens for work done on the church.[13]

Again, wills were potentially crucial documents. The ability to write them, or to check them, was doubtless valued. In the dispute which rent the Rochester family in the 1590s, the whole issue turned on whether or not a single word had been interlined in a will.[14] That there was an increasing ability and willingness on the part of villagers to use their literacy to these various ends is shown not only by the tradesman's bills but by the extent to which the villagers were freed from reliance on the clergy and

---

[12] P. R. O. Req. 2 48/22.
[13] E. R. O. D/P 299/5/1A.
[14] P. R. O. STAC 5 A54/13.

schoolmasters in their will-making. In 1539 the ability to write a will was so rare that one testator had to make his will by word of mouth "for default of a scribe."[15] This situation changed slowly. Between 1560 and 1579 there was only one scribe of Terling wills—the vicar. In the years 1580 to 1599 there were ten different scribes but the vicar and schoolmaster together accounted for three-quarters of the wills made. In the first two decades of the seventeenth century there were again ten scribes, but by now the vicar and the principal lay scribe made only a little over half the surviving wills. In the remaining two decades before the Civil War, no fewer than eighteen villagers acted as scribes, and the vicar's and schoolmaster's share had fallen to only a quarter of all wills. Dependence upon the village's handful of official intellectuals had been decisively broken.

Literacy also certainly had its uses for the men involved in local administration. The ability to read a warrant or a precept, or to write a presentment or a petition, was doubtless of great help. Indeed, over time literacy may almost have become a necessary qualification for parish office. This was almost certainly so by the last decades of the seventeenth century, by which time churchwardens and overseers were expected to keep minutely detailed accounts, which were entered up annually in beautifully kept parish account books. The illiteracy of churchwardens was reduced from 50 to 8% between the 1580s and the 1660s, that of sessions jurymen from 50 to 16% over the same period. Perhaps by the later seventeenth century, the status that literacy conferred was part and parcel of the complex of distinctions of wealth, reputation, and the like which raised a man to the level of a vestryman.

All this is well enough, yet we must go further if we are to account fully for the very real desire among the more wealthy villagers to acquire literacy for themselves or their children which fueled the seventeenth-century transformation in Terling. Tom Laqueur and Margaret Spufford are surely correct in their reminders that at bottom may often have been a desire on the part of individuals to participate independently in the literate culture of the period.[16] A village craftsman could get by without writing bills; a man was not called on to write deeds or wills frequently enough to warrant the achievement of literacy for that end alone. Perhaps more men wrote wills and bills and accounts were better kept, largely because individuals had *already* moved into the ranks of the literate for other reasons. In every village there were some who simply wanted to read. To read what? Ballads and almanacs, perhaps, but above all they wanted to

[15] E. R. O. D/ACR 4/68.

[16] T. Laquer, "The Cultural Origins of Popular Literacy in England," *passim;* M. Spufford, *Contrasting Communties,* chapter 8.

read the Bible. They desired to be participants in a literate culture that was still primarily a religious culture. The few references to books that occur in village wills are to religious works. John Rochester left in 1583 his "great bible of the Geneva translation." He was a Calvinist. Thomas Shaw had "my booke of actes and monuments." He was familiar with John Foxe's portrayal of England's divinely appointed place in the cosmic war between Christ and Antichrist.[17] Wills in which villagers expressed aspirations for the education of their heirs commonly coupled religious and secular reasons for education. An example is provided by John Wood, a pious yeoman who wanted his grandchild brought up "in good and Christian education" and also "in the trade of a glover." Cyprian Cornwell, an illiterate Quaker, wanted his grandchild "brought upp to larne to writte and read and to larne a trade."[18]

The development of a lay reading public in Terling of some sophistication among the more substantial villagers is amply demonstrated by the prefaces that John Stalham, Puritan vicar from 1632 to 1662, addressed to the villagers of Terling in his published works. His catechism of 1644 was published "at the desire of divers for the private instruction of their little children and most ignorant servants, . . . because sufficient written copies cannot be procured." Clearly there was a considerable demand. In his *Vindiciae Redemptionis* (1647), directed against sectarian preachers who had influenced some of his flock, he urged his parishioners to "Read and pray, read and meditate" and to "peruse all . . . with a Bible in [your] hand." He referred to his people rather patronizingly as "country-readers" with "country understandings," but they were readers nonetheless and their understandings were sufficiently independent to make him fear for their souls. Again in *The Reviler Rebuked* (1657), a book against the Quakers, he urges his parishioners rather peevishily to "redeem some time for the reading of it; especially such of you as have allowed spare hours for the reading of the Adversaries Pamphlets."[19]

It is surely not fanciful to see those villagers who desired to open to themselves and their children the literate culture of the Reformation era as the leading edge of the newfound popular literacy of the village. They may have set the tone of future development, making the way clear for a broader literacy and a broader application of the skill. For those who did not follow, the oral culture remained alive enough. There were sermons

---

[17] E. R. O. D/ACW 7/240, D/ACW 3/321.

[18] E. R. O. D/ACW 11/37, D/ACW 10/189.

[19] J. Stalham, *A Catechisme for Children in yeeres and Children in understanding*, To the Reader and Teacher in the Family; *Idem, Vindiciae Redemptionis*, To My Beloved Brethren and Neighbours in Terling; *Idem, The Reviler Rebuked: or a Re-inforcement of the Charge against the Quakers*, To the Church of Christ which is at Terling.

aplenty in the church (though not so appealing to itching curiosities as those of the sects). There were political proclamations read aloud in church (the churchwardens recorded paying for them). But their effect was the less on men who had acquired independent purchase on religious and political affairs. The advent of popular literacy had caused the scales to drop from the eyes of many a villager. They could strike out alone into the currents of national life. Nowhere was this more apparent than in religion.

Well-placed as it was to feel the influence of London, of Cambridge, and of continental ideas entering England through the ports of East Anglia, Essex was in the vanguard of religious change in the period. The county had its pockets of surviving Lollard heresy on the eve of the Reformation and was rapidly penetrated by early Protestantism. By the reign of Mary, radical Protestantism was deeply enough rooted for Essex to provide ordinary men and women willing to face the horror of the stake for their beliefs. Later, as the Elizabethan settlement was consolidated, the county became noted for the activity of its Puritan ministers. Puritanism was well established, particularly in the northeast of the county, by 1604 when a group of godly ministers published their critical survey of the state of the clergy in Essex. Its hold was consolidated and extended in the early decades of the seventeenth century by the joint action of lay patrons and preaching ministers. By the 1630s perhaps half the parishes of Essex had ministers of broadly Puritan sympathies and, as the Laudian reaction gathered momentum, Essex provided both its clerical nonconformists and a steady stream of lay emigrants to the freer air of New England. The civil wars and Interregnum saw the high tide of Puritan advance under the commonwealth church, and after the restoration of the Anglican Church in 1662 a permanent legacy of religious nonconformity remained in the county.[20]

Terling played its part in these developments. Initially the changes wrought by the Henrician and Edwardian reformations were more institutional than theological. The Trinity Guild, an association for religious purposes and mutual aid, active in 1524, was dissolved together with the parish chantry. The gift of the living of Terling passed from the Bishop of Norwich to the Crown, thus beginning the journey that was to bring it into the hands of the lords of the manor of Terling, the Mildmay family.[21] Nevertheless the religious universe of the parishioners was slow to change. Prior to 1550 the piety expressed in the preambles to the wills of the

[20] H. Smith, *The Ecclesiastical History of Essex Under the Long Parliament and Commonwealth, passim* (a work of much broader timespan than its title implies); K. W. Shipps, "Lay Patronage of East Anglian Puritan Clerics in Pre-Revolutionary England," pp. 142–43. We would like to thank Dr. Shipps for permission to refer to his unpublished dissertation.

[21] P. R. O. E 301 19/96, E 179 108/154; P. Morant, *The History and Antiquities of the County of Essex*, vol. 2, p. 128.

villagers remained solidly Catholic. Souls were bequeathed to "almighti god to our blessed lady virgin and moder and to all the glowious saynts in hevyn." Sums were laid aside for masses for the souls of the departed. Only in the later years of Edward VI's reign did Protestant theology make its appearance in dedications of souls to God alone. Indeed, some wills of these years indicate the uncertainty of the villagers as to how best to provide for their spiritual good. In 1550 Robert Hare, lacking the sure knowledge of the best path to heaven which had characterized earlier villagers, instructed his children only "to dispose for my soule as they shall thynke good."[22] The reign of Mary saw divided opinion in the parish. Some testators turned with relief to fully Catholic dedications; others remained Protestant. The parish was divided.

The triumph of at least conventional Protestantism was the work of the first decade of the reign of Elizabeth. The last Catholic vicar of Terling was deprived in 1560 and the last hint of Catholicism in a will came in 1562.[23] For the remainder of the century the two vicars who usually acted as scribes for the villagers' wills provided their parishioners with impeccably Protestant dedications of their souls "to almightie god", or to "Almighty god my maker, saviour and redeemer." No signs of more radical commitment to Protestantism are to be found before 1583, though thereafter a number of testators bequeathed their souls in terms sufficiently unusual to persuade us that we have in them the stamp of an unusual personal piety. In 1583 John Rochester Esq., owner of a Geneva Bible, wrote a will in his own hand in which he express his hope

> to dwell and eternally to rest with holy and blessed saintes in the Joyes of blisse prepared by god for his anngells and elected as yt is written. I believe that my redeemer liveth and that in the last daye I shall rise owt of the earth and in my fleshe shall se my saviour. This my hope is layd uppe in my bosome.[24]

This was conviction indeed and a similar piety, though less lavishly expressed, breathes from the wills of a handful of yeomen and husbandmen of the 1580s and 1590s. Thomas Fish, for example, was the first villager to leave money "to make an sermon at my berryal" in 1599, dedicating his soul to "almighty god my maker and redeemer not doughtying butt that he will for his suferring sake resceive me to his glorie."[25]

If the 1580s provide the first sure evidence of the establishment in the village of a Protestantism of conviction, as distinct from that of conven-

---

[22] E. R. O. D/ABW 18/109.
[23] C. A. Barton, *Historical Notes and Records of the Parish of Terling, Essex*, p. 85; E. R. O. D/AER 8/44.
[24] E. R. O. D/ACR 7/240.
[25] E. R. O. D/ACW 4/114.

tion, the same years saw the initiation of attempts to enforce a stricter ecclesiastical conformity which were to persist well into the next century. From 1583 the church courts saw an upsurge of Terling prosecutions for failure to receive the communion. Of the thirty-five prosecutions known for this offence in the whole of our period, thirty-one were made before 1600—most of them between 1583 and 1597. On occasion it can be established that the persons prosecuted had been unable to communicate as a result of excommunication for one offence or another. In most cases, however, we appear to be dealing with a real attempt to tighten up on the parishioners' standards of ritual conformity to the Anglican Church. As the seventeenth century opened, these prosecutions were supplemented by the regular harrying of parishioners who were "standing excommunicate," usually as a result of defying the church courts' sanctions. Such presentments appear to have been intended to prevent such contempt from passing unremarked, even though in some cases the person concerned persisted in his or her formal alienation from the Christian community. Finally, from 1610 the parish officers showed a novel concern, in their presentments to both Quarter Sessions and the Archdeacon's court, with the prosecution of persons who were simply failing to attend church. Initially they concentrated upon a handful of known or suspected recusants, but from 1617 onward the courts saw an annual crop of prosecutions of simple neglectors of church attendance which continued through to the early 1630s.

This mounting initiative in the prosecution of religious offences was undoubtedly aimed at persons low in the social scale for the most part. Some 70% of those prosecuted for failing to take communion were drawn from the laboring poor, while husbandmen and craftsmen provided a further 18%. Two-thirds of those who stood excommunicate came from the lowest level of village society, while all save two of the remainder were husbandmen or modest craftsmen. If we exclude the handful of known or suspected recusants (all of them relatively high in the social scale), those prosecuted for failure to attend church prior to 1640 were again overwhelmingly drawn from Categories IV (53%) and III (29%).

In these prosecutions we have the evidence of pressure exerted by the parish officers to establish new standards of religious conformity among the mass of the parishioners. For many of them, regular church attendance must have been an unfamiliar ideal. It was certainly not one that had been insisted upon by the medieval church. Some simply failed to turn up more than occasionally, like Edward Melford and John Joslin, both prosecuted "for verie seldome coming to Church." Some presented a more obstinate opposition to the churchwardens' desires, like Thomas Mead who "doth verye negligentlye and wilfullye absent himself from churche and amongeste the rest upon sundaye last being requested to come in he obstinately refused and went his way."[26] The establishment of habits of weekly church attendance and of communion at least once in the year required some effort from the village officers. It was supplemented by the prosecution of other activities inimical to the new standards of devotional conformity. Sunday work was the subject of a steady trickle of prosecutions from the end of the sixteenth century and more regular presentments in the 1610s. Thus we find the presentment of William Ball "for reaping of his corne upon the Saboth daye," of Thomas Every "for that he did sett his mill woorke on the Saboth daye," of Richard Kingsom for ploughing, of John Hanbury for carting, and of Edward Melford for having "trymd" or "barbd" a customer upon the day required by the Lord.[27] Sunday sports and pastimes were also under attack. Richard Gaymer found himself in trouble for fishing on the Sabbath in service time, Richard Oughan "for hunting coneyes," the latter pleading lamely that "he was absent from the Church upon one Saboth day and going through a wood with a dog he putt up a cony and the churchwardens came."[28] Dancing on the green in service time was attacked in 1588, and both pipers and dancers found themselves again before the courts in 1594 and 1600. Indeed, by 1616 public dancings on Sundays seem to have been driven off the green and into the village alehouses. In that year Robert Melford was brought before the justices for going "with a tabor and pipe from alehowse to alehowse upon the Sabothe dayes and often times he hath had warninge of it."[29] By then, as we have seen, the alehouses themselves were under vigorous attack, the more so if they tolerated Sunday disorders. With the decline of communal recreations and the attack upon the more fragmented sociability of the alehouses, the only collective activity remaining to the villagers was church attendance.

By 1630, when Mathew Warren made his presentment to the justices, these measures were certainly beginning to bite. One left-handed compliment to the achievement of the parish officers was paid by Mathew Mitchell, a frequent object of the churchwardens' attentions. When prosecuted in 1630 for coming to church only after the sermon was over, he pleaded with a naïve irony worthy of Svejk that "he could not get into the church by reason of the crowde of people." He was admonished and dismissed.[30]

We can be sure that Mathew Mitchell made less effort to push his way into the church than he would have done to find room at Widow Lamson's alehouse, where he commonly spent Sundays. But no one denied that ser-

---

[26] E. R. O. D/ACA 44 fo. 176, 30 fo. 261v.

[27] E. R. O. D/ACA 22 fo. 131, 34 fo. 182, 40 fos. 12, 70v, 96, 98v.

[28] E. R. O. D/ACA 25 fo. 100, 43 fo. 28v.

[29] E. R. O. D/ACA 16 fos. 111v, 149, 157; D/ACA 22 fo. 130; D/ACA 25 fo. 103; Q/SR 214/31.

[30] E. R. O. D/ACA 47 fo. 167v.

mons in Terling were well attended. Indeed, by 1630 we have other evidence of the appearance among the parishioners of a group exhibiting a distinctly Puritan piety, not least among those parish officers who had been instrumental in seeing through the general tightening-up on religious offences in the second and third decades of the seventeenth century. Such evidence comes in the first place from the dedicatory preambles of the villagers' wills. As in earlier years, a great many wills bore the stereotyped preambles associated with particular scribes. As the seventeenth century advanced, however, strikingly individual wills became increasingly common, with complex, essentially personal clauses being added to the conventional formulae. Such wills were particularly frequent in the 1620s and bore witness to the individual religious commitment of a growing number of testators. William Gutch, for example, bequeathed his soul in 1626 "into the hands of almighty God my maker and redeemer," which was conventional enough, but then went on, "by whose merits precious deathe and bloudshedding [I] steadfastlie believe to have free pardon and remission of all my sins . . . and hope to have a Joyfull resurrection with the just in the last daie." He also left 10s. for a sermon at his funeral. A year earlier, William Cornwell bequeathed his soul "into the hands of Almighty God my creator and in Jesus Christ my loveinge father and of Jesus Christ my Saviour and redeemer through whose al sufficient satisfaction I look to have eternall life." The tortuous wording makes the dedication the more striking. Among the witnesses was the Puritan vicar, Thomas Weld, a man who—unlike his predecessors—rarely appeared as scribe of or witness to the wills of his flock.[31]

In the wills of these years we see the passing of a whole generation of parish notables of striking personal piety. Moreover, the men concerned can be said to have formed a quite distinct group within village society. Earlier testators had left evidence of unusual religious conviction; yet they appeared as rather isolated individuals. Here at last we have a coherent group. The ten men whose wills in the 1620s and 1630s showed such signs of special devotion left evidence in the course of their active lives of thirty-five will-making relationships with other parishioners. Of these, twenty were with other men known to have been of deep piety. In addition, some showed themselves closely linked to the ministers of the parish. Thomas Weld, as we have seen, witnessed William Cornwell's will; he was also left as guardian of John Wood's grandchild and was entrusted with a charitable bequest by John Green.[32] These pious men were thus intimately interconnected by willmaking relationships, which must surely bear witness to a

---

[31] E. R. O. D/ACW 10/39; D/ACW 10/126.
[32] E. R. O. D/ACW 10/66; D/ACW 11/37.

considerable degree of mutual friendship and trust. Furthermore, they possessed a strong social identity. Eight of the ten were yeomen, the remaining two being husbandmen. Five had served as churchwardens, seven as sessions jurymen. Indeed, the group included every key figure in parish government between 1615 and 1629. Finally, seven of the ten were literate.

The emergence of this godly group was the result of a combination of factors. There is little evidence of either kinship ties between the men concerned or of lineal descent from earlier villagers of known piety, though one at least had a father as godly as himself. Some had spent their childhood, and presumably undergone religious education, in other parishes and were to this extent products less of religious development in Terling than of the mounting tide of Protestant lay piety in Essex as a whole. Others may have been influenced or confirmed in their faith during adult life by Thomas Rust and Thomas Weld, vicars of Terling. Rust, vicar from 1604 to 1625, was a preacher and a man of Puritan leanings in ethical matters, though no nonconformist.[33] Weld, vicar from 1625 to 1631, was a Puritan zealot and an uncompromising opponent of the Anglican establishment. But whatever the origins of their piety, these men had come together and been consolidated into a distinct group within Terling itself. They shared a social position and a faith. Moreover, they were demonstrably prepared to put their beliefs into action in the steps they took, far beyond those of their predecessors, to discipline the religious and moral lives of their fellow parishioners.

Further consolidation of the local "reformation" achieved by 1630 was to be disturbed by the advent, under Archbishop Laud, of the Arminian reaction in the Church of England. Terling's experience in the 1630s further reveals the extent to which the parish had been penetrated by Puritanism. For if Thomas Rust had helped to consolidate a sober lay piety in the parish, puritanism with a small *p*, Thomas Weld led the way into an active nonconformity, which meant open conflict with the ecclesiastical establishment.

The situation in Terling first attracted the attention of the ecclesiastical authorities in 1629, when the churchwardens were required to answer to the archdeacon "for suffering Mr. Peter a suspended minister to preache in their Churche." The churchwardens replied that Mr. Peter had preached in the church on a Thursday "and that they did not knowe either that he was suspended or should preach there till he was in the pulpitt and who procured him to preach there or gave him leave to doe so they knowe not."[34] If

---

[33] J. and J. A. Venn eds., *Alumni Cantabrigiensis.* Part I. Rust was listed as a preacher in the puritan survey of 1604, *A Viewe of the State of the Clargie within the Countie of Essex,* p. 7.

[34] E. R. O. D/ACA 47 fo. 5.

the churchwardens pretended ignorance, the archdeacon knew better. Not long afterward Mr. Weld himself was summoned "to show by what authority he reads a lecture in his parish church upon the weeke day." Soon Laud himself was to act against Weld who, after defying Laud to his face and refusing to conform to the Prayer Book service, was first suspended and then in 1631 deprived of his living. Weld made his escape first to the Netherlands and then to New England, where he was to plunge into the controversy surrounding Mrs. Hutchinson and to become pastor of the church of Roxbury, Massachusetts. He returned to England in 1641 and, after an unpleasant taunting of his former enemy Laud in the Tower of London, went on eventually to trouble the peace of Gateshead during The Interregnum.[35]

Weld's whole life showed him to be a bigot and zealot of the first order, even by seventeenth-century standards. Yet his powerful personality left its mark in Terling. Even while his case hung before the church authorities, his parishioners were following in his footsteps. In 1630 a conventicle met "betweene 4 and 5 of the morninge" at the house of the schoolmaster's widow, attended by a number of men and women and led by "a younge scholar that then lived at Mr. Welles his house" and by John Cullin who "did preach or expound the Scriptures to them." Meanwhile, the curate Nathaniel Bosse continued to officiate in the parish, declining in doing so to wear the surplice, read the whole Prayer Book service, or use the cross in baptism and "administering the communion to some that will not kneele." The authorities soon struck, and in 1631 both Bosse and the conventiclers whose names were known were called before the archdeacon. Bosse soon left the parish.[36]

By late 1631 and early 1632 the authorities appeared to have won and Terling was in some disarray. The churchwardens were ordered "to certifie for the church ornaments" and duly appeared in the church court to report that they had spent £15 in reedifying the church. The extent of sullen local alienation from the authorities was evidenced in May, 1632, when they were cited again to answer the charge "that they had neither divine service nor sermon in their church on Easter day last, nor on lowe sunday nor on most of the holy daies in the yeare last past and for that they had no service nor ringing on the kings Coronation day last past."[37] However, the selfconfidence of the godly soon returned. In 1632 the new minister, John Stalham, made his appearance. Stalham, too, was a man of Puritan piety, attracted to Terling as later recalled to his congregation by "that inviting

---

[35] E. R. O. D/ACA 47 fo. 94v. For an account of Weld's turbulent life, see R. Howell, "Thomas Weld of Gateshead. The return of a New England Puritan."

[36] E. R. O. D/ACA 48 fos. 13v, 29v.

[37] E. R. O. D/ACA 48 fos. 52v, 77v, 166.

report which was given of you that you were a fasting and a praying people: which I found true, among the best of you, who gave me a call hither." Initially, however, Stalham "through inconsiderate timidity and temerity" was content to reintroduce the Prayer Book ceremonies, though his people held out to him Weld's "example of Non-Conformity to Prelaticall injunctions." Later he confessed himself "convinc'd . . . of my folly" and satisfied lay demand by taking his own stand against the prelates.[38]

The first signs of renewed nonconformity came in 1634 when the churchwardens were called to report "whether the parishioners receive the communion kneeling." Two years later the archdeacon discovered that the communion table in Terling was still not railed-in in the chancel and ordered the churchwardens to see to it. This was done, but in 1638 Stalham was cited before the archdeacon "for goinge out of the rayle and administering the communion to most of the principall parishioners out of the rayle." At the same time it was revealed that on the eve of Easter communion the communion table had been removed from behind its rails and placed in the middle of the church. The churchwardens pleaded ignorance as to who could have committed the offence. Stalham was in trouble again in 1639 for not reading "his majesties proclamation" and "for not wearing the surplice" and was required to answer "howe the communion is received."[39] This was the situation when the constitutional crisis which preceded the Civil War intervened, perhaps saving Stalham from a fate much like that of Weld.

In later years Stalham was to recall how he had survived "in weaknesse and in fear and in much trembling" these years of persecution, but to rejoice that he enjoyed "Preaching liberties (with some success) all the Prelates times." It does indeed seem probable that in these difficult early years of his ministry Stalham was able to consolidate the "goodly heritage" left to him by Weld. Puritan godliness was now well established among the leading families of the parish, though of realities lower in the social scale we know much less. The socially biased nature of the evidence provided by wills prevents any deep exploration of the religious commitment of the poor. Certainly some relatively humble villagers were among the godly but at the same time it seems likely that the first generation of Puritan villagers was recruited mainly from the upper and middling ranks of village society. It was the "principall inhabitants" who declined to take the communion kneeling. Stalham's own references to "the best of you who gave me a call" and his pointed distinction of "Professours" from "the ignorant and profane

---

[38] J Stalham, *Vindiciae Redemptionis*, To My Beloved Brethren and Neighbors in Terling.
[39] E. R. O. D/ALV fo. 24; D/ACA 51 fo. 157, 52 fos. 226v, 227, 53 fo. 195v, 54 fos. 88v, 152.

multitude" seem to imply something of a social as well as a spiritual and behavioral differentiation.[40] Puritanism, in at least its first phase, would appear to have inserted a cultural wedge, a radical sense of dissociation, between "the better part" and "the greater part," the "few" and the "multitude." By 1640 distinctions of religious outlook, education, and manners had been superimposed on the existing distinctions of wealth, status, and power in the village.

Whatever the situation in the years before the country's slide into civil war, the changed situation of the years during and immediately after the war seemed to hold out the prospect of a fuller, further reformation in Terling. Stalham was to write with enthusiasm in 1647 of how, in the immediately preceding years, "some competent number of you have fallen in with me in a time of Publique Reformation, to witnesse against Popery, Prelacy, Superstition, Schisme, Heresie, Prophanenesse and Formality and have helpt towards their Extirpation according to Covenant." The godly had joined him in "casting out of Ceremonies and Service-book as a menstruous cloth" and had sought "with joynt consent" the true institutions of Christ's church. In Terling they recognized "a true Church here in being."[41] As the institutions of a congregational church were set up in the parish the war against profaneness and ignorance was continued. Stalham was one of fifteen ministers who in 1643 communicated to the Committee at Chelmsford their "serious and sad thoughts upon the grounds of the growth of profanes" in Essex. In their diagnosis it was the village alehouses that were "one of the cheife rootes upon which a world of diabolicall wickednes growes" and they recomended "that all alehouses may be suppressed and then those that shall be judged fitt for scitutation and have persons fitly qualified for the keepinge them may be licensed uppon the approbation of the ministers and other cheife inhabitants and the rest finally suppressed." As a result, the justices initiated in 1644 a county-wide purge of alehouses—including those of Terling that had slipped from control during the war years.[42] While the sword of the magistrate punished the ungodly, new steps were taken to spread the word. Stalham preached energetically and, in addition, produced in 1644 his *Catechisme for children in yeeres and Children in understanding*, an abridged version of a number of catechestical sermons first preached, then circulated, among the parishioners in manuscript. In it he set out the doctrines of sin, justification, reconciliation, sanctification, and redemption in plain terms. He expounded "the right way of government in Families, Schooles and Churches" and expressed the hope that, by daily calling to account of their

---

[40] J. Stalham, *Vindiciae Redemptionis*, To My Beloved Brethren and Neighbours in Terling.
[41] J. Stalham, *Vindiciae Redemptionis*, To My Beloved Brethren and Neighbours in Terling.
[42] E. R. O. Q/S Ba 2/48; Q/S Ba 6.

families, his readers might make "all your Households as so many little Churches."[43] As the work continued, Stalham himself received unexpected help from the state in the form of a financial augmentation of his living, initially granted in 1646 and periodically renewed up to 1659. His income was thus brought up close to the £100 a year regarded by Parliament as most fitting for an educated minister. When the commissioners of the commonwealth church survey reported in 1650, they found all well in Terling under its pastor, "a godly a painefull minister who preacheth constantly."[44]

Not all, however, was as well as might appear. For in the very years of triumph, Terling, like all England, began to feel the effects of the centrifugal forces of Puritan individualism. As early as 1643 Stalham found that a number of his parishioners had become infected with Baptist ideas. Having conferred with them and failed to persuade them, he organized a public debate in the church between three orthodox ministers and two Baptists from London, one of them a physician, the other a soapboiler. The arguments of the ministers prevailed and when the congregation were asked whether or not they accepted them "they gave their general attestation by a shout with Yes, Yes" and proceeded to sing Psalm 117[45]. Three years later a more serious situation arose. Terling, in common with some other Essex parishes, was visited by the wandering Baptist preacher Samuel Oates, described by Stalham's close friend John Maidstone as "a man of lovely and desirable parts" but "apt to deceive and delude all the silly souls he meets with." Oates preached in a private house without Stalham's consent and announced "an universall . . . Redemption by the death of Christ . . . for all." This was plain heresy to Stalham, who insisted upon the position that "Christ died but for some" and that "most men will lose their souls." By 1647, when Stalham went into print to refute Oates' message, several of the parish were "nibbling at the bait" led, it would appear from Stalham's punning allusions, by the yeoman Cyprian Cornwell. Some were "persisting in a way of needlesse separation from me and your Brethren and that privately as publikely," as Stalham complained. "Some," he claimed, "have taken upon you the office of teaching, and re-baptising; others have hearkened after you and you with them after false teachers, who have drawn disciples after them, not only to another Baptisme, but to another Gospel."[46]

This time neither private discussions, sermons, nor printed books

---

[43] J. Stalham, *A Catechisme for Children in yeeres and Children in understanding*, To the Reader and Teacher in the Family and *passim*.

[44] Bodleian Library MS. 323 fo. 104, 327 fo. 179; Lambeth Palace Library Comm VIa/3 fo. 114, Comm VIb/2 fo. 50; H. Smith, *The Ecclesiastical History of Essex*, p. 305.

[45] J. Stalham, *The Summe of a Conference at Terlinge in Essex*, p. 36

[46] J. Stalham, *Vindiciae Redemptionis*, To My Beloved Brethren and Neighbours in Terling, To My Christian Reader in generall, To the Christian Reader.

prevailed and the wayward independence of some of the parish decisively broke Stalham's monopoly to spiritual guidance. In 1656 the situation was compounded by the appearance of Quaker ideas which were adopted by a handful of villagers, this time certainly led by Cyprian Cornwell. In the preface to his *The Reviler Rebuked* (1657) Stalham adopted a tone of earnest but moderate concern. He rejected the solution of those who "cry up nothing but Club Law against the men called Quakers," preferring to put forward arguments that showed his close familiarity with the teachings of George Fox, James Naylor, and other Quaker apostles. To such teachings as "that the Scriptures are not the word of God," "that they have no sin dwelling in them and that their warfare is at an end," that "there is no Baptism of water," and that the Lord's Supper was "a humane invention," he patiently put forward the orthodox alternative. Clearly, such close argument was needed to deal with villagers of some theological sophistication. But it was of no avail. When Stalham urged his flock to "take heed of curiosity and an itching desire of Novelty or of knowing any new way to Christ and Heaven," he was trying to shut the stable door after the horse had bolted. A century of educational advance and religious debate had bred up individuals ready enough to find their own paths of the spirit, to ponder alone the mysteries of salvation.[47]

If the Interregnum saw the disintegration of Puritan unity in Terling, the Restoration saw the final blasting of godly hopes. Stalham was deprived for nonconformity to the restored Anglican Church in 1662, though he lived on in Terling as nonconformist pastor. He was replaced by a conforming vicar, Robert Ridgeway. Ridgeway's inheritance was scarcely one to be envied, but he appears to have conducted himself with a degree of moderation in dealing with his disaffected parishioners. Alternatively, the fact that he was also vicar of Thorpe and not resident in Terling may have inhibited any close supervision of his flock. The field remained open for Stalham.[48] A number of nonconformists were prosecuted in the ecclesiastical courts, Quarter Sessions, and Assizes in the years 1663 to 1672, but it seems certain that no attempt was made to deal with more than the most prominent or most recalcitrant offenders. Those appearing most regularly were the village Quakers, perhaps because their activities were as much disliked by the much larger body of orthodox dissenters as by the established church. The Quaker men—two yeomen, two husbandmen, an innkeeper, a millwright, and grocer—appeared time and again in the court

---

[47] J. Stalham, *The Reviler Rebuked: or a Re-inforcement of the Charge against the Quakers*, To His Highness Oliver, Lord Protector, To the Church of Christ which is at Terling, and *passim*.

[48] A. G. Matthews, *Calamy Revised*; T. W. Davids, *Annals of Evangelical Nonconformity in the County of Essex from the time of Wycliffe to the Restoration*, p. 487.

records, sometimes joined by their womenfolk. For the rest, thirteen non-conformists of unspecified theological affiliation were presented on single occasions up to 1672, either for failing to attend church services or for attending conventicles in other parishes. It seems likely that the remainder of Stalham's former congregation observed some limited kind of conformity. A number of former Baptists or Quakers were also won back in the course of the 1670s, bringing in droves of children to be baptized all at once and to have their dates of birth and baptism entered in the parish register.

This evidence might give an impression of nonconformity in Terling as a fairly marginal phenomenon, an impression that might be reinforced by the absence of any Terling return to the Compton Census of 1676. This impression would be utterly false, for Terling was probably one of the most strongly nonconformist parishes in an area swarming with religious dissidents. Of the twenty-seven parishes in Witham deanery that made returns to the Compton Census, twenty-three numbered nonconformists among their parishioners. Overall, some 7% of the parishioners returned for the deanery were Protestant dissenters, while Terling's neighbors, Witham and Fairstead, were both over 14% nonconformist in 1676.[49] The reality of the situation in Terling was revealed only in 1679 when, at the time of the arrival of a new vicar, Mr. Blower, a massive presentment was made to the court of the Archdeacon of Colchester. It listed thirty men as persons "not comeing to divine service" and a further twenty-seven men as persons "not comeing to Church at all."[50] This meant that approximately 25% of the householders of Terling were practising only a very severely limited conformity to the restored Church of England, while in addition something over 20% of householders were failing to attend church at all.

The presentment of 1679, while undoubtedly representing the bones of the religious state of the parish in 1679, is nonetheless somewhat difficult to interpret. It seems to us most probable that it presents the results of a full investigation of the extent of religious dissent in the parish. The men listed as "not comeing to divine service" may well have been dissenters sufficiently hostile to the Prayer Book service to absent themselves from part of church services. Indeed, five of those listed had been prosecuted on other occasions for failing to attend church or actually attending dissenting conventicles, while another two were among those who had failed to have their children baptized at birth. Those men listed as "not comeing to Church at all," however, might be either hard-core nonconformists or, alternatively, simple neglecters of church. We are inclined to accept the former interpretation for several reasons. First, prosecutions of simple

[49] E. R. O. T/A 420.
[50] E. R. O. D/ACV 7 unfoliated (20 June 1679).

casual neglectors of church of the type common enough before 1640 had been absent since 1662. The authorities of the Restoration church were more concerned with dissent than with simply erratic church attendance, and those prosecuted for religious offences from Terling up to 1679 had all been dissenters. Second, the list of names includes those of ten men who had been repeatedly in trouble for nonconformity prior to 1679, five of them being known Quakers. Of the others named we cannot of course be sure, but it seems reasonable to regard them as religious dissenters. A final argument in favor of our regarding the 1679 presentment as a whole as being a survey of nonconformity is provided by the fact that some years later Stalham's former congregation was described as 200 strong and including a score of county voters and a number of gentlemen.[51] The figure tallies well with the numbers of men presented in 1679 when allowance is made for their wives and children. Again, the social composition of those presented fits the description. Why such a survey should have been undertaken, presumably by the incoming vicar, is a mystery. Pehaps the answer lies in the fact that Terling was one of the few parishes in Witham deanery that had neglected to make a return to the Compton Census of 1676. Mr. Blower may have decided to conduct his own enquiry into the state of his new parish or may have been prompted to do so by his ecclesiastical superiors.

Terling in the reign of Charles II was thus a parish deeply divided in matters of religion. The long years of Puritan influence and the turmoil of the Interregnum had left their mark. Yet the influence of radical religion had not been diffused equally in village society. As we have seen, the initial impact of Puritanism in Terling had been felt chiefly among the leaders of parish society and may be said to have had the effect of superimposing a cultural and spiritual differentiation on to the existing hierarchy of wealth and status in the village. By the later 1670s this situation had been modified to a degree, but not overcome. Over the whole period of persecution between 1662 and 1685 we know of seventy-five villagers prosecuted for their failure to conform to the restored church, only three of them being women. In almost all cases, the wealth and social position of the men concerned is known to us and is set out in detail in Table 6.3.

As Table 6.3 makes clear, nonconformity was spread across the whole social scale. But, significantly, the laboring poor of Category IV were markedly underrepresented. The appeal of the puritan gospel had proved universal but it was not *equally* powerful at all social levels. Nonconformity in Terling, be it Stalham's Congregationalism or the gospel of the Quakers, was essentially an affair of the middling sort of villager. Perhaps

[51] T. W. Davids, *Annals of Evangelical Nonconformity in the County of Essex*, p. 487.

TABLE 6.3
The Social Position of Terling Dissenters[a]

Social category	Men presented	
	1663–1685	1679 only
I	6 8.3%	4 7.0%
II	18 25.0%	14 24.6%
III	26 36.1%	22 38.6%
IV	18 25.0%	14 24.6%
?	4 5.6%	3 5.2%
	72 100%	57 100%

[a] Data refer to men only.

the matter of the best road to salvation in the next world exercised only a limited appeal over the imaginations of those hardest put to keep body and soul together on earth. Perhaps the social bias of puritan reforming zeal served to alienate the "profane multitude" which was perennially on the receiving end of the cultural aggression of the godly. Perhaps, also, their educational inadequacy rendered the poor less receptive than their social superiors to the theological niceties of the preachers. The dissenters of Terling were undoubtedly considerably in advance of their neighbors in this respect. Those of them for whom we have evidence were only 27% illiterate; they were for the most part villagers of middling rank, with the literacy of the middling sort. Their educational superiority cannot be said to have caused their nonconformity but it was doubtless an important enabling skill for those villagers psychologically disposed towards a more intense concern with the question of their salvation. It may also have been a means of giving added strength and resilience to the convictions of the converted.

Such strength and resilience were needed in the years after 1662 when the godly, instead of setting the tone of village society, found themselves disvalued by hostile authorities in both church and state. Stalham's "little flock" had become the "absenters" of 1679. Yet the extent of their alienation from the village community, from the church itself, should not be exaggerated. In discussing nonconformity we have been forced by the evidence available to lump together individuals practising various degrees of nonconformity to the Established Church. With the exception of the small group of Quakers, the exact theological allegiance of the people concerned is unknown to us, though the vast majority must certainly have been Stalham's Congregationalists. As we have seen, the majority of those presented in 1679 were still maintaining some kind of relationship to the parish church. The fact that not only they, but also most of those listed as "not comeing to Church at all," were prepared to accept some of the sacraments of the Established Church can be demonstrated by examining the registrations of baptisms, marriages, and burials brought together in the family reconstitution forms of the men concerned. It will perhaps be both surprising and a welcome relief to historical demographers to learn that the vast majority of all dissenters known to us in the period 1662 to 1685 continued to bring in their children for baptism, or at least registration, and their dead for burial, throughout the period of their persecution. This was as true of those listed in 1679 as "not comeing to Church at all" as of those who simply absented themselves from divine service. Where the two differed was in the respect that the former seem to have been unwilling to marry in the Anglican Church. The only exceptions to be found to these general rules were the known Quakers, who appear to have had no dealings whatsoever with the church, and the few individuals (also Quakers, perhaps?) who withheld children from baptism but later conformed and brought them in. These findings can be further confirmed by the checking of the wills of dissenters against their family reconstitution forms. Children named in wills were rarely unknown to the baptismal register. The omission of occasional children as a result of their having been baptized elsewhere was certainly no more common among dissenters than among conformist villagers. Only three cases of gross underregistration were found, all of the men concerned being known Quakers.[52]

This evidence, with its suggestion that (the Quakers excepted) Terling dissenters were only partly alienated from normal parish life, is reinforced by other findings. For example, it is clear that they continued to play their proportionate part in parish government. Eleven served as churchwardens, seven as sessions jurymen, six as constables, eight as overseers of the poor, and four as vestrymen in the period 1662 to 1688. Still others were to hold office after 1688. Especially striking is the fact that over one-third of the churchwardens of the reigns of Charles II and James II were men who had been in trouble at Quarter Sessions or Assizes or before the church courts for their nonconformity. Clearly religious considerations did not prevent the majority of the wealthier dissenters from playing the part in parish affairs to which their social standing naturally entitled them. Moreover, in doing so they interacted as equals with their conformist neighbors among the ruling group of the parish. The Quaker Cyprian Cornwell was debarred

---

[52] This evidence would support E. A. Wrigley's interesting suggestions in his note, "Clandestine marriage in Tetbury in the late 17th century," that later seventeenth-century registers tend to be deficient not in baptisms or burials, but in marriages only.

from serving as constable on one occasion because of his understandable refusal to take an oath. More normal was the case of Richard Yeldham. He was complained of by the visitation court of the archdeacon in 1676 for his negligence and as "one that speaks slightly of the corte." Yet he served that year as churchwarden nonetheless.[53]

Having established that the dissenters were for the most part little fenced off by their beliefs from participation in parish life, it comes as less as a surprise to find that they did not form a distinct group within the village in terms of their ties of kinship. Of the forty-three identifiable nonconformist householders on the 1671 Hearth Tax listing, only a maximum of twenty-six had kin among the other householders. Of their thirty-seven possible kin links, only fifteen were to other nonconformists. Both the absolute and the relative kinship densities of nonconformists in Terling were low, much as was the case with the population at large. Of course, some kinsmen showed a common nonconformity. The Huccaby brothers were both dissenters, while there were some dissenting marriages—between the Price and Abbot families, for example. But, equally, some families with several representatives in the village were divided by religion—the Birchalls, Palmers, and Fannings, for example. Again, population turnover in the period was such that there are few signs of lineal descent from the religious radicals of the earlier seventeenth century to the nonconformists of the later seventeenth century. Only five of the nonconformist householders of 1671 had even the remotest family connection to earlier puritans in the village. In any case, such connections could work both ways: The descendants of the godly Augustine Norrell were conformists. Of course, it would be foolish to deny that the family was a major agency in the transmission of religious affiliation, but it would appear that this role was played by the nuclear family rather than by the extended kin. The subsequent emigration of children militated against the building up of more than a few nonconformist dynasties in the village in the seventeenth century. Where family traditions existed, they must have extended over a much broader area than that of the single parish. Most of the nonconformist householders of late seventeenth-century Terling were first-generation villagers. As in the case of literacy, that of nonconformity reminds us that village conditions were as much a product of broader processes within Terling's social area as of purely local development.

If the kinship ties of nonconformists showed no peculiar density, however, their neighborly ties indicate a real preference for one another. While they interacted a good deal with conformist villagers in matters of local government and in economic affairs, when it came to the making,

---

[53] E. R. O. Q/SR 375/46; D/ACV 7 unfoliated, (6 April 1676).

witnessing, and overseeing of wills they preferred their coreligionists. This preference, however, varied according to the social position of the men concerned, as is indicated in Table 6.4

The density of neighborly interaction among nonconformists as measured by will-making relationships was thus greatest among men high in the social scale of the village. Persons in Categories I and II, and to a lesser extent III, demonstrated a preference for other nonconformists that was not evident among nonconformist laborers. Individually, some had these relationships with nonconformists only, while others were linked to conformist villagers also. As is shown in Table 6.5, it was men in Category II who were most likely to be linked to nonconformists only, and men in Category IV who were least likely to be so. It is probably of significance that, of those who had will-making relationships to other nonconformists only, all save one were among the minority of hard-core nonconformists who were prosecuted in the courts on more than one occasion; two of them were Quakers.

The preferences exhibited here were not limited to particular grades of nonconformity. A Quaker might have a will-making relationship with a probable Congregationalist and vice versa. Preferences do, however, seem to have been influenced even more deeply by social position than has been indicated hitherto. As we have seen, social position influenced the degree to which individuals showed a consistent preference for other nonconformists. When the actual social direction of links is examined it also emerges that, while nonconformists of Categories I to III were very closely connected to one another, only one nonconformist laborer was linked by a will relationship to a person higher in the social scale than the husbandman-craftsman level. Religious affiliation was, on this evidence, rarely strong enough to overcome social distance in the village.

In 1688 the churchwardens John Dawson (one of the nonconformists of

TABLE 6.4
Will-making Relationship of Dissenting Villagers[a]

Social category	Number of dissenters	Number of will relationships	Number and percentage of will relationships with other dissenters	
I	4	9	5	56%
II	10	26	17	65%
III	7	22	10	45%
IV	5	13	4	31%
Totals	26	70	36	51%

[a]Data refer to men only.

TABLE 6.5
Will-making Preferences of Dissenting Villagers[a]

Social category	Number of dissenters	Relationships with other dissenters only	Relationships with dissenters and conformists	Relationships with conformists only
I	4	1	2	1
II	10	5	4	1
III	7	1	4	2
IV	5	1	1	3
Totals	26	8	11	7

[a]Data refer to men only.

1679) and Andrew Hall recorded in their accounts the purchase of "two papers of Prayers for the Prince of Orange" and subsequently of "his Majesties Declaration for Liberty of Conscience." The time of trial was over for the dissenters of Terling and, as is usual in social history, freedom from persecution meant their disappearance from the public records available to us. Some perhaps returned to the fold of a nonpersecuting church. Others certainly stayed outside and in 1714 obtained their own meetinghouse in Terling.[54] The religious development of the parish in the period from the Reformation to the Glorious Revolution had borne its final fruit in the formal religious division of the parish. The dissenters lived on, far from alienated from their community but forming a distinct group within it, a permanent legacy of the seventeenth century.

The century between the Armada and the Revolution of 1688 had seen a momentous extension of the cultural horizons of the villagers. A new popular literacy had enabled some of them to participate in the literate culture of the nation. Some parishioners had been drawn into the currents of religious change and had then struck out for themselves, adopting in the process new conceptions of the relationship of God to man and of men to one another. A popular culture of communal dancings, alehouse sociability, and the like had retreated before a more sober ideal of family prayer, neighborly fellowship, and introspective piety. All this had taken place within the context of a social structure that persisted relatively unchanged. Indeed, the outcome of change was to a very large extent moulded by the persistence of the structures of wealth, status, and power. Illiteracy had been banished only at the top of the social scale; it remained solidly hierarchical. Religious innovation again worked its way down from the leaders

[54] E. R. O. D/P 299/5/1A fos. 13v, 14; D/DRa T 83.

of the parish and even by 1679 had made only a limited impact on the village poor. New conceptions of order came to prevail because they had taken root among the village élite. Customary norms of behavior loosened their hold when they were proscribed and attacked by the same ruling group. The essentials of the traditional social system persisted unchanged. Yet a new complexity had been given to village society. New distinctions of education and religion, of attitudes and manners, had come into being, sometimes to cut across, but more often to reinforce, the existing distinctions between men.

7

THE "BETTER SORT" AND THE LABORING POOR

Human experience is never uniform, yet it has its regularities. From the individual fortunes of each family, of every villager, in sixteenth- and seventeenth-century Terling emerge patterns of shared experience shaped by broad similarities of circumstances and of opportunity. In this book we have sought to delineate some of the characteristic forms of behavior, some of the common aspirations of the villagers of Terling as a whole. At the same time, we have attempted to establish wherever possible the distinctions that can be discerned between the experience of individuals occupying different places in the hierarchies of wealth, status, and power within the village community. For this we make no apologies, since to analyze is to make distinctions. Only by so doing can we hope to recapture the full richness and texture of life in our period. Only thus can we avoid the pitfall of regarding the villagers as an undifferentiated mass. Of equal importance is the fact that only by establishing the nature of the distinctions that existed between villagers can we uncover the subtleties of the processes of development and change in Terling. For social change is almost always selective. It does not descend on whole communities like an avalanche carrying all before it, but is infiltrated slowly by the agency of individuals and social groups occupying strategic positions in the structure of local society. In Terling, as elsewhere, the key to the understanding of the structure of society lies in an appreciation of the distinctions between men as well as of those ties that held them together. Equally, our understanding of the complexities of social change depends on the extent to which we are able to discern the differences in the nature and chronology of the experience of particular individuals and groups.

Village society in Terling was highly stratified. Hierarchy was a fundamental fact of life. Relative position in the village's own pattern of social inequality exercised a pervasive influence over the lives of the villagers. It influenced the size and structure of their households, their varying degrees of geographical mobility, the density of their kinship networks, and the range of their recognition of kinsmen. It shaped the structure of their neighborly relations, their relative dependency or freedom of action. It went far to determine the opportunities and life-chances of individuals, their differing abilities to set up independent family units, to put bread in their children's bellies, to provide for their children's futures, and to ease their transition into the adult world. At the same time, social position was the single most important structural influence on the villagers' openness and receptiveness to change. Market outlets were for men with a surplus to sell. Education was for those who could afford it and were prepared to see that their children acquired it because its advantages were tangible to persons of their rank. Administrative activity was the prerogative of those whose inherited or achieved social position entitled them to rule. Involvement in religious change was open to all, yet the response of the villagers to the demanding creed of the Puritans was, for whatever complex of reasons, markedly socially selective. The enduring structures of social inequality thus patterned both the characteristic life experiences of the villagers as generation succeeded generation and the advent among them of social changes peculiar to particular generations. In the preceding chapters we have sought to analyze the enduring characteristics of economy and society in Terling and to describe the social changes that emerged in the sixteenth and seventeenth centuries. Our task now is to focus attention on the overall process of change in the village, to highlight the forces involved, to examine the nature of their interaction, and to interpret their distinctive local chronology.

Social change in Terling was the outcome of two convergences. The one was chronological; the peaking within the early decades of the seventeenth century of forces of demographic, economic, cultural, and administrative change. The other was sociological; the peculiar involvement as the beneficiaries of these changes of the upper and middling ranks of village society, of the yeomanry, the more substantial husbandmen and craftsmen of Terling, the "principal inhabitants" or "better sort" as they sometimes described themselves. Let us examine these processes in more detail.

Between 1524 and 1671 the population of Terling rose by some 75%; from a total of something over 300 inhabitants to one of almost 600. The evidence of our demographic study suggests that this expansion was essentially completed by the 1620s, by which decade a stabilization of population was setting in. The results of such a demographic expansion were perhaps predictable. While the absolute numbers of yeoman, husbandman, and craftsman households in the village remained fairly stable, the numbers of families of the laboring poor doubled. This development, which might in itself be expected to have had profound effects on village society, was made the more significant by the fact that not only had the numbers of the poor increased, but their increase had been accompanied by a widening of the gap between their living standards and those of their more substantial neighbors. The new prosperity of the commercial farmers of the village and of the craftsmen who supplied their needs stood in sharper contrast to the deteriorating economic position of their laborers. The houses rebuilt and refurnished so splendidly by the yeomen and craftsmen of Terling were surrounded by the mushroom growth of the bare cottages of the poor, the gulf between the fortunes of the two sections of society being probably at its greatest in the three decades which followed the catastrophic harvests of the 1590s. For the market-oriented yeomen these were the years of opportunity. For the laboring poor and for those least fortunate or able among the smallholders of the parish, these were years of chronic insecurity. The interconnected demographic and economic development of the parish was producing a polarization of wealth and poverty to a degree unknown since the late thirteenth century.

The villagers cannot have failed to have been aware of this situation, however confused their perception of their case may have been. As the machinery of the Tudor poor laws became established in the parish at the turn of the century the more substantial inhabitants must have felt in their purses the new and heavier burden of the poor rate. This in itself may be said to have symbolized the radical divergence of the fortunes of the villagers and to have stimulated a novel form of group consciousness. If this was indeed the case, then such a sense of differentiation was complemented by the effects of processes of change that gathered momentum in the closing decades of the sixteenth century and came to a head in the early decades of the seventeenth. The educational achievements of the more substantial villagers opened up a new divide between them and their poorer neighbors which was consolidated in these years. Selective involvement in religious change resulted in the same years in the emergence of a group of firmly committed Puritans among the yeomen of the parish. Together these changes helped promote a further sense of social distance between the literate and the " proffessors" of Terling and what Stalham dismissed as "the ignorant and profane multitude."[1] Finally, the decades after 1595 saw a further influence brought to bear on the ruling group of Terling as the national authorities of the period, anxious to contain the perplexing problems of a fluid social reality within a stable framework of traditional values and relationships, urged forward a general tightening of local administration and social regulation aimed at the safeguarding of order.

The coincidence in time of these various forces of change, each of which made a peculiar impact on the upper ranks of village society, may be said to have promoted a widening differentiation between the prinicipal inhabitants of the village and the laboring poor that had both economic and cultural dimensions. Of course, not all of the leading villagers were equally involved in this complex of changes, just as not all of their poorer neighbors were excluded from the benefits of change. Yet the socially selective nature of the villagers' response and experience was sufficiently clear to permit us to speak of the emergence of increasingly marked and progressively more divergent group identities within the village. As some members of the one group became more deeply involved in the material, cultural, and administrative innovations of the age, most members of the other were sunk more profoundly in the age-old struggle for subsistence. As the few aspired toward new senses of identity, new conceptions of their relationship to man and God, the many remained rooted in the attitudes and manners of the customary culture of their forefathers. In the face of such processes there was little to hold together the polarizing village community. Terling had no communal agriculture; it was manorially divided. After the demise of the parish religious guild in the mid-sixteenth century the parish had no communal institutions save the church and the machinery of the poor laws—and these were as prone to highlight as to overlay the distinctions between men. Even the recreations of the villagers, the dancings, and the sociability of the alehouses, were more likely to provoke conflict between those who sought to uphold them and those who sought their suppression in the name of order and godliness than to act as forces for social cohesion. As a result, the atmosphere of the early decades of the seventeenth century was one of strain and conflict, of tension and hostility, between parish notables and the poor, between the successful and the declining, between the erstwhile guardians of custom and the thrusting bearers of innovation.

The situation that had thus developed by the second decade of the seventeenth century bred two reactions among the villagers of Terling. On the one hand there was the beginning of a demographic adjustment to meet the

---

[1] J. Stalham, *Vindiciae Redemptionis*, To My Beloved Brethren and Neighbors in Terling.

deteriorating economic circumstances of the mass of the population. This adjustment was no doubt hardly conscious, a compound of the individual response of dozens of couples. On the other hand, however, there was the quite conscious attempt by the leaders of the parish to impose upon the community a social discipline that would preserve social stability, while at the same time bringing the comportment of the villagers more firmly into conformity with their own novel conceptions of order and reformation. The former initiative was doubtless to contribute greatly to the more stable demographic and improved economic climate of the village in the later seventeenth century. The latter movement, witnessed in the attack on the alehouses, the enforcement of more regular religious observances, the tightening of control over sexual behavior and over immigration, was aimed quite deliberately at the poor and at those of their social superiors who countenanced or shared their "disorders." It was to set the tone of social relations for the future.

This use of the courts by the ruling group of the village to redefine and mark out anew the boundaries of permitted behavior in Terling was in all likelihood made necessary by the particular state of the institutional development of the village at this period. The manor court, the traditional and wholly local instrument of social regulation in English rural society, was of little use to the village officers. Terling was manorially divided. The courts of the various manors met infrequently and exercised no regulative authority. In any case, they had jurisdiction over only the minority of villagers who were manorial tenants. The innovating yeomen had perforce to turn to the local courts of church and state for the imposition of formal sanctions upon those whose behavior they regarded as morally and socially reprehensible. If the forum of their efforts was thus decided, however, the nature and detailed chronology of their initiative owed more to the form and the timing of social differentiation in Terling and to the coming to power of the individual villagers who were the leading actors in the process of innovation.

To take the latter issue first, the men responsible for the mounting use of the courts for regulative prosecutions after 1607 can be quite clearly identified by simply examining the lists of churchwardens and of presentment jurymen provided by the court records in order to establish which Terling men were most active in the prosecution of the misdemeanours of their neighbors. A group of twenty-one activists emerges. Five were drawn from the great farmers of the parish, fifteen from the lesser yeomen and wealthier tradesmen, and one from among the husbandmen and craftsmen. They included both natives of the village and immigrants, but the most active among them were rather more likely to have been born to Terling families than not. Whatever their origins, they were a distinct group, densely interlinked to one another by ties of friendship and mutual aid, by common service in village office, and, of course, by common action against disorders. They were only 20% illiterate. Finally, at least nine of them (including all the leading figures) were men of peculiar personal piety: known Puritans.

The rise to power of these men can be clearly traced. In 1607 when Richard Rochester, Augustine Norrell, and John Wood launched their attack on Thomas Holman and on a group of alleged drunkards, they were acting as private individuals. None of them held at this time a key position in parish government—and indeed the leading parishioners were more likely to be found among the petitioners whom we have seen defending Thomas Baker from prosecution. The activists were accused of malice and were resisted. This situation changed slowly. From 1609, Augustine Norrell began to serve occasionally as a sessions juryman. When he did so, he prosecuted alehousekeepers for unlicensed selling and disorder. In this he was backed by two other jurymen, Richard Mason and Robert Frank. Yet still these men were not among the core of parish leaders. They could act only when they chanced to be selected as presentment jurymen, and meanwhile older and more prominent parish notables showed little inclination to follow their lead. From 1616, however, the innovators were at last able to set the pace. The older generation had died away and Norrell, John Wood, John Green, and Richard Tabor had emerged as the key figures within the ruling group of the village. Together, with a group of supporters, they pushed up the rate of prosecutions from Terling. The petition against alehouses of 1620 represents their final winning over of the parish elite. It was signed by every leading parish officer except, significantly, George Cannon, a yeomen whose unwillingness to take part in such regulative activity has already been commented upon. As the 1620s advanced, the victory of the innovators was consolidated. At no other period of the seventeenth century was there such a marked overlap of personnel between the churchwardens and the sessions jurymen. They cooperated smoothly, prosecuting offenders with a will in both the church courts and Quarter Sessions. A new tone had been established in parish government. As the original innovators died out in the later 1620s and the 1630s, they were replaced by men who had learned their duties in the new school and who continued to prosecute offenders, defending the ground that had been so painfully won in the preceding decades.

What prompted these men to act as they did? Why were they willing to provoke and, if necessary, to face down the conflict that their actions almost inevitably aroused? What led them to act so firmly against forms of behavior previously tolerated in the village and seek to establish new standards of order? In the first place they were deeply preoccupied with the problem of the poor, both because of the expense of poor relief and because of the threat that the poor seemed to constitute to good order. As the Elizabethan poor laws became established and institutionalized in the village, the parish leaders became increasingly sensitive to the threat of further impoverishment and insistent that their paupers should conform to the statutory stereotype of the deserving poor. Hence we find the disorderly alehousekeeper John Aldridge prosecuted on one occasion,

> for harboringe and sufferinge to play at the bords ends, drinkinge and tipplinge at all tymes such persons that do sweare and dishonor god and soe poore that many of them have almes of the parishe and theire wifs and children beg in the parishe.

Two years later Aldridge was presented again "for sufferinge of pore men to sit tiplinge and drinkenge in his house for the space of halfe a daye and all nighte together."[2] Even more striking as evidence of the new determination to discipline the behavior of the poor were the terms of Henry Smith's charity, set up in 1626 for the relief in "Clothing, Bread, Flesh or Fish" of the able-bodied poor and administered by the parish officers. Laudable as was his foundation, its stipulations were significant. Relief was to be granted only to such poor people as had lived in the parish for five years or more. Further regulations laid down that:

> No poor person that takes Almes of the Parish or those that are guilty of excessive drinkinge, profane swearing, pilfering and other scandalous crimes or are Vagrants or are Idle Persons or have been incorrigible when Servants or do entertain Inmates shall have any of this charity.

In addition, it was laid down that persons relieved in clothing were to be given "upper Garments on the right arm of which shall be a badge with the letters H.S.."[3] Seventy years before the final humiliation of wearing badged clothing was inflicted upon the paupers of the nation at large, the poor of Terling were singled out and badged.

The association of poverty with actual or potential disorder in the minds of the parish officers received further reinforcement from their religious hostility to the "disorders" of the traditional popular culture and their further tendency to associate ungodliness with the poor. The explicit sense of spiritual dissociation from the rude multitude expressed in John Stalham's words to his "little flock" has already been quoted. Equally striking are the terms in which Thomas Weld wrote to his followers in Terling from his exile in New England in 1633. After commenting upon the excellent system

---

[2] E. R. O. Q/SR 279/17, 284/12.
[3] E. R. O. D/P 299/5/1B

of government in the Puritan colony, where he found "scandals prevented, censured" and all things done "according to the precise rule," Weld continued:

> The greater part are the better part here. . . . Here, blessed be the Lord, our ears are not beaten, nor the air filled with oaths, swearers nor railers, nor our eyes and ears vexed with the unclean conversation of the wicked. Here it is counted an honour by the worst to lay hold on the skirt of the few. Here the rudest have a charge and dare not break it.[4]

Presumably such sentiments found an echo among the "better sort" of Terling. Indeed, we know that they did from the petition against alehouses of 1620 in which the innovating village notables had urged the magistrates ordained by God "to take punishment on them that do evil" and in particular to stamp out the drunkenness, swearing, idleness, ungodliness, and impoverishment occasioned by the alehouses of Terling.[5]

Poverty, idleness, ungodliness, disorder: These were the key themes underlying the sense of dissociation that fueled the actions of the innovating "better sort" of Terling. The course of their slow withdrawal from the traditional popular culture of their forefathers can be simply demonstrated by considering the behavior of the men who served as churchwardens and sessions jurymen in three separate decades. Of the twenty-four men who held these offices in the 1590s, two-thirds were themselves prosecuted in the courts in the course of their adult lives, eight of them on more than one occasion. Five were guilty of sexual misdemeanors, three of crimes of violence, while the remainder found themselves presented along with their poorer neighbors for drunkenness, sabbath-breaking, dancing in service time, and failure to attend church or to take communion. Among them were two of the most generally "disorderly" householders in the village. They were 75% illiterate and included only a handful of men marked out by their wills as men of advanced piety. In their recorded behavior these officers were hardly distinguishable from the neighorhood at large. Turning to their twenty-two counterparts among the officers of the 1620s, we find that half had themselves been prosecuted in the courts, though only three of them on more than one occasion. Moreover, the offences of which they were accused had changed significantly. Though there were still three sexual offenders among them, their other offences consisted of harboring inmates, of maintaining cottages without four acres of land, and of failing to pay parish rates. These were the offences of farmers and employers, quite distinct in kind from the misdemeanors of the poor which

---

[4] The letter is reproduced in full in C. A. Barton, *Historical Notes and Records of the Parish of Terling, Essex*, pp. 89–91.

[5] See chapter 5, note 27, above.

these same officers were so active in prosecuting. The single drunkard among the parish officers was Robert Gosse, a man whose response to his presentment was as unusual and revealing as his offence was by now rare for one of his station. Appearing before the Archdeacon, he confessed "that he was overtaken with drinke . . . through weakness and that he is very sorry for it and humbly submitteth himselfe to the Judges order."[6] Gosse's evident shame at his lapse was a sign of the changing times. For the rest, his fellow officers were only 24% illiterate, while seven were men whose wills indicated perculiar piety and eight were signatories of the parish petition against alehouses of 1620. Finally, we may consider the officers of the 1670s. Of these nineteen men, two-fifths had been prosecuted in the courts. Two had commited sexual misdemeanors. All of the others appeared for religious nonconformity, save one who had failed to perform his share of labor on the highways. Some two-fifths of the officers were either dissenters or left very pious will. They were only 15% illiterate.

As they themselves gradually withdrew from the traditional popular culture, the parish notables attacked it where it seemed to be strongest still, in the alehouses of the village and among the poor. In part their actions were crudely instrumental, an attempt to impose a new form of social discipline that would reinforce their own position as masters, employers, ratepayers, and pillars of the church. Yet we would not wish to overstress this element of direct social control, for there were always limits to their coercive power. Of the effectiveness of Quarter-sessions sanctions we know little, though the unlicensed ale trade was certainly brought under control. In the case of the church courts it is clear that those prosecuted could and sometimes did either ignore the court completely or fail to perform its orders and stand excommunicate for years on end. The effectiveness of the moral censures of the ecclesiastical courts depended above all upon the extent to which they were backed by the informal pressures of public opinion in the community. What is clear is that as the early seventeenth century advanced an ever greater proportion of offenders was brought to obey the orders of the Archdeacon for moral offences. In 1620, for example, the year of the sharpest attack in the church courts upon drinking offences, seventeen of those presented quickly obeyed the court's orders, while the remaining six were excommunicated: a success rate of 70%. Were we to include those who eventually submitted—sometimes after subsequent prosecutions—then the general rate of success in enforcing obidience would be higher. Yet formal obedience, confession of error, even public penance, are inadequate indicators of real success. There were those among the villagers who were perfectly willing to manipulate the formal

---

[6] E. R. O. D/ACA 44, fo. 50v.

processes of the courts. They submitted, were admonished, and were dismissed, yet soon enough they might appear again charged with the like offences.

The coercive efficiency of the sanctions brought to bear by the parish notables is clearly of some significance. Their rising rate of formal success may indicate a groundswell of general support over time. Yet ultimately the actions of the village officers must be seen as symbolic. In their activity they were engaged in the marking out of new boundaries of acceptable social behavior. More, they were expressing their own dissociation from the practice of their poorer neighbors. Indeed, given the nature of their beliefs concerning the willingness of their jealous God to visit his judgements upon an errant people, the symbolic and instrumental ends of their efforts were closely interwined. They feared the consequences of the dishonoring of God and they sought to avoid contracting the guilt of sin by inactivity. The motivation of the "better sort" of Terling was therefore complex. They were innovators straddling two worlds, brokers between the broader society of seventeenth-century England and a polarizing village community. They owed their prosperity to their commercial farming, their novel attitudes and perceptions to their involvement in the currents of administrative, educational, and religious change, their power to their role as the local officers of church and state, their social identity to their withdrawal from and hostility to a popular culture that was slowly being transformed into a culture of poverty.

The new pattern of social relations between the yeomanry of Terling and their laborers, hammered out in the earlier seventeenth century and admirably symbolized in the terms of Henry Smith's charity, passed intact into the later seventeenth century and beyond. Demographic stabilization and the rising real wages of laborers after 1650 helped to reduce the problem of poverty, but the poor remained as a permanent class in village society. The seventeenth century saw no reversal of the situation such as had been brought about by the demographic collapse of the fourteenth century. While the second half of the seventeenth century saw a seepage donward in society of the educational achievement and religious radicalism that had introduced new cultural distinctions among the villagers, these developments were so limited in their impact among the laboring population as to modify rather than to overcome the cultural differentiation of the community. Though the Interregnum and Restoration were to witness the breakdown of the religious solidarity of the parish leaders, they continued to stand together in the administration of the parish, united by a shared social position and identity of interests which was demonstrably stronger than their differences of theological emphasis. That they displayed much less cultural aggression than their predecessors is scarcely surprising. That battle had been fought and won. Besides, they had new and entirely local instruments of regulation at their disposal in the parish vestry, which kept a careful watch over village affairs, and in the now fully institutionalized and smoothly functioning machinery of the poor laws.

The neatly kept parish books of the later seventeenth century breathe an air of calm confidence on the part of the rulers of Terling in their ordering of parish affairs, a confidence that stemmed from the consolidation of the new social equilibrium which their predecessors had struggled to establish fifty years before. The bond that united them to those who had gone before was the continued prominence of the problem of the poor in their deliberations. But what had required initiative and aggression now required only administration. Year by year the meticulously kept overseers' books recorded the regular maintenance of a score of widows and old men and a dozen or so orphans, and the occasional relief of the able-bodied poor when sick or under the provisions of Henry Smith's charity. In the 1690s some sixty ratepayers were taxed annually and between £130 and £170 was laid out for the poor, more being spent in winter than in summer. From time to time new names were added to the overseers' lists as vestry resolutions were passed for the relief of new paupers. Other accounts were closed with the brief entries relating to pauper burials. So far as can be ascertained, the officers of the parish performed their duties conscientiously and well and their administrative costs were very small. Their books bring out the very real nature of the positive achievement of the English poor law. Yet its effects are equally evident in such entries as the payment made on 25 September 1697 "for cutting out two dozen and a halfe of Letters and setting them on to the poor."[7] The badging of the poor, however justified by the demands of administrative efficiency, was the enduring symbol of the social transformation of the seventeenth century.

Terling had its own history. How far was its experience shared in England? Ultimately this is a question to which we can give no positive answer. We might point to the fact that some of the general influences that shaped Terling's experience—demographic, economic, administrative, religious, and educational—were undoubtedly at work in the nation at large. On the question of shifts in social relations, however, we have no fully comparable studies on which to draw. Our expectation would be that Terling provides one example, one variant, of a social process that was active elsewhere, though subject to considerable local variation in chronology and consequences. As for Terling itself, the parish entered the eighteenth century as a near classic example of the carefully regulated

---

[7] E. R. O. D/P 299/1/0.

"closed parish." It needed only the final consolidation of the tenant system under a single dominant landlord to complete the pattern and that was to come. By the mid-eighteenth century the parish was sufficiently established as a model of its kind for a gentleman to write to the squire of Terling complimenting the "prudent and necessary regulations" that were observed in Terling's one remaining alehouse and lamenting the lack of such control in his own township, "where every man is unfortunately his own master, and no one can be found to regulate the actions of the ignorant and unthinking."[8] The developments of the seventeenth century had seen the crystallization in Terling of the distinctive agrarian class system of "traditional" lowland England. In that process the prime movers had not been the landlords of the village, who exercised little direct influence over parish affairs in the period. The initiative for change lay rather with the parish yeomanry, the local worthies who had been subject to influences that distanced them from their neighbors and, at the same time, assimilated them more closely to the values and interests of their social superiors and religious mentors. Our task is not to judge them but to comprehend their motivation. According to their lights, they served local needs. Ironically, the heirs of their achievements were not their lineal descendants, for few of these remained in Terling, while those who did could not always retain their fathers' social standing. Their true heirs were the inheritors of their social position.

In all of this the poor appeared rarely as actors in the social drama of the age, though their mass presence was an essential prolegomenon to the process of change. As we have seen, they were neither passive nor submissive in the face of the aggressiveness of their betters. Some resisted openly where they could muster sufficient support. Others learned to manipulate the prejudices of the rulers of the parish in order to preserve to themselves a measure of freedom of action. Yet in the main they endured rather than shaped the changes that determined the terms of their existence. For them the period which we have tried to illuminate saw a worsening of their poverty which was alleviated only late in the seventeenth century, increased social regulation, new forms of dependency and public humiliation and, for the most part, exclusion from an elite culture that was not only novel but aggressive. We write of them in the mass, for few of them stand revealed to us as individuals. We have seen Robert Whitehead, who stole a sheep to feed his family. We have listed the pathetic possessions of Richard and Priscilla Sizer, left to the parish in the hope that they might provide a sufficient sum to see their two small boys apprenticed to trades. Others of

---

[8] Letter to J. Strutt Esq., 21 August 1768. We must thank Hon. C. R. Strutt for providing us with this reference.

their class were Abraham Handley, James Crowe, Daniel Frank, Susan Aldridge, Sarah Rowell, and Thomas Todd. These and many others had in common the fact that they were unable to afford the small costs of interring a wife, husband, or child and were beholden to the parish for pauper burials.[9] The qualities of the principal inhabitants of Terling, their enterprise, their educational and religious aspirations, their moral courage under persecution, the care with which they endeavoured to provide for their widows and children, established a bond of human sympathy across more than 300 years. The plight of those who worked their fields, whose present poverty rendered them unable to bury their own dead, and whose future, if they trod carefully, was an almshouse and a badged coat, is its essential complement. A shudder of pain vibrates across the centuries.

[9] E. R. O. D/P 299/12/0, unfoliated.

REFERENCES

MANUSCRIPT SOURCES

Essex Record Office

Quarter Sessions Records

Q/SR 1–555	Quarter Sessions Rolls, 1555–1713
Q/SO 1–4	Quarter Sessions Order Books, 1651–1717
Q/S Ba 1	Uncalendared loose indictments, 1610–1623
Q/S Ba 2	Quarter Sessions Bundles, 1621–1689
Q/S Ba 4	Presentments of Roads and Bridges, 1618
Q/S Ba 5	Presentments of Recusants, 1641
Q/S Ba 6	Presentments of Alehouses, 1644
Q/AA 1	Wage assessments, 1612

Ecclesiastical Court Records

Archdeaconry of Colchester

D/ACA 1–55	Act Books, 1540–1666
D/ACC 1–16	Causes, 1571–1640
D/ACV 1–12	Visitations, 1586–1703
D/ACD 1–7	Depositions, 1587–1641

Bishop of London's Commissary in Essex and Hertfordshire
D/ABA 1–12   Act Books, 1616–1670
D/ABC 1–8   Causes, 1618–1665
D/ABD 1–8   Depositions, 1618–1665

Bishop of London's Consistory Court
D/ALV 1–2   Visitations, 1624–1638

Taxation Records

Q/R Th 1   Hearth Tax, 1661
Q/R Th 5   Hearth Tax, 1671
Q/R Th 8/9   Hearth Tax, 1673

Parochial Records

T/R 60   Parish Registers of Terling, (Microfilm of Transcript)
D/P 299/5/1A   Churchwardens' Accounts, 1668–1719
D/P 299/5/1B   Churchwardens' Accounts, 1720
D/P 299/12/0   Overseers' Accounts and Rates, 1694–1713
D/P 299/13/1A,1B   Settlement Certificates, 1697–1787
D/P 299/13/2, 3   Removal Orders, 1703–1837
D/P 299/14/1   Apprenticeship Indentures
T/B 54   Tithe Account, 1713, (Photocopy)

Manorial and Estate Records

Manor of Terling Place
D/DM M 69   Rental, 1475
D/DM M 170   Court Book, 1609–1613
D/DQS 64   Fee Farm Rents, c. 1650
T/M 63   Photocopy of 1597 Map and Survey
T/P 87   Rental, c. 1692

Manor of Ringers
D/DRa M 79   Court Rolls, 1698–1705

Manor of Terling Hall
D/DRa M 89   Rental, 1722

Manor of Ockendon Fee
D/DRa M 91   Court rolls, 1581–1719
D/DRa M 92   Court Book, 1690–1719
D/DRa M 93   Rentals, 1632,1670
D/DRa M 94   Rentals, 1705–1715

Manor of Ridley Hall
D/DRa M 98   Court Rolls, 1675–1681
D/DRa M 102   Survey, undated, later seventeenth century
D/DRa M 104   Rental, 1677–1678

Deeds
D/DRa T 59–251   Bundles of deeds of property in Terling, 1492–1903

Wills

Terling wills 1503–1715 from D/ABW 1–34, D/ACW 2–24 and D/ACR 1–26, as listed in F.G. Emmison ed., *Wills at Chelmsford*, Vols I and II, *British Record Society, Index Library*, 78, 79, (1958–1959)

GREATER LONDON RECORD OFFICE

DL/C/303–327, 615–626   Bishop of London's Consistory Court, Office Act Books, 1574–1706

PUBLIC RECORD OFFICE

E 179   108/154, 174, 180   Lay Subsidy Returns, 1524–1629, and Hearth Tax, 1666
        109/262
        110/419
        111/509, 523
        112/588, 607, 638
        246/19

E 301 19/96   Chantry Certificates, 1547

SP 28/290   Accounts of Trustees for the Maintenance of Ministers, 1655–1657

Req 2   32/20, 48/22, 107/47,   Court of Requests
        245/44, 245/45,
        299/44, 306/33,
        415/63, 404/2

STAC 5   A7/30, A8/1, A8/13,   Court of Star Chamber
         A19/9, A27/35,
         A33/20, A33/39,
         A39/18, A54/13,
         A55/23, A57/6

BODLEIAN LIBRARY

Ms Bodley 323   Augmentations granted by the Committee for the Relief of Plundered Ministers, 1646

Ms Bodley 324–329   Minutes of the Committee for the Relief of Plundered Ministers, 1646–1653

LAMBETH PALACE LIBRARY

Comm V1a/1–10   Augmentation Books of the Committee for the Reform of the Universities and of the Trustees for the Maintenance of Ministers, 1650–1660.

Comm V1b/1-2   Tabular accounts of sums to be paid and abstracts of augmentations
                    granted, 1655-1659.

PRINTED SOURCES

CONTEMPORARY PRINTED BOOKS

1606 *A Viewe of the State of the Clargie within the Countie of Essex.* London
Baxter, R.
    1656   *The Reformed Pastor.* London
Bolton, R.
    1639   *Two Sermons Preached at Northampton.* London.
Bownde, N.
    1595   *The Doctrine of the Sabbath plainely layde forthe.* London
Hammond, S.
    1659   *Gods Judgements upon Drunkards etc.* London.
Proffett, N.
    1645   *Englands Impenitencie under Smiting.* London.
Stalham, J.
    1644   *A Catechisme for Children in Yeares and Children in understanding.* London
    1644   *The Summe of a Conference at Terling in Essex.* London.
    1647   *Vindiciae Redemptionis.* London
    1657   *The Reviler Rebuked: or a Re-inforcement of the Change against the Quakers.*
        London.

EDITIONS OF MANUSCRIPTS AND EARLY PRINTED BOOKS

"Calendar of Queen's Bench Indictments Ancient Relating to Essex, 1558-1603" (With continu-
    ation for the reign of James I). Essex Record Office typescript calendar.
Fishwick, H., ed.
    1878   *Lancashire and Cheshire Church Surveys.* Lancashire and Cheshire Record So-
        ciety, 1. Manchester.
Macfarlane, A., ed.
    1976   *The Diary of Ralph Josselin, 1616-1683.* Records of Social and Economic History.
        New Series III. London: Oxford University Press for The British Academy.
Merrill, T.F., ed.
    1966   *William Perkins, 1558-1602: English Puritanist. His Pioneer Works on Casuistry.*
        The Hague: B. De Graaf, Nieuwkoop.
O'Farrell, N. McNeil, ed.
    Calendar of Essex Assize Files in the Public Record Office, 1559-1714. 4 Vols.
        Essex Record Office typescript calendar.
Tawney, R.H. and Power, E., eds.
    1924   *Tudor Economic Documents.* 3 Vols. London: Longmans.
Thirsk, J. and Cooper, J.P., eds.
    1972   *Seventeenth-Century Economic Documents.* Oxford University Press.

UNPUBLISHED DISSERTATIONS

Burley, K.H.
    1957   "The Economic Development of Essex in the Later Seventeenth and Early Eigh-
        teenth Centuries." Ph.D. dissertation. University of London.

Cressy, D.
  1972 "Education and Literacy in London and East Anglia, 1580–1700." Ph.D. dissertation. University of Cambridge.
Hull, F.
  1950 "Agriculture and Rural Society in Essex, 1560–1640." Ph.D. dissertation. University of London.
Sheail, J.
  1968 "The Regional Distribution of Wealth in England as Indicated in the Lay Subsidy Returns of 1524/5." Ph.D. dissertation. University of London.
Shipps, K.W.
  1971 "Lay Patronage of East Anglian Puritan Clerics in Pre-Revolutionary England." Ph.D. dissertation. Yale University.
Todd, E.
  1976 "Seven Peasant Communities in Pre-Industrial Europe. A comparative study of French, Italian and Swedish rural parishes." Ph.D dissertation. University of Cambridge.
Walker, J.C.M.
  1971 "Crime and Capital Punishment in Elizabethan Essex." B.A. dissertation, Faculty of Mediaeval and Modern History. University of Birmingham.

BOOKS AND ARTICLES

Appleby, A.B.
  1975 "Agrarian Capitalism or Seigneurial Reaction? The Northwest of England, 1500–1700." *American Historical Review*, 80:574–594.
Barnes, T.G.
  1961 *Somerset, 1625–1640. A county government during 'the personal rule'*. Oxford: Oxford University Press.
Barton, C.A.
  1953 *Historical Notes and Records of the Parish of Terling, Essex*. Privately published.
Beresford, M.W.
  1958 "The Common Informer, the Penal Statutes and Economic Regulation." *Economic History Review*, Second Series, X:221–237.
Bowden, P.J.
  1976 "Agricultural Prices, Farm Profits, and Rents," in *The Agrarian History of England and Wales, Vol. IV. 1500–1640*, edited by J. Thirsk, pp. 593–695. Cambridge: Cambridge University Press.
Brigg, M.
  1962 "The Forest of Pendle in the Seventeenth-Century." *Transactions of the Historic Society of Lancashire and Cheshire*, 115: 65–89.
Britton, E.
  1977 *The Community of the Vill. A Study in the History of the Family and Village Life in Fourteenth-Century England*. Toronto: Macmillan of Canada.
Campbell, M.
  1942 *The English Yeoman under Elizabeth and the Early Stuarts*. New Haven: Yale University Press.
Chambers, J.D.
  1972 *Population, Economy and Society in Pre-Industrial England*. Oxford: Oxford University Press.
Clark, P.
  1977 *English Provincial Society from the Reformation to the Revolution: Religion, Politics and Society in Kent, 1500–1640*. Hassocks: Harvester Press.

Clark, P. and Slack, P.
  1976   *English Towns in Transition, 1500–1700*. Oxford: Oxford University Press.
Cliffe, J.T.
  1969   *The Yorkshire Gentry From the Reformation to the Civil War*. London: Athlone Press.
Cockburn, J.S.
  1972   *A History of English Assizes, 1558–1714*. Cambridge: Cambridge University Press.
  1977   "The Nature and Incidence of Crime in England, 1559–1625: A Preliminary Survey." In *Crime in England, 1550–1800* edited by J.S. Cockburn, pp. 49–71. London: Methuen.
Curtis, M.H.
        Oxford and Cambridge in Transition, 1558–1642. Oxford: Oxford University Press.
Davids, T.W.
  1863   *Annals of Evangelical Nonconformity in the County of Essex from the time of Wycliffe to the Restoration*. London.
DeWindt, E.B.
  1972   *Land and People in Holywell-cum-Needingworth. Structures of Tenure and Patterns of Social Organization in an East Midlands Village, 1252–1457*. Toronto: Pontifical Institute of Mediaeval Studies.
Dickens, A.G.
  1967   *The English Reformation*. London: Collins—Fontana edition.
Dyer, A.D.
  1973   *The City of Worcester in the sixteenth century*. Leicester: Leicester University Press.
Emmison, F.G.
  1973   *Elizabethan Life: Morals and the Church Courts*. Chelmsford: Essex County Council.
Everitt, A.M.
  1970   *Change in the Provinces: the Seventeenth Century*. Occasional Papers of the Department of Local History, Second Series, 1. Leicester: Leicester University Press.
Fisher, F.J.
  1935   "The Development of the London Food Market, 1540–1640." *Economic History Review*, v. Reprinted in *Essays in Economic History*, Vol. 1, edited by E.M. Carus-Wilson, pp. 135–151. London: Edward Arnold.
Goody, J. and Watt, I.
  1968   "The Consequences of Literacy." In *Literacy in Traditional Societies*, edited by J. Goody, pp. 27–68. Cambridge: Cambridge University Press.
Goubert, P.
  1968   "Legitimate Fecundity and Infant Mortality in France During the Eighteenth Century: A Comparison." *Daedalus*, 97: 593–603.
Hajnal, J.
  1965   "European Marriage Patterns in Perspective." In *Population in History. Essays in Historical Demography*, edited by D.V. Glass and D.E.C. Eversley, pp. 101–143. London: Edward Arnold.
Harrison, C.J.
  1971   "Grain Price Analysis and Harvest Qualities, 1465–1634." *Agicultural History Review*, XIX: 138–155.
Hey, D.G.
  1974   *An English Rural Community. Myddle under the Tudors and Stuarts*. Leicester: Leicester University Press.

Hill, C.
1956 *Economic Problems of the Church, from Archbishop Whitgift to the Long Parliament.* Oxford: Oxford University Press.
1963 "Puritans and the Dark Corners of the Land." *Transactions of the Royal Historical Society,* Fifth Series, XIII: 77–102.
1970 *God's Englishman. Oliver Cromwell and the English Revolution.* London: Weidenfeld and Nicolson.

Hilton, R.H.
1975 *The English Peasantry in the Later Middle Ages.* Oxford: Oxford University Press.

Hirst, D.
1976 *The representative of the people? Voters and voting in England under the early Stuarts.* Cambridge: Cambridge University press.

Holderness, B.A.
1975 "Credit in a Rural Community, 1660–1800." *Midland History,* III: 94–116.

Hoskins, W.G.
1950 "The Leicestershire Country Parson in the Sixteenth Century." In *Essays in Leicestershire History,* pp. 1–22. Liverpool: Liverpool University Press.
1957 *The Midland Peasant. The economic and social history of a Leicestershire village.* London: Macmillan.
1964 "Harvest fluctuations and English Economic History, 1480–1619." *Agricultural History Review,* XII: 28–46.
1968 "Harvest fluctuations and English Economic History, 1620–1759." *Agricultural History Review,* XVI: 15–31.

Howell, C.
1976 "Peasant inheritance customs in the Midlands, 1200–1700." In *Family and Inheritance. Rural Society in Western Europe, 1200–1800,* edited by J. Goody, J. Thirsk and E.P. Thompson, pp. 112–155. Cambridge: Cambridge University Press.

Howell, R.
1970 "Thomas Weld of Gateshead. The Return of a New England Puritan." *Archaeologia Aeliana,* Fourth Series, XLVIII: 304–332.

James, M.E.
1974 *Family, Lineage and Civil Society. A Study of Society, Politics and Mentality in the Durham Region, 1550–1640.* Oxford: Oxford University Press.

Johnston, J.A.
1971 "The Probate Inventories and Wills of a Worcestershire Parish, 1676–1775." *Midland History,* 1: 21–33.

Jordan, W.K.
1962 *The Social Institutions of Lancashire.* Manchester: Chetham Society, 3rd Series, XI.

Knodel, J.
1968 "Infant Mortality and Fertility in Three Bavarian Villages." *Population Studies,* 22:297–318.
1970 "Two and a Half Centuries of Demographic History in a Bavarian Village." *Population Studies,* 24:353–376.

Laqueur, T.
1976 "The Cultural Origins of Popular Literacy in England, 1500–1850." *Oxford Review of Education,* 2:255–275.

Laslett, P.
1972 "Mean household size in England since the sixteenth century." In *Household and family in past time,* edited by P. Laslett and R. Wall, pp. 125–158. Cambridge: Cambridge Univeristy Press.

1977   "Clayworth and Cogenhoe." In *Family Life and illicit love in earlier generations. Essays in historical sociology*, pp. 50–101. Cambridge: Cambridge University Press.

Laslett, P. and Oosterveen, K.
1973   "Long-term Trends in Bastardy in England, 1561–1960." *Population Studies*, 27: 255–286.

Ledermann, S.
1969   *Nouvelles Tables Types de Mortalité*. Paris: Presses Universitaires de France.

Lévine, D.
1977   *Family Formation in an Age of Nascent Capitalism*. New York and London: Academic Press.

Macfarlane, A.
1970   *The Family Life of Ralph Josselin. A Seventeenth-Century Clergyman. An Essay in Historical Anthropology*. Cambridge: Cambridge University Press.

Macfarlane, A., Harrison, S., and Jardine, C.
1977   *Reconstructing Historical Communities*. Cambridge: Cambridge Univeristy Press.

Matthews, A.G.
1934   *Calamy Revised*. Oxford: Oxford University Press.

Morant, P.
1768   *The History and Antiquities of the County of Essex*. 2 Vols. London.

Morrill, J.S.
1974   *Cheshire, 1630–1660: County Government and Society During the 'English Revolution'*. Oxford: Oxford University Press.

Outhwaite, R.B.
1969   *Inflation in Tudor and Early Stuart England*. London: Macmillan.

Plumb, J.H.
1973   *The Commercialisation of Leisure in Eighteenth-Century England*. Reading: University of Reading Press.

Raftis, J.A.
1964   *Tenure and Mobility. Studies in the Social History of the Social History of the Medieaval English Village*. Toronto: Pontifical Institute of Mediaeval Studies.

Rogers, H.B.
1956   "The Market Area of Preston in the Sixteenth and Seventeenth Centuries." *Geographical Studies*, 3: 46–55.

Royal Commission on Historical Monuments.
1921   *An Inventory of the Historical Monuments in Essex*. London: H.M.S.O.

Rylands, W.H.
1885   "Booksellers and Stationers in Warrington, 1639 to 1657." *Transactions of the Historic Society of Lancashire and Cheshire*, New Series, I: 67–115.

Samaha, J.
1974   *Law and Order in Historical Perspecitve. The Case of Elizabethan Essex*. New York and London: Academic Press.

Schofield, R.S.
1968   "The Measurement of Literacy in Pre-Industrial England." In *Literacy in Traditional Societies*, edited by J. Goody, pp. 311–325. Cambridge: Cambridge University Press.

1972   "Age-specific Mobility in an Eighteenth Century Rural English Parish." *Annales de Démographie Historique:* 261–274.

1973   "Dimensions of Illiteracy, 1750–1850," in *Explorations in Economic History*, Second Series, 10: 437–454.

1977   "The relationship between demographic structure and environment in pre-industrial western Europe". In *Sozialgeschichte Der Familie in Der Neuzeit Europas*, edited by W. Conze, pp. 147-160. Stuttgart: Klett.

Smith, H.
1932 *The Ecclesiastical History of Essex Under the Long Parliament and Commonwealth.* Colchester: Privately published.

Smith, D.S.
1977 "A Homeostatic Demographic Regime. Patterns in West European Family Reconstitution Studies." In *Population Patterns in the Past*, edited by R.D. Lee, pp. 19-51. New York and London: Academic Press.

Spufford, M.
1974 *Contrasting Communities. English Villagers in the Sixteenth and Seventeenth Centuries.* Cambridge: Cambridge University Press.
1976 "Peasant inheritance customs and land distribution in Cambridgeshire from the sixteenth to the eighteenth centuries." In *Family and Inheritance. Rural Society in Western Europe, 1200-1800*, edited by J. Goody, J. Thirsk and E. P. Thompson, pp. 156-176. Cambridge: Cambridge University Press.

Stone, L.
1964 "The Educational Revolution in England, 1560-1640." *Past and Present*, 28: 41-80.
1965 *The Crisis of the Aristocracy, 1558-1641.* Abridged edition. Oxford: Oxford University Press.
1975 "The rise of the nuclear family in early-modern England: The Patriarchal Stage." In *The Family in History*, edited by C.E. Rosenberg, pp. 13-57. Philadelphia: University of Pennsylvania Press.

Thompson, E.P.
1974 "Patrician Soceity Plebeian Culture." *Journal of Social History*, VII: 382-405.

Tupling, G.H.
1927 *The Economic History of Rossendale.* Manchester: Chetham Society, New Series 86.

Venn J. and Venn J.A., eds.
1922 *Alumni Cantabrigiensis, Part I.* 4 Vols. Cambridge: Cambridge University Press.

Walter, J. and Wrightson, K.
1976 "Dearth and the social order in early-modern England." *Past and Present*, 71: 22-42.

Williams, W.M.
1956 *The Sociology of an English Village: Gosforth.* London: Routledge and Kegan Paul.
1963 *A West Country Village: Ashworthy. Family, Kinship and Land.* London: Routledge and Kegan Paul.

Wrigley, E.A.
1966 "Family Reconstitution." In *An Introduction to English Historical Historical Demography*, edited by E.A. Wrigley, pp. 96-159. London: Weidenfeld and Nicolson.
1966 "Family Limitation in Pre-Industrial England." *Economic History Review*, Second Series, XIX: 82-109.
1967 "A Simple Model of London's Importance in Changing English Society and Economy, 1650-1750." *Past and Present*, 37: 44-70.
1968 "Mortality in Pre-Industrial England: The Example of Colyton, Devon, Over Three Centuries." *Daedalus*, 97: 546-580.
1972 "Clandestine marriage in Tetbury in the late 17th century." *Local Population Studies*, 10:15-21.
1972 "Some problems of family reconstitution using English parish register material.

The example of Colyton." In *Communications, Third International Conference of Economic History, 1965*, pp. 199–221. Paris: Mouton.
Wrightson, K.
1975 "Infanticide in earlier seventeenth-century England." *Local Population Studies*, 15: 10–22.
1979 "Alehouses, order and reformation in rural England, 1590–1660," In *Class Relations and Cultural Forms. Essays on the working class and Leisure*, edited by E. and S. Yeo. London: Croom Helm.

INDEX

All references to Terling villagers and other Essex villages have been noted only when they occur more than once.

STUDIES IN SOCIAL DISCONTINUITY

Under the Consulting Editorship of:

CHARLES TILLY
University of Michigan

EDWARD SHORTER
University of Toronto

David Levine. Family Formations in an Age of Nascent Capitalism

Dirk Hoerder. Crowd Action in Revolutionary Massachusetts, 1765-1780

Charles P. Cell. Revolution at Work: Mobilization Campaigns in China

Frederic L. Pryor. The Origins of the Economy: A Comparative Study of Distribution in Primitive and Peasant Economies

Harry W. Pearson. The Livelihood of Man by Karl Polanyi

Richard Maxwell Brown and Don E. Fehrenbacher (Eds.). Tradition, Conflict, and Modernization: Perspectives on the American Revolution

Juan G. Espinosa and Andrew S. Zimbalist. Economic Democracy: Workers' Participation in Chilean Industry 1970-1973

Arthur L. Stinchcombe. Theoretical Methods in Social History

Randolph Trumbach. The Rise of the Egalitarian Family: Aristocratic Kinship and Domestic Relations in Eighteenth-Century England

Tamara K. Hareven (Ed.). Transitions: The Family and the Life Course in Historical Perspective

Henry A. Gemery and Jan S. Hogendorn (Eds.). The Uncommon Market: Essays in the Economic History of the Atlantic Slave Trade

Keith Wrightson and David Levine. Poverty and Piety in an English Village: Terling, 1525-1700

In preparation

Michael Haines. Fertility and Occupation: Population Patterns in Industrialization

Harvey L. Graff. The Literacy Myth: Literacy and Social Structure in the Nineteenth-Century City

Elizabeth Hafkin Pleck. Hunting For a City: Black Migration and Poverty in Boston, 1865-1900

Lucile H. Brockway. Science and Colonial Expansion: The Role of the British Royal Botanic Gardens